Security Onion Documentation

Release 16.04.6.1

May 14, 2019

Foreword

Richard Bejtlich

If you're reading documentation for the Security Onion project, you probably agree that network security monitoring (NSM) is a necessity for anyone who owns a network.

When might NSM not be a necessity? The only non-NSM situation I can imagine involves a complete lack of ownership, as would be the case for users accessing public Wi-Fi (or an increasingly less common wired equivalent). Public WiFi users are supposed to be responsible for their own activity, a fact that is usually reinforced by accepting some sort of acceptable use policy (AUP) upon connecting to a wireless access point. Public WiFi users are also not capable of introducing separate monitoring hardware and software, as their scope for action is limited to their individual endpoints.

Let's imagine the questions that a network owner wants answered about his or her asset. One could imagine many more questions that relate to the health and security of a network, but this list is a good one with which to start.

- Is the network operational?
    - If no, prepare to answer a myriad of operational questions about the outage.
    - If yes, are there signs that the network might not work in the future?
- Is the available bandwidth suitable for the network users?
    - If no, what devices are using the most bandwidth?
    - If yes, are there signs that the network might not have enough capacity in the future?
- Is the network usage consistent with the acceptable use policy?
    - If no, what devices are violating the AUP?
    - If yes, are there signs that devices may violate the AUP in the future?
- Is the network infrastructure sound (i.e., is the infrastructure not compromised)?
    - If no, prepare to answer a myriad of incident detection and response questions.
    - If yes, are there signs that the infrastructure is vulnerable to compromise, or that threats are trying to compromise the infrastructure?

Note that other levels of detail could be investigated here. Beyond talking in terms of devices, we could try to identify the users operating the devices. Even if users are operating within the AUP, they may become victims of intruder activity. An attacker could encrypt a user's endpoint via ransomware and demand payment. An intruder could try to leverage network misconfigurations to launch a distributed denial of service attack against a third party. An intruder could extract tokens from an endpoint that allow unauthorized access to a third party's cloud infrastructure. All of these scenarios are within scope in real networks.

If one accepts that these are worthy questions for network owners to consider, the next step is to decide how best to answer them. Network infrastructure itself can provide data for many of these questions. However, the more data requested of the infrastructure, the less capacity for the infrastructure to fulfill its primary purpose -- providing connectivity to users.

If understanding the network becomes the purpose of the network, then it has lost its utility. Therefore, most network infrastructure providers limit, or encourage owners to limit, the ability to answer the more detailed of these questions. Up/down status, bandwidth usage, and generic error detection are expected of most network devices out-of-the-box, but network usage and security operations are generally add-ons that operators must apply themselves. Even gaining access to network traffic can be problematic, as network vendors often discourage operators from configuring span ports to mirror traffic to collection platforms.

If the network operator happens to also own all of the endpoints for which the network provides connectivity, then he or she might be able to leverage that authority to introduce endpoint-centric security and utility monitoring solutions. This does not work, however, if the endpoints are closed systems that neither export logs nor allow installation of third-party monitoring solutions.

Interestingly enough, this is similar to the situation one finds with some network infrastructure. While many devices will export logs, doing so may limit the device's ability to perform its primary network function. Furthermore, network devices are also generally closed systems, unfriendly to installation of third-party monitoring solutions.

We have now found ourselves in a situation where we still have questions to answer about the network, but we may not be able to answer them by relying on the endpoints, nor on the infrastructure devices. Even if we could "rely" on the endpoints, how well would our trust endure once those endpoints or infrastructure fail to enemy hands? Besides simply terminating endpoint-centric security logging, intruders could subvert or otherwise tamper with such measures. We appear to be in a bind.

This is the logical progression that should bring a skeptic to the point where he or she recognizes that NSM isn't optional. NSM, in fact, is mandatory for any network owner.

NSM may not be able to answer every question about the network and its assets, but it's clear that the limitations of previously discussed approaches leave network owners no choice. By introducing NSM into the network ownership equation, operators give themselves the best chance to not only answer their key questions, but to defend their methods should they be challenged as a result of any standards of diligence and due care.

I started using Doug Burks' Security Onion NSM distro in late 2010. I was building my third iteration of my TCP/IP Weapons School, and for the previous two editions I had provided students my own FreeBSD-based virtual machine running NSM applications like Sguil, Snort, and Wireshark. I was thrilled to see that Doug had created an Ubuntu-based NSM distro that was under active development, unlike the FreeBSD VM I created once every other year for teaching purposes.

When I joined Mandiant in the spring of 2011, I knew I needed someone like Doug working with me to monitor a network that was surely attracting too much attention from global threat actors. I heard from many consultants who were amazed that Doug had tracked down suspicious or occasionally malicious activity involving their endpoints, thanks to his NSM approach. Thankfully, during our tenure as chief security officer and deputy, we did not suffer any serious incidents and we were both able to later transition to other roles and companies with clean security records.

If you've made it to the end of this foreword, then I know you probably appreciate a key aspect of Security Onion that makes it stand out among many open source projects, whether security-centric or not. Security Onion's documentation has always been, in my opinion, second to none. It is always exceptionally well-organized, clearly written, and supported by an ever-growing number of helpful people via Google Groups, Reddit, and other social media. When Doug asked me to write this section, I was very happy to add my own small contribution to what I consider to be one of the best documented open source projects available.

Security Onion recently celebrated its ten year anniversary, and I wish Doug and the project another wonderful ten years!

Richard Bejtlich
@taosecurity
Principal Security Strategist, Corelight
Vienna, VA
7 April 2019

Table of Contents

1 About   **1**
- 1.1   Security Onion 1
- 1.2   Security Onion Solutions, LLC 1
- 1.3   Documentation 1

2 Introduction   **3**
- 2.1   Core Components 3
- 2.2   Analysis Tools 4
- 2.3   Deployment Scenarios 5
- 2.4   Conclusion 5

3 Getting Started   **7**
- 3.1   Use Cases 7
- 3.2   Architecture 8
- 3.3   Hardware Requirements 17
- 3.4   HWE 21
- 3.5   Download 22
- 3.6   VMWare 22
- 3.7   VirtualBox 23
- 3.8   Booting Issues 24
- 3.9   Installation 25
- 3.10   ISO Release Notes 25
- 3.11   Quick Evaluation using Security Onion ISO image 26
- 3.12   Quick Evaluation on Ubuntu 26
- 3.13   Production Deployment 27
- 3.14   After Installation 31
- 3.15   Secure Boot 33

4 Analyst Tools   **35**
- 4.1   Kibana 35
- 4.2   CapME 38
- 4.3   CyberChef 39
- 4.4   Squert 40
- 4.5   Sguil 43
- 4.6   NetworkMiner 46
- 4.7   Wireshark 48

5 Network Visibility — 51
- 5.1 NIDS — 51
- 5.2 Snort — 52
- 5.3 Suricata — 53
- 5.4 Bro — 54
- 5.5 netsniff-ng — 58

6 Host Visibility — 61
- 6.1 Beats — 61
- 6.2 Wazuh — 63
- 6.3 Sysmon — 64
- 6.4 Autoruns — 65
- 6.5 Syslog — 66

7 Elastic Stack — 69
- 7.1 Elasticsearch — 69
- 7.2 Logstash — 74
- 7.3 ElastAlert — 77
- 7.4 Curator — 79
- 7.5 FreqServer — 80
- 7.6 DomainStats — 88
- 7.7 Docker — 89
- 7.8 Redis — 92
- 7.9 Data Fields — 93
- 7.10 Alert Data Fields — 94
- 7.11 Bro Fields — 94
- 7.12 Elastalert Fields — 111
- 7.13 Re-Indexing — 111

8 Updating — 113
- 8.1 Updating — 113
- 8.2 MySQL Upgrade Errors — 115
- 8.3 apt-cacher-ng — 117
- 8.4 End Of Life — 117

9 Customizing for Your Environment — 119
- 9.1 Network Configuration — 119
- 9.2 Proxy Configuration — 121
- 9.3 Firewall — 122
- 9.4 Email Configuration — 122
- 9.5 Changing IP Addresses — 125
- 9.6 NTP — 127

10 Tuning — 129
- 10.1 BPF — 129
- 10.2 Managing Rules — 131
- 10.3 Adding Local Rules — 133
- 10.4 Managing Alerts — 134
- 10.5 PF-RING — 143
- 10.6 AF-PACKET — 144
- 10.7 High Performance Tuning — 145
- 10.8 MySQL Tuning — 147
- 10.9 Trimming PCAPs — 148
- 10.10 Disabling Processes — 150

11 Tricks and Tips   153
- 11.1 Airgapped Networks 153
- 11.2 Analyst VM 153
- 11.3 Best Practices 154
- 11.4 Cloud Client 155
- 11.5 Connecting to Sguild 160
- 11.6 Disabling Desktop 161
- 11.7 DNS Anomaly Detection 161
- 11.8 ICMP Anomaly Detection 162
- 11.9 MetaPackages 163
- 11.10 Adding a new disk 164
- 11.11 PCAPs for Testing 167
- 11.12 Removing a Sensor 168
- 11.13 Salt 170
- 11.14 Sensor Stops Seeing Traffic 175
- 11.15 SSH 176
- 11.16 UTC and Time Zones 176

12 Services   179
- 12.1 All services 179
- 12.2 Server services 180
- 12.3 Sensor services 180
- 12.4 Elastic services 180

13 Utilities   183
- 13.1 jq 183
- 13.2 Setup 183
- 13.3 so-allow 184
- 13.4 so-import-pcap 185

14 Help   187
- 14.1 FAQ 188
- 14.2 Directory Structure 198
- 14.3 Tools 199
- 14.4 Passwords 203
- 14.5 Support 204
- 14.6 Mailing Lists 204
- 14.7 Help Wanted 206

15 Integrations   209
- 15.1 AlienVault-OTX 209
- 15.2 Etherpad 210
- 15.3 FIR 211
- 15.4 GRR 211
- 15.5 TheHive 213
- 15.6 MISP 214
- 15.7 NtopNG 216
- 15.8 RITA 216
- 15.9 Strelka 217
- 15.10 Syslog Output 218

16 Security   221

17 Appendix   223
- 17.1 ELSA to Elastic 223

17.2 Upgrading from 14.04 to 16.04 227

18 Cheat Sheet **233**

CHAPTER 1

About

1.1 Security Onion

Security Onion is a free and open source Linux distribution for intrusion detection, enterprise security monitoring, and log management. It includes Elasticsearch, Logstash, Kibana, Snort, Suricata, Bro, Wazuh, Sguil, Squert, CyberChef, NetworkMiner, and many other security tools. The easy-to-use Setup wizard allows you to build an army of distributed sensors for your enterprise in minutes!

For more information about Security Onion not contained in this Documentation, please see our community site at https://securityonion.net.

1.2 Security Onion Solutions, LLC

Doug Burks started Security Onion as a free and open source project in 2008 and then founded Security Onion Solutions, LLC in 2014.

Security Onion Solutions, LLC is the only official provider of training, professional services, and hardware appliances for Security Onion.

For more information about these products and services, please see our corporate site at https://securityonionsolutions.com.

1.3 Documentation

1.3.1 Formats

This documentation is published online at https://securityonion.net/docs. If you are viewing an offline version of this documentation but have Internet access, you might want to switch to the online version at https://securityonion.net/docs to see the latest version.

This documentation is also available in PDF format:
https://readthedocs.org/projects/securityonion/downloads/pdf/latest/

1.3.2 Authors

Security Onion Solutions is the primary author and maintainer of this documentation. Some content has been contributed by members of our community. Thanks to all the folks who have contributed to this documentation over the years!

1.3.3 Contributing

We welcome your contributions to our documentation! We will review any suggestions and apply them if appropriate.

If you are accessing the online version of the documentation and notice that a particular page has incorrect information, you can submit corrections by clicking the `Edit on GitHub` button in the upper right corner of each page.

To submit a new page, you can submit a pull request (PR) to the following repo:
https://github.com/Security-Onion-Solutions/securityonion-docs

1.3.4 Naming Convention

Our goal is to allow you to easily guess and type the URL of the documentation you want to go to.

For example, if you want to read more about Suricata, you can type the following into your browser:
https://securityonion.net/docs/suricata

To achieve this goal, new documentation pages should use the following naming convention:

- all lowercase
- `.rst` file extension
- ideally, the name of the page should be one simple word (for example: `suricata.rst`)
- try to avoid symbols if possible
- if symbols are required, use hyphens (NOT underscores)

CHAPTER 2

Introduction

Network Security Monitoring (NSM) is, put simply, monitoring your network for security related events. It might be proactive, when used to identify vulnerabilities or expiring SSL certificates, or it might be reactive, such as in incident response and network forensics. Whether you're tracking an adversary or trying to keep malware at bay, NSM provides context, intelligence and situational awareness of your network. Enterprise Security Monitoring (ESM) takes NSM to the next level and includes endpoint visibility and other telemetry from your enterprise. There are some commercial solutions that get close to what Security Onion provides, but very few contain the vast capabilities of Security Onion in one package.

Many assume NSM is a solution they can buy to fill a gap; purchase and deploy solution XYZ and problem solved. The belief that you can buy an NSM denies the fact that the most important word in the NSM acronym is "M" for Monitoring. Data can be collected and analyzed, but not all malicious activity looks malicious at first glance. While automation and correlation can enhance intelligence and assist in the process of sorting through false positives and malicious indicators, there is no replacement for human intelligence and awareness. I don't want to disillusion you. Security Onion isn't a silver bullet that you can setup, walk away from and feel safe. Nothing is and if that's what you're looking for you'll never find it. Security Onion will provide visibility into your network traffic and context around alerts and anomalous events, but it requires a commitment from you the administrator or analyst to review alerts, monitor the network activity, and most importantly, have a willingness, passion and desire to learn.

2.1 Core Components

Security Onion seamlessly weaves together three core functions:

- full packet capture;
- network-based and host-based intrusion detection systems (NIDS and HIDS, respectively);
- and powerful analysis tools.

Full-packet capture is accomplished via netsniff-ng, "the packet sniffing beast". netsniff-ng captures all the network traffic your Security Onion sensors see and stores as much of it as your storage solution will hold (Security Onion has a built-in mechanism to purge old data before your disks fill to capacity). Full packet capture is like a video camera for your network, but better because not only can it tell us who came and went, but also exactly where they went and what they brought or took with them (exploit payloads, phishing emails, file exfiltration). It's a crime scene recorder that can tell us a lot about the victim and the white chalk outline of a compromised host on the ground. There is certainly valuable evidence to be found on the victim's body, but evidence at the host can be destroyed or manipulated; the camera doesn't lie, is hard to deceive, and can capture a bullet in transit.

Network-based and host-based intrusion detection systems (IDS) analyze network traffic or host systems, respectively, and provide log and alert data for detected events and activity. Security Onion provides multiple IDS options:

NIDS:

- Rule-driven NIDS. For rule-driven network intrusion detection, Security Onion offers the choice of Snort or Suricata. Rule-based systems look at network traffic for fingerprints and identifiers that match known malicious, anomalous or otherwise suspicious traffic. You might say that they're akin to antivirus signatures for the network, but they're a bit deeper and more flexible than that.

- Analysis-driven NIDS. For analysis-driven network intrusion detection, Security Onion offers Bro (Zeek). Unlike rule-based systems that look for needles in the haystack of data, Bro says, "Here's all your data and this is what I've seen. Do with it what you will and here's a framework so you can." Bro monitors network activity and logs any connections, DNS requests, detected network services and software, SSL certificates, and HTTP, FTP, IRC SMTP, SSH, SSL, and Syslog activity that it sees, providing a real depth and visibility into the context of data and events on your network. Additionally, Bro includes analyzers for many common protocols and by default has the capacity to check MD5 sums for HTTP file downloads against Team Cymru's Malware Hash Registry project. Beyond logging activity and traffic analyzers, the Bro framework provides a very extensible way to analyze network data in real time. The input framework allows you to feed data into Bro, which can be scripted, for example, to read a comma delimited file of C-level employee usernames and correlate that against other activity, such as when they download an executable file from the Internet. The file analysis framework provides protocol independent file analysis, allowing you to capture files as they pass through your network and automatically pass them to a sandbox or a file share for antivirus scanning. The flexibility of Bro makes it an incredibly powerful ally in your defense.

HIDS:

- For host-based intrusion detection, Security Onion offers Wazuh, a free, open source HIDS for Windows, Linux and Mac OS X. When you add the Wazuh agent to endpoints on your network, you gain invaluable visibility from endpoint to your network's exit point. Wazuh performs log analysis, file integrity checking, policy monitoring, rootkit detection, real-time alerting and active response. As an analyst, being able to correlate host-based events with network-based events can be the difference in identifying a successful attack.

In addition to the above, Security Onion can collect data via syslog or other agent transport.

2.2 Analysis Tools

With full packet capture, IDS logs and Bro data, there is a daunting amount of data available at the analyst's fingertips. Fortunately, Security Onion integrates the following tools to help make sense of this data:

- Sguil, created by Bamm Visscher, is "The Analyst Console for Network Security Monitoring." It is the analyst's right hand, providing visibility into the event data being collected and the context to validate the detection. Sguil provides a single GUI in which to view Snort, Suricata, and Wazuh alerts. More importantly, Sguil allows you to pivot directly from an alert into a packet capture (via Wireshark or NetworkMiner) or a transcript of the full session that triggered the alert. So, instead of seeing only an individual packet associated with an alert and being left with the unanswerable question, "What now?" or "What happened next?," you can view all of the associated traffic and actually answer that question. Sguil differs from other alert interfaces in that it allows collaboration among analysts by allowing alerts to be commented on and escalated to more senior analysts who can take action on the alerts.

- Squert, originally developed by Paul Halliday, is a web application interface to the Sguil database. Although it is neither meant to be a real-time (or near real-time) interface nor a replacement for Sguil, it allows querying of the Sguil database and provides several visualization options for the data such as "time series representations, weighted and logically grouped result sets" and geo-IP mapping. Squert can pivot to full packet capture via CapMe.

- Kibana, created by the team at Elastic, allows us to quickly analyze and pivot between all of the different data types generated by Security Onion through a "single pane of glass". This includes not only NIDS/HIDS alerts, but also Bro logs and system logs collected via syslog or other agent transport. Kibana can pivot to full packet capture via CapMe.
- CapMe, originally developed by Paul Halliday, allows you to view PCAP transcripts and download full PCAP files. Squert and Kibana are pre-configured to pivot to CapMe to retrieve full packet capture.

2.3 Deployment Scenarios

Analysts around the world are using Security Onion today for many different use cases and architectures. The Security Onion Setup wizard allows you to easily configure the best installation scenario to suit your needs.

2.4 Conclusion

So we have full packet capture, Snort or Suricata rule-driven intrusion detection, Bro event-driven intrusion detection and Wazuh host-based intrusion detection, all running out of the box once you run Security Onion setup. These disparate systems with various dependencies and complexities all run seamlessly together and would otherwise take hours, days or weeks to assemble and integrate on their own. What was once a seemingly impossible task is now as easy as answering a few questions.

CHAPTER 3

Getting Started

This section will give you an overview of different use cases for Security Onion and how you might install and configure Security Onion to handle those use cases.

3.1 Use Cases

Security Onion is designed for many different use cases! Here are just a few examples.

3.1.1 Pcap Forensics

One of the easiest ways to get started with Security Onion is using it to forensically analyze one or more pcap files. Just install Security Onion and then run so-import-pcap on one or more of the pcap files in `/opt/samples/`.

3.1.2 Classroom

`Evaluation Mode` is ideal for classroom or small lab environments.

Install Security Onion. Run Setup and configure network interfaces. Reboot, run Setup again, and then choose `Evaluation Mode`.

For more information, please see the Quick Evaluation section.

3.1.3 Production Server - Standalone

Install Security Onion. Run Setup and configure network interfaces. Reboot, run Setup again, choose `Production Mode`, choose `New Deployment`, and enable network sensor services.

For more information, please see the Production Deployment section.

3.1.4 Production Server - Distributed Deployment

Install Security Onion on the master server box. Run Setup and configure network interfaces. Reboot, run Setup again, choose `Production Mode`, and then choose `New Deployment`.

Install Security Onion on one or more nodes and then on each one: run Setup, configure network interfaces, reboot, run Setup again, choose `Production Mode`, and then choose `Existing Deployment` to join to master.

For more information, please see the Production Deployment section.

3.1.5 Analyst VM

If you've built a Production Server as described above, you may want to connect to it using an Analyst VM. Install Security Onion in a VM on your local desktop or laptop. You do NOT need to run Setup in the Analyst VM since this VM won't be running any services, only applications such as Sguil, Wireshark, NetworkMiner, and a web browser.

For more information, please see the Analyst-VM section.

3.1.6 Sending Logs to Separate SIEM

You can install Security Onion and then configure it to send logs to a separate SIEM.

For more information, please see the Syslog Output section.

3.2 Architecture

Below are several diagrams to represent the current architecture and deployment scenarios for Security Onion and the Elastic Stack.

3.2.1 High-Level Architecture Diagram

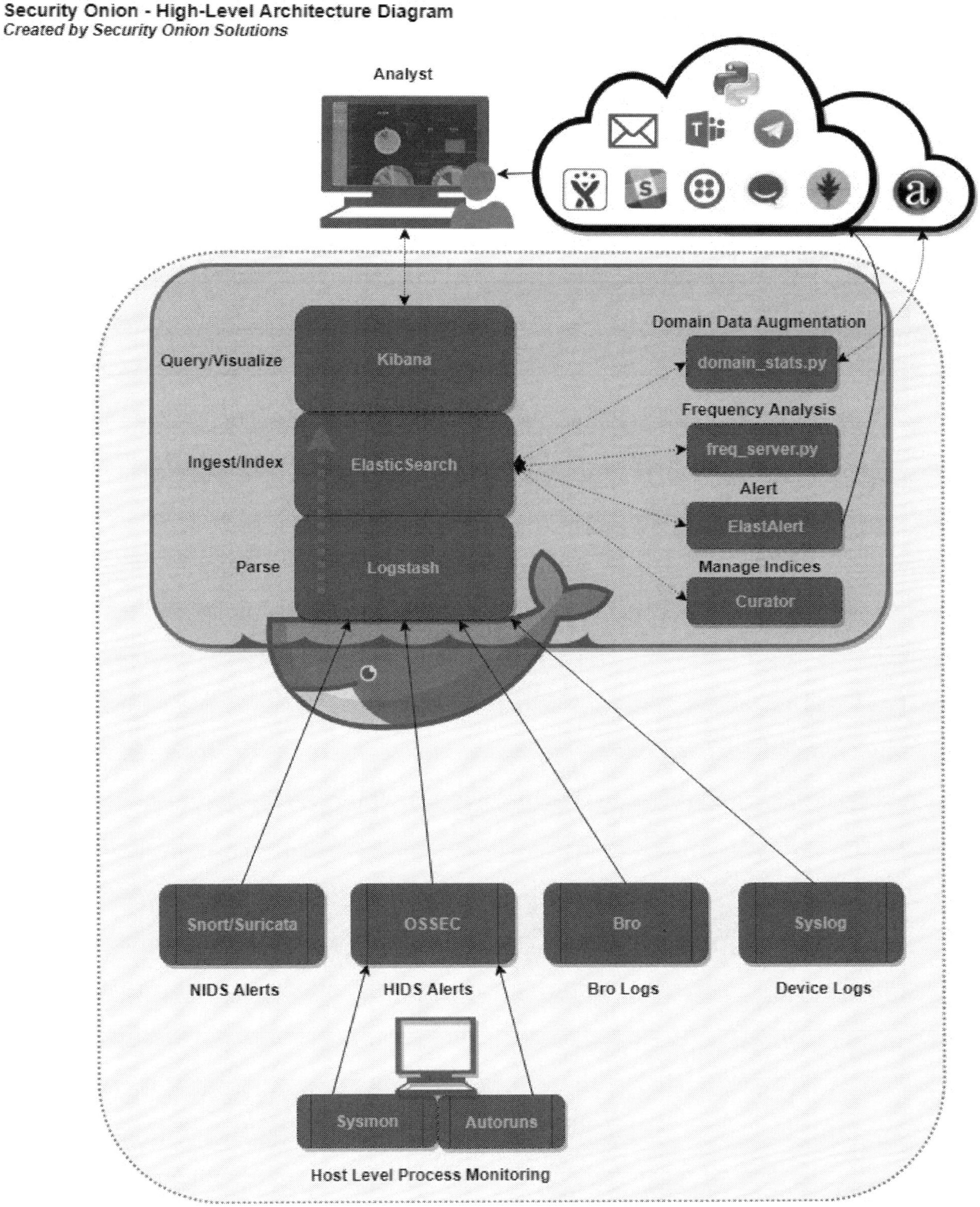

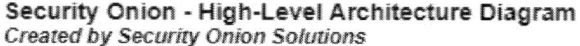

3.2.2 Core Components

Logstash

- Parse and format logs.

Elasticsearch

- Ingest and index logs.

Kibana

- Visualize ingested log data.

3.2.3 Auxilliary Components

Curator

- Manage indices through scheduled maintenance.

ElastAlert

- Query Elasticsearch and alert on user-defined anomalous behavior or other interesting bits of information.

FreqServer -Detect DGAs and find random file names, script names, process names, service names, workstation names, TLS certificate subjects and issuer subjects, etc.

DomainStats

- Get additional info about a domain by providing additional context, such as creation time, age, reputation, etc.

3.2.4 Detailed Data Flow Diagram

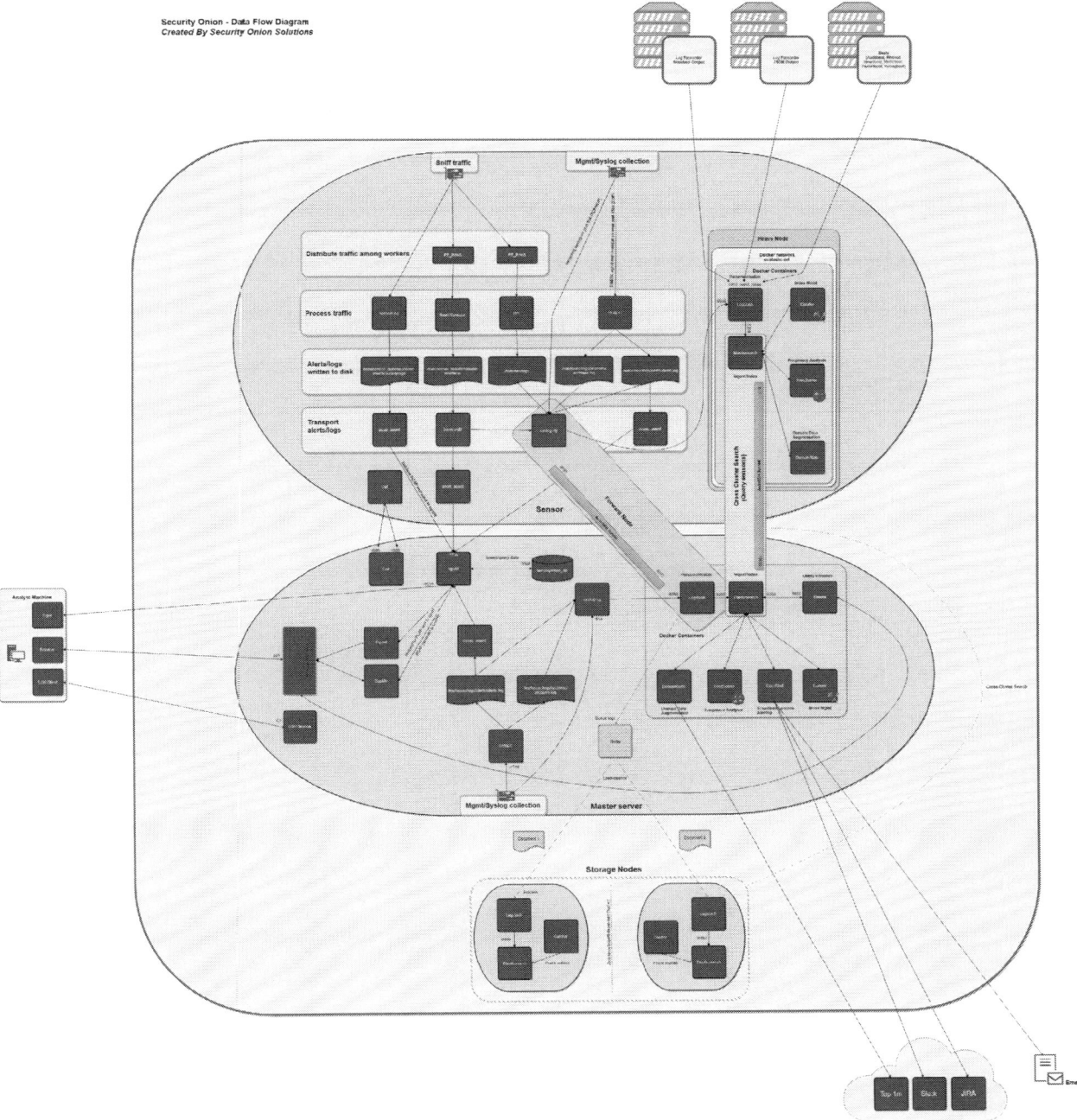

If you're viewing the online version of this documentation, you can click the image to zoom in.

3.2.5 Deployment Types

Security Onion is built on a modified distributed client-server model. In the past, Security Onion relied solely on the use of a "sensor" (the client) and a Security Onion "server" (the server). With the inclusion of the Elastic Stack, the distributed architecture has since changed, and now includes the use of Elastic components and separate nodes for processing and storing Elastic stack data.

This means that a standard distributed deployment is now comprised of the **master server**, one or more **forward nodes** (previously called a sensor – runs sensor components), and one or more **storage nodes** (runs Elastic components). This architecture is ideal; while it may cost more upfront, this architecture provides for greater scalability and performance down the line, as one can simply "snap in" new storage nodes to handle more traffic or log sources.

There is the option to utilize only two node types – the **master server** and one or more **heavy nodes**, however, this is not recommended due to performance reasons, and should only be used for testing purposes or in low-throughput environments.

Last, similar to before, users can run a **standalone**, which combines the functions of a **master server**, **forward node**, and **storage node**. The same caveats with performance apply here. This type of deployment is typically used for testing, labs, POCs, or **very** low-throughput environments.

More detail about each deployment and node type can be found below.

Distributed

- Recommended deployment type
- Consists of a master server, one or more forward nodes, and one or more storage nodes.

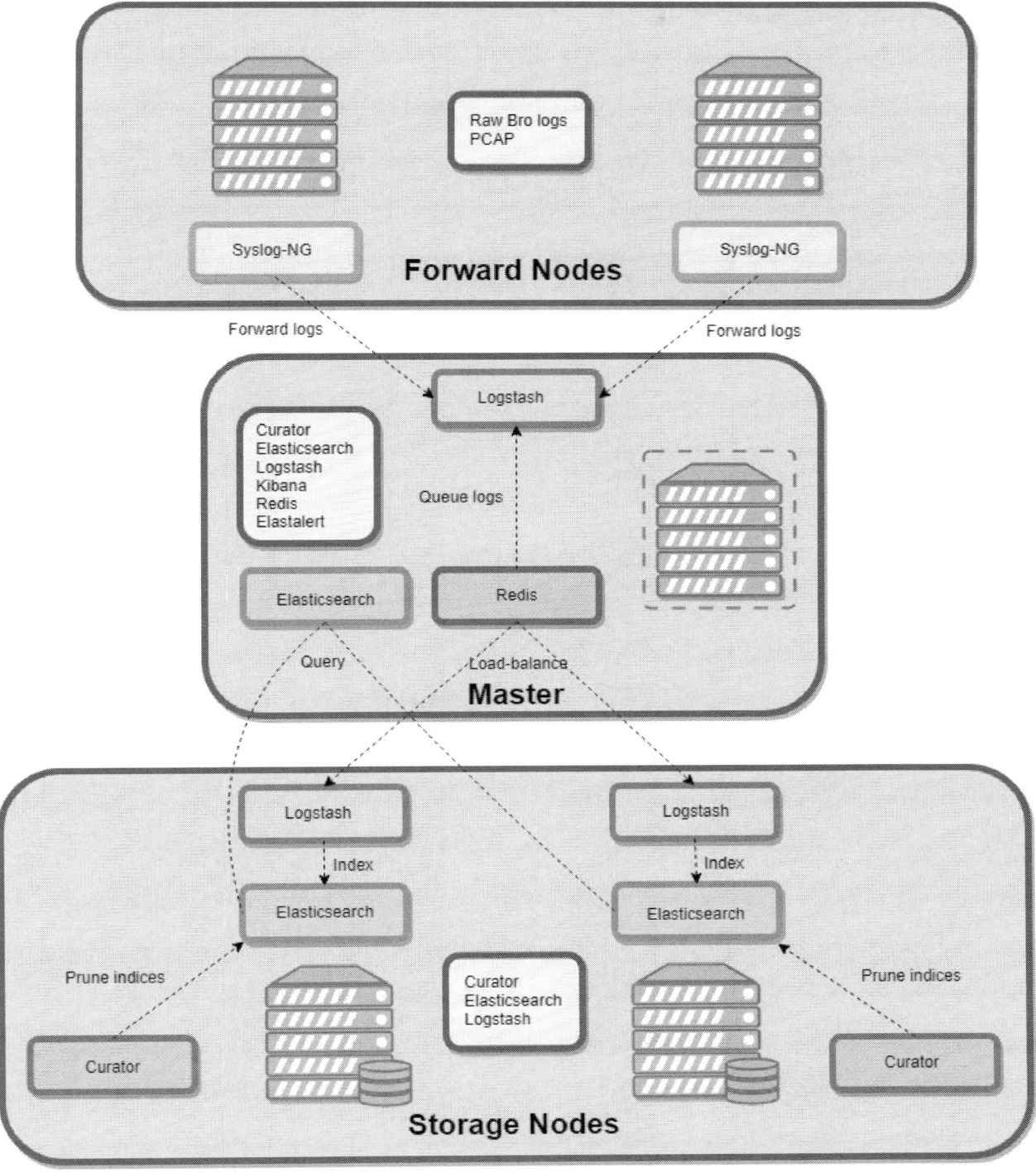

Heavy Distributed

- Recommended only if a standard distributed deployment is not possible.
- Consists of a master server, and one or more heavy nodes.

Security Onion - Heavy Distributed Deployment
Created by Security Onion Solutions

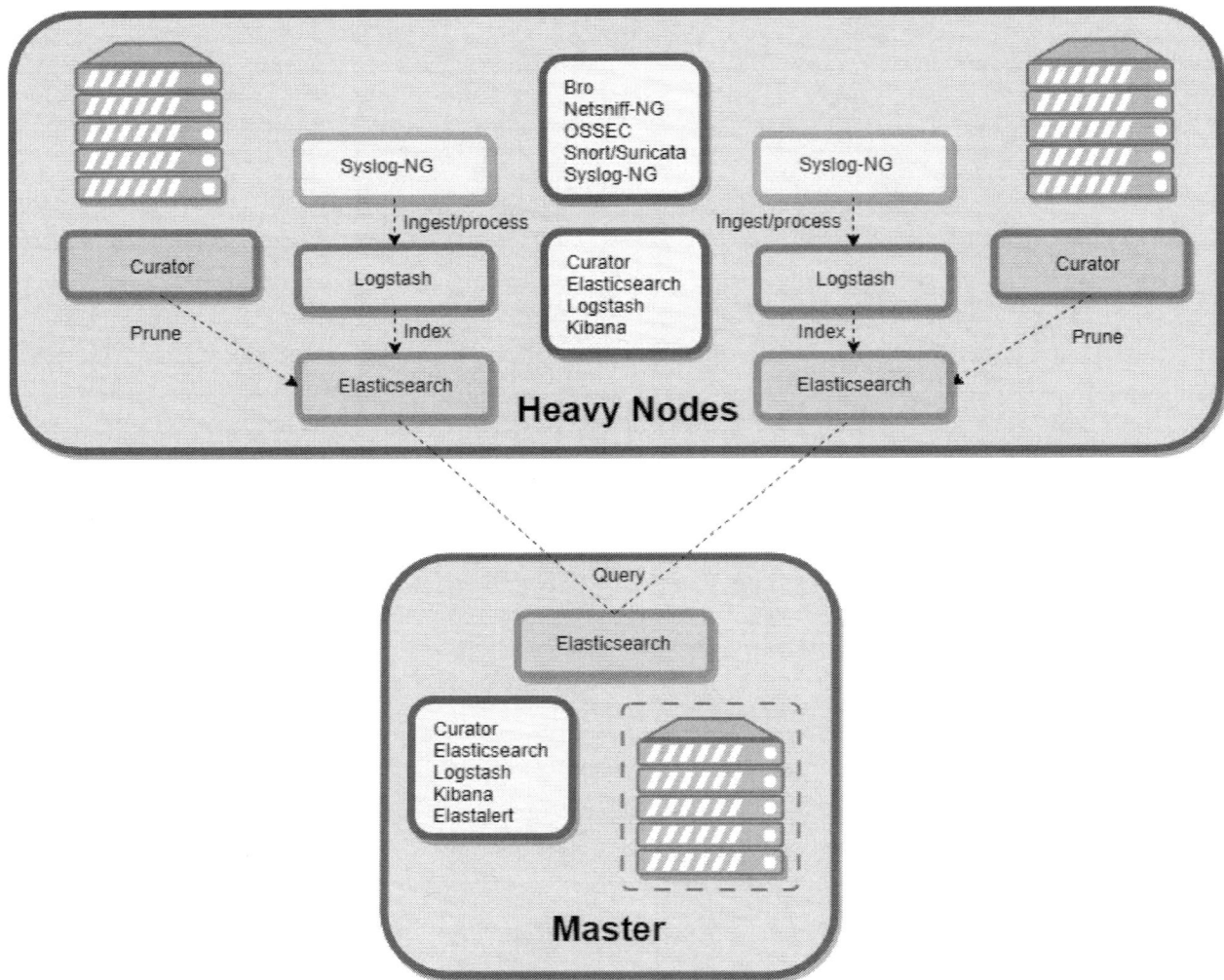

Standalone

- Not recommended for monitoring high-throughput links
- Consists of a single server running master server components, sensor, and Elastic stack components.

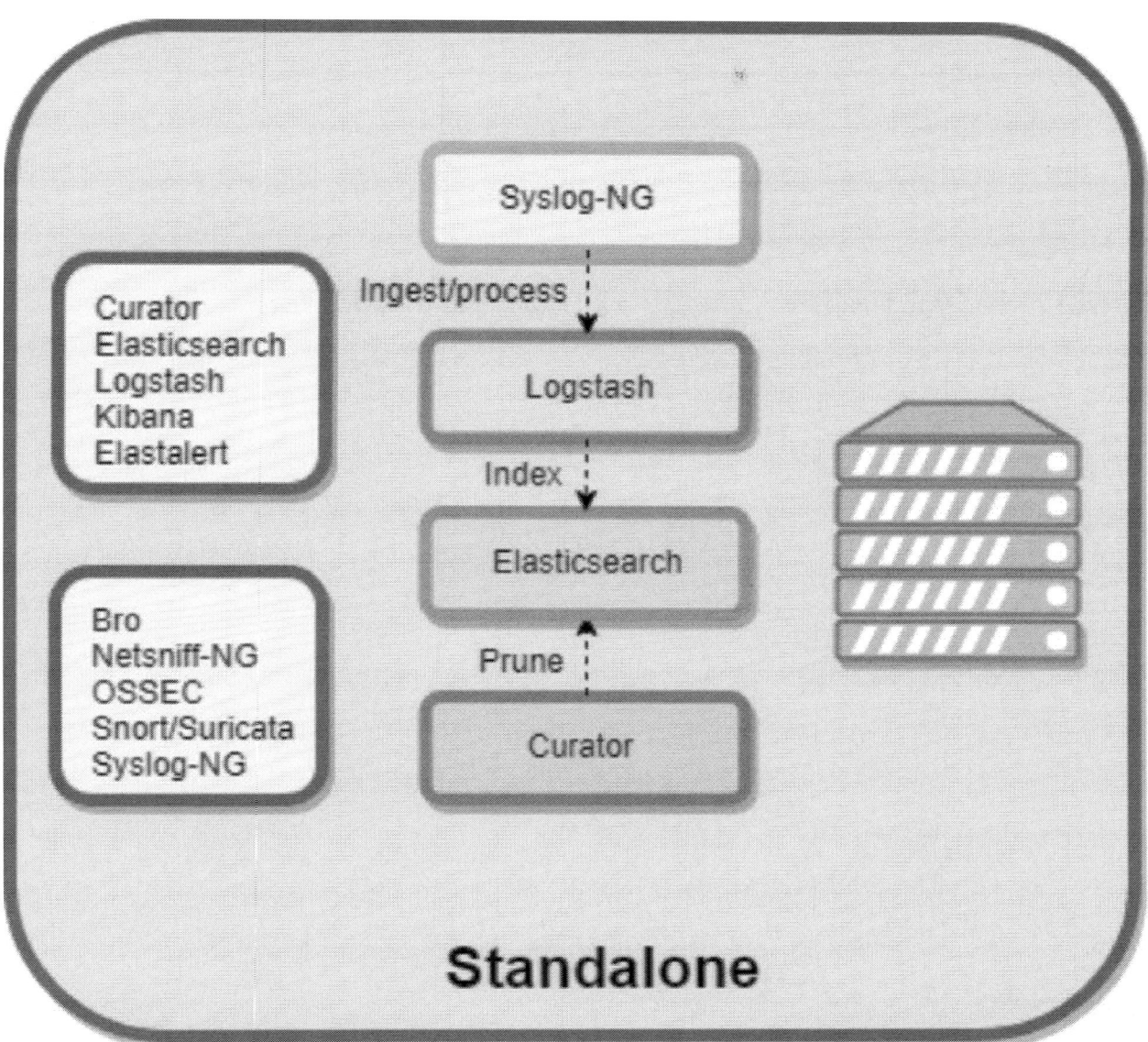

3.2.6 Node Types

Master

The `master server` runs it's own local copy of Elasticsearch, which manages cross-cluster search configuration for the deployment. This includes configuration for `heavy nodes` and `storage nodes` (where applicable), but not `forward nodes`, as they do not run Elastic Stack components. An analyst connects to the server from a client workstation (typically a Security Onion virtual machine installation) to execute queries and retrieve data.

The Master Server runs the following components (Production Mode w/ Best Practices):

- Elasticsearch

- Logstash
- Kibana
- Curator
- Elastalert
- Redis (Only if configured to output to a storage node)
- OSSEC
- Sguild

Forward Node

When using a `forward node`, Elastic Stack components are not installed. Syslog-NG forwards all logs to Logstash on the master server via an autossh tunnel, where they are stored in Elasticsearch on the master server, or forwarded to storage node's Elasticsearch instance (if the master server has been configured to use a storage node). From there, the data can be queried through the use of cross-cluster search.

Forward Nodes run the following components (Production Mode w/ Best Practices):

- Bro
- Snort/Suricata
- Netsniff-NG
- OSSEC
- Syslog-NG

Heavy Node

When using a `heavy node`, Security Onion implements distributed deployments using Elasticsearch's cross cluster search. When you run Setup and choose `Heavy Node`, it will create a local Elasticsearch instance and then configure the master server to query that instance (similar to ELSA distributed deployments). This is done by constructing an autossh tunnel from the heavy node to the master server, configuring reverse port forwarding to allow the master server to connect to the local Elasticsearch instance, and updating _cluster/settings on the master server so that it will query the local Elasticsearch instance.

- Elasticsearch
- Logstash
- Curator
- Bro
- Snort/Suricata
- Netsniff-NG
- OSSEC
- Syslog-NG (forwards logs locally to Logstash)

Storage Node

`Storage nodes` extend the storage and processing capabilities of the master server. Just like heavy nodes, storage nodes are added to the master's cluster search configuration, so the data that resides on the nodes can be queried from the master.

Storage Nodes run the following components (Production Mode w/ Best Practices):

- Elasticsearch
- Logstash
- Curator
- OSSEC

3.3 Hardware Requirements

3.3.1 32-bit vs 64-bit

Security Onion only supports 64-bit hardware.

3.3.2 UEFI

If your hardware has UEFI, please see https://help.ubuntu.com/community/UEFI.

3.3.3 UEFI Secure Boot

If your hardware has UEFI Secure Boot enabled, please see the Secure Boot section.

3.3.4 UPS

Like most IT systems, Security Onion has databases and those databases don't like power outages or other ungraceful shutdowns. To avoid power outages and having to manually repair databases, please consider a UPS.

3.3.5 Elastic Stack

If you're going to enable the Elastic Stack, please note that the MINIMUM requirements are 4 CPU cores and 8GB RAM. These requirements increase as you monitor more traffic and consume more logs.

Please refer to our Architecture Page for detailed deployment scenarios.

We recommend placing all Elastic storage on SSD or fast spinning disk in a RAID 10 configuration. This includes `/nsm/elasticsearch` and `/nsm/logstash`.

3.3.6 Standalone Deployments

In a standalone deployment, the master server components and the sensor components all run on a single box, therefore, your hardware requirements will reflect that. This deployment type is recommended for evaluation purposes, POCs (proof-of-concept) and small to medium size single sensor deployments. Although you can deploy Security Onion in this manner, it is recommended that you separate the backend components and sensor components.

- CPU: Used to parse incoming events, index incoming events, search metatadata, capture PCAP, analyze packets, and run the frontend components. As data and event consumption increases, a greater amount of CPU will be required.
- RAM: Used for Logstash, Elasticsearch, disk cache for Lucene, Snort/Suricata, Bro, Sguil, etc. The amount of available RAM will directly impact search speeds and reliability, as well as ability to process and capture traffic.
- Disk: Used for storage of indexed metadata. A larger amount of storage allows for a longer retention period. It is typically recommended to retain no more than 30 days of hot ES indices.

Please refer to our Architecture Page for detailed deployment scenarios.

3.3.7 Master server with local log storage

In an enterprise distributed deployment, a master server will store logs from itself and forward nodes. It can also act as a syslog destination for other log sources to be indexed into Elasticsearch. An enterprise master server should have 8 CPU cores at a minimum, 16-128GB RAM, and enough disk space (multiple terabytes recommended) to meet your retention requirements.

- CPU: Used to parse incoming events, index incoming events, search metadata. As consumption of data and events increases, more CPU will be required.
- RAM: Used for Logstash, Elasticsearch, and disk cache for Lucene. The amount of available RAM will directly impact search speeds and reliability.
- Disk: Used for storage of indexed metadata. A larger amount of storage allows for a longer retention period. It is typically recommended to retain no more than 30 days of hot ES indices.

Please refer to our Architecture Page for detailed deployment scenarios.

3.3.8 Master server with storage nodes

This deployment type utilizes storage nodes to parse and index of events. As a result, the hardware requirements of the master are reduced. An enterprise master server should have 4-8 CPU cores, 8-16GB RAM, and 100GB to 1TB of disk space. Many folks choose to host their master server in their VM farm since it has lower hardware requirements than sensors but needs higher reliability and availability.

- CPU: Used to receive incoming events and place them into Redis. Used to run all the front end web components and aggregate search results from the storage nodes.
- RAM: Used for Logstash and Redis. The amount of available RAM directly impacts the size of the Redis queue.
- Disk: Used for general purposes, as well as storing dashboards and Sguil components.

Please refer to our Architecture Page for detailed deployment scenarios.

3.3.9 Storage Node

Storage nodes increase search and retention capacity with regard to Elasticsearch. These nodes parse and index events, and provide the ability to scale horizontally as overall data intake increases.

- CPU: Used to parse incoming events and index incoming events. As consumption of data and events increases, more CPU will be required.
- RAM: Used for Logstash, Elasticsearch, and disk cache for Lucene. The amount of available RAM will directly impact search speeds and reliability.

- Disk: Used for storage of indexed metadata. A larger amount of storage allows for a longer retention period. It is typically recommended to retain no more than 30 days of hot ES indices.

Please refer to our Architecture Page for detailed deployment scenarios.

3.3.10 Forward Node (Sensor)

A forward node runs sensor components only, and forwards metadata to the master server. All PCAP stays local to the sensor, and is accessed through use of an agent.

- CPU: Used for analyzing and storing network traffic. As monitored bandwidth increases, a greater amount of CPU will be required. See below.
- RAM: Used for write cache and processing traffic.
- Disk: Used for storage of PCAP and metadata . A larger amount of storage allows for a longer retention period.

Please refer to our Architecture Page for detailed deployment scenarios.

3.3.11 Heavy Node (Sensor with ES components)

A heavy node Runs all the sensor components AND Elastic components locally. This dramatically increases the hardware requirements. In this case, all indexed metadata and PCAP are retained locally. When a search is performed through Kibana, the master server queries this node's Elasticsearch instance.

- CPU: Used to parse incoming events, index incoming events, search metadata . As monitored bandwidth (and the amount of overall data/events) increases, a greater amount of CPU will be required.
- RAM: Used for Logstash , Elasticsearch, and disk cache for Lucene. The amount of available RAM will directly impact search speeds and reliability.
- Disk: Used for storage of indexed metadata. A larger amount of storage allows for a longer retention period. It is typically recommended to retain no more than 30 days of hot ES indices.

Please refer to our Architecture Page for detailed deployment scenarios.

3.3.12 Sensor Hardware Considerations

The following hardware considerations apply to sensors. If you are using a heavy node or standalone deployment type, please note that it will dramatically increase CPU/RAM/Storage requirements.

Virtualization

We recommend dedicated physical hardware (especially if you're monitoring lots of traffic) to avoid competing for resources. Sensors can be virtualized, but you'll have to ensure that they are allocated sufficient resources.

CPU

Snort, Suricata, and Bro are very CPU intensive. The more traffic you are monitoring, the more CPU cores you'll need. A very rough ballpark estimate would be 200Mbps per Snort instance, Suricata worker, or Bro worker. So if you have a fully saturated 1Gbps link and are running Snort and Bro, then you'll want at least 5 Snort instances and 5 Bro workers, which means you'll need at least 10 CPU cores for Snort and Bro with additional CPU cores for netsniff-ng and/or other services.

RAM

RAM usage is highly dependent on several variables:

- the services that you enable
- the **kinds** of traffic you're monitoring
- the **actual amount of traffic** you're monitoring (example: you may be monitoring a 1Gbps link but it's only using 200Mbps most of the time)
- the amount of packet loss that is "acceptable" to your organization

For best performance, over provision RAM so that you can fully disable swap.

The following RAM estimates are a rough guideline and assume that you're going to be running Snort/Suricata, Bro, and netsniff-ng (full packet capture) and want to minimize/eliminate packet loss. Your mileage may vary!

If you just want to quickly evaluate Security Onion in a VM, the bare minimum amount of RAM needed is 8GB. More is obviously better!

If you're deploying Security Onion in production on a small network (50Mbps or less), you should plan on 8GB RAM or more. Again, more is obviously better!

If you're deploying Security Onion in production to a medium network (50Mbps - 500Mbps), you should plan on 16GB - 128GB RAM or more.

If you're deploying Security Onion in production to a large network (500Mbps - 1000Mbps), you should plan on 128GB - 256GB RAM or more.

If you're buying a new server, go ahead and max out the RAM (it's cheap!). As always, more is obviously better!

Storage

Sensors that have full packet capture enabled need LOTS of storage. For example, suppose you are monitoring a link that averages 50Mbps, here are some quick calculations: 50Mb/s = 6.25 MB/s = 375 MB/minute = 22,500 MB/hour = 540,000 MB/day. So you're going to need about 540GB for one day's worth of pcaps (multiply this by the number of days you want to keep on disk for investigative/forensic purposes). The more disk space you have, the more PCAP retention you'll have for doing investigations after the fact. Disk is cheap, get all you can!

We highly recommend using local storage whenever possible! SAN/iSCSI/FibreChannel/NFS can be made to work, but they increase complexity, points of failure and have serious performance implications. By using local storage, you keep everything self-contained and you don't have to worry about competing for resources. Local storage is most times the most cost efficient solution as well.

NIC

You'll need at least two wired network interfaces: one for management (preferably connected to a dedicated management network) and then one or more for sniffing (connected to tap or span). Make sure you get good quality network card, especially for sniffing. Most users report good experiences with Intel cards.

Packets

You need some way of getting packets into your sensor interface(s). If you're just evaluating Security Onion, you can replay pcaps. For a production deployment, you'll need a tap or SPAN/monitor port. Here are some inexpensive tap/span solutions:

Sheer Simplicity and Portability (USB-powered):
http://www.dual-comm.com/port-mirroring-LAN_switch.htm

Dirt Cheap and Versatile:
https://mikrotik.com/product/RB260GS

Netgear GS105E (requires Windows app for config):
https://www.netgear.com/support/product/GS105E.aspx

Netgear GS105E v2 (includes built-in web server for config):
https://www.netgear.com/support/product/GS105Ev2

low cost TAP that uses USB or Ethernet port:
http://www.midbittech.com

More exhaustive list of enterprise switches with port mirroring:
http://www.miarec.com/knowledge/switches-port-mirroring

Enterprise Tap Solutions:

- Net Optics / Ixia
- Arista Tap Aggregation Feature Set
- Gigamon
- cPacket
- Bigswitch Monitoring Fabric
- Garland Technologies Taps
- APCON
- Profitap

Further Reading

For large networks and/or deployments, please also see https://github.com/pevma/SEPTun.

3.4 HWE

HWE stands for Hardware Enablement and is Ubuntu's term for kernel and graphics driver support.

3.4.1 Security Onion ISO Image

In order to provide the latest hardware support, our Security Onion 16.04 ISO image includes the HWE stack, which is the kernel and graphics support from Ubuntu 18.04 (Linux kernel 4.15).

3.4.2 Building from Ubuntu

If you choose to use an Ubuntu image instead the Security Onion image and want the latest hardware support, you'll want to choose an image that includes the HWE stack. Some Ubuntu images (like Ubuntu Server), provide a boot menu option to enable the HWE stack.

3.4.3 More information

For more information, please see https://wiki.ubuntu.com/Kernel/LTSEnablementStack.

3.5 Download

To install Security Onion, you can either download our Security Onion ISO image **or** download a standard Ubuntu 16.04 ISO image and then add our Security Onion PPA and packages. **Please keep in mind that our PPA and packages are only compatible with Ubuntu 16.04**.

ALWAYS verify the checksum of ANY downloaded ISO image! Regardless of whether you're downloading our Security Onion ISO image or whether you're starting with an Ubuntu 16.04 ISO image, you should ALWAYS verify the downloaded ISO image.

- If downloading our Security Onion 16.04 ISO image, please verify using these instructions: https://github.com/Security-Onion-Solutions/security-onion/blob/master/Verify_ISO.md
- If downloading an Ubuntu 16.04 ISO image, please verify using these instructions: https://help.ubuntu.com/community/VerifyIsoHowto

3.6 VMWare

3.6.1 Overview

In this section, we'll cover creating a virtual machine (VM) for Security Onion 16.04 in VMWare Workstation Pro 12 (although this should be similar for most VMWare installations).

If you don't have VMWare Workstation, you could also use VMWare Player, found here:

http://www.vmware.com/products/player/playerpro-evaluation.html

3.6.2 Creating VM

Follow the steps below to install our Security Onion ISO image in VMware:

1. From VMWare, select File >> New Virtual Machine.
2. Select Typical installation >> Click `Next`.
3. Installer disc image file >> SO ISO file path >> Click `Next`.
4. Choose Linux, Ubuntu 64-Bit and click `Next`.
5. Specify virtual machine name and click `Next`.
6. Specify disk size (min 40GB), store as single file, click `Next`.
7. Customize hardware:

8. Memory – 8GB or more

9. Processors – 4 CPU cores or more

10. Network Adapter (NAT or Bridged – if you want to be able to access your Security Onion machine from other devices in the network, then choose Bridged, otherwise choose NAT to leave it behind the host) – in this tutorial, this will be the management interface.

11. Add >> Network Adapter (Bridged) - this will be the sniffing (monitor) interface.

12. Click `Close`.

13. Click `Finish`.

14. Power on the virtual machine.

3.6.3 Sniffing

- With the sniffing interface in "bridged" mode, you will be able to see all traffic to/from the host machine's physical NIC. If you would like to see **ALL** the traffic on your network, you will need a method of forwarding that traffic to the interface to which the virtual adapter is bridged. This can be achieved by switch port mirroring (SPAN), or through the use of a tap.

3.7 VirtualBox

In this section, we'll cover installing Security Onion on VirtualBox. You'll need a computer with at least 16GB of RAM (so that we can dedicate at least 8GB RAM to the VM) for best results. You can download a copy of VirtualBox for Windows, Mac OS X or Linux at http://www.virtualbox.org.

3.7.1 Creating VM

Launch VirtualBox and click the "New" button. First we'll provide a name for our virtual machine ("Security Onion" for example) and specify the type ("Linux") and version ("Ubuntu" or "Ubuntu 64 bit"), then click "Continue." We'll next define how much memory we want to make available to our virtual machine. You should dedicate at least 8GB RAM to the Security Onion VM.

Next we'll create a virtual hard drive. Specify "Create a virtual hard drive now" then click "Create" to choose the hard drive file type "VDI (VirtualBox Disk Image)" and "Continue." For storage, we have the options of "Dynamically allocated" or "Fixed size." For a client virtual machine, "Dynamically allocated" is the best choice as it will grow the hard disk up to whatever we define as the maximum size on an as needed basis until full, at which point Security Onion's disk cleanup routines will work to keep disk space available. If you happen to be running a dedicated sensor in a virtual machine, I would suggest using "Fixed size," which will allocate all of the disk space you define up front and save you some disk performance early on. Once you've settled on the storage allocation, click "Continue" and provide a name from your hard disk image file and specify the location where you want the disk file to be created if other than the default location. For disk size, you'll want enough disk capacity for retrieving/testing packet captures and downloading system updates. At a minimum for a client, I would designate at least 40GB. Click "Create" and your Security Onion VM will be created.

At this point, you can click "Settings" for your new virtual machine so we can get it configured. You might want to increase your display virtual memory to 128MB of RAM, but most other settings should be fine. We do, however, need to do a couple of things. First, mount the Security Onion 16.04 ISO file so our VM can boot from it to install Linux. Click the "Storage" icon, then under "Controller: IDE" select the "Empty" CD icon. To the right, you'll see "CD/DVD Drive" with "IDE Secondary" specified with another CD icon. Click the icon, then select "Choose a virtual CD/DVD disk file" and browse to where you downloaded the Security Onion 16.04 ISO file, select it then choose "Open." Next click "Network" then "Adapter 2." You'll need to click the checkbox to enable it then attach it to "Internal Network."

Under the "Advanced" options, set "Promiscuous Mode" to "Allow All." Click "Ok" and we are ready to install the operating system.

Hit the "Start" button with your new virtual machine selected and after a few seconds the boot menu will load.

3.7.2 VirtualBox Guest Additions

At the top of your virtual machine window you'll notice menu items for VirtualBox. Click on your virtual machine window, then on the menu click "Devices" then "Install Guest Additions..." Doing so will mount the VirtualBox guest additions CD on your virtual machine and it will open the folder showing you the files now available. Click on your terminal window and type "cd /media/VBOX" then press the Tab key key to autofill the folder name and press Enter to change to that directory. To install the Guest Additions type:

```
sudo ./VBoxLinuxAdditions.run
```

The installation will launch and after a few minutes you'll return to the command prompt when it's complete.

3.7.3 Snapshots

You'll notice two icons on the top right in VirtualBox Manager when you select your virtual machine: Details and Snapshots. Click "Snapshots" then click the camera icon and give your snapshot a name and description. Once we have a snapshot, we'll be able to make changes to the system and revert those changes back to the state we are preserving.

3.8 Booting Issues

- Did you verify the downloaded ISO image as described on the Installation page?
- Does your machine support 64-bit? (If you're trying to run a 64-bit VM, then your 64-bit processor must support virtualization and virtualization must be enabled in the BIOS.) If not, then you'll need to obtain a 64-bit machine to use our 64-bit ISO image (recommended).
- If you think your machine does support 64-bit, but you're still having problems with our 64-bit ISO image, try downloading the Ubuntu 16.04 64-bit ISO image and seeing if it runs. If it doesn't, then you should verify your 64-bit compatibility.
- If the ISO image boots, but it does not get past the splash screen, try pressing the "Esc" key to see the current status.
- If the ISO image boots, but the Live Desktop doesn't appear properly, it may be a video card/driver issue. Try changing `modeset` options:
  https://groups.google.com/d/topic/security-onion/FTEecyn4uJ4/discussion
  https://groups.google.com/d/topic/security-onion/UKE5-dqybQ4/discussion
  https://groups.google.com/d/topic/security-onion/51JZWXZfBho/discussion
- If all else fails but standard Ubuntu 16.04 installs normally, then you can always install our packages and Docker images on top of your Ubuntu 16.04 installation as described on the following pages:
  InstallingOnUbuntu
  ProductionDeployment

3.9 Installation

3.9.1 Language

Please note that we only support the English language at this time.

3.9.2 Choose your Installation Guide

We have different Installation Guides to cover various use cases. Please choose the appropriate Installation Guide for your use case.

Quickly Evaluating Security Onion

If you just want to **quickly evaluate** Security Onion, choose one of the following two options. If you're a first time user, we recommend the first option.

- To quickly evaluate using **our Security Onion ISO image**, please see the QuickISOImage section.

OR

- To quickly evaluate using **your preferred flavor of Ubuntu 16.04**, please see the InstallingOnUbuntu section.

Production Deployment

If you're deploying Security Onion in **production**, please see the Production Deployment section.

3.10 ISO Release Notes

- As always, make sure you verify the downloaded ISO image: https://github.com/Security-Onion-Solutions/security-onion/blob/master/Verify_ISO.md
- When the ISO boots, choose the default boot menu option.
- Once the live desktop appears, double-click the `Install SecurityOnion` icon.
- On the "Installation type" screen, you may want to select the `Use LVM` option, as this will automatically create a `/boot` partition at the beginning of the drive and will give you more flexibility later. Check to see if the installer allocates a large amount of space to `/home`. If this is the case, you may want to shrink `/home` to give more space to `/`.
- If prompted with an encrypt home folder or encrypt partition option, DO NOT enable this feature.
- If asked about automatic updates, DO NOT enable automatic updates.
- The Keyboard Layout screen may be larger than your screen resolution and so the Continue button may be off the screen to the right as shown at https://launchpadlibrarian.net/207213663/Screenshot_wilyi386deskmanual_2015-05-22_13%3A05%3A41.png. You can simply slide the window over until you see the Continue button. For more information, please see https://bugs.launchpad.net/ubuntu/+source/ubiquity/+bug/1458039.
- Once the installer completes, it should prompt to remove installation media and press ENTER. If instead it appears to hang, simply press the ENTER key to reboot. If that doesn't work, you may forcibly restart the machine.

- Once you've logged into your newly installed Security Onion, you'll notice that there is only a Setup icon on the desktop. Other icons will be created when you complete both phases of Setup. So you'll run Setup, configure your network interfaces, reboot, run Setup again to configure services, and then you'll see desktop icons for user interfaces.
- Setup now defaults to enabling the Elastic Stack. We recommend a BARE MINIMUM of 4 CPU cores and 8GB RAM.
- When choosing Evaluation Mode, the following services are enabled by default: Snort, Bro, netsniff-ng, pcap_agent, snort_agent, barnyard2.
- When choosing Production Mode, you then have the option of Best Practices or Custom. Best Practices asks a smaller number of questions and chooses the services that most folks want (Snort or Suricata, Bro, netsniff-ng, pcap_agent, snort_agent, barnyard2, salt). Custom gives you more control over your system but requires more in-depth knowledge about services and their functions.
- Once you've completed both phases of Setup, you should see new icons on your Desktop.
- For more information, please refer to the full Installation guide and other documentation.

3.11 Quick Evaluation using Security Onion ISO image

If you just want to quickly evaluate Security Onion using our ISO image:

1. Review the Hardware Requirements and Release Notes pages.
2. Download and verify our Security Onion ISO image.
3. Boot the ISO image and choose the default boot menu option.
4. Once the live desktop appears, double-click the `Install SecurityOnion` icon.
5. Follow the prompts in the installer. If prompted with an `encrypt home folder` or `encrypt partition` option, **DO NOT** enable this feature. If asked about automatic updates, **DO NOT** enable automatic updates.
6. Once the installer completes, rebooot into your new installation and login using the username and password you specified during installation.
7. Double-click the Setup icon. The Setup wizard will walk you through configuring `/etc/network/interfaces` and will then reboot.
8. After rebooting, log back in and start the Setup wizard again. It will detect that you have already configured `/etc/network/interfaces` and will walk you through the rest of the configuration. When prompted for `Evaluation Mode` or `Production Mode`, choose `Evaluation Mode`.
9. Once you've completed the Setup wizard, use the Desktop icons to login to Sguil, Squert, or Kibana.
10. Finally, review the Post Installation page.

3.12 Quick Evaluation on Ubuntu

If you want to quickly evaluate Security Onion on your preferred flavor of Ubuntu 16.04 64-bit (not using our ISO image), follow these steps:

- Review the Hardware Requirements page.
- Download the ISO image for your preferred flavor of Ubuntu 16.04 64-bit, verify the ISO image, and boot from it.

- Follow the prompts in the installer. If prompted to `encrypt home folder` or `encrypt partition`, **DO NOT** enable either of these. When asked about automatic updates, **DO NOT** enable automatic updates.
- Reboot into your new installation.
- Login using the username and password you specified during installation.
- Verify that you have Internet connectivity. If necessary, configure your proxy settings.
- Log back in (using `ssh -X` if you're installing on Ubuntu Server or a headless distro).
- Configure `MySQL` not to prompt for root password (Setup will generate a random password later):

```
echo "debconf debconf/frontend select noninteractive" | sudo debconf-set-
↪selections
```

- Clean apt list repository:

```
sudo rm -rf /var/lib/apt/lists/*
```

- Update package list:

```
sudo apt-get update
```

- Install software-properties-common if necessary:

```
sudo apt-get -y install software-properties-common
```

- Add the Security Onion stable repository:

```
sudo add-apt-repository -y ppa:securityonion/stable
```

- Update package list:

```
sudo apt-get update
```

- Install the securityonion-all metapackage:

```
sudo apt-get -y install securityonion-all syslog-ng-core
```

- Run the Setup wizard (if you're using Ubuntu Server with no GUI and are doing this over SSH, you will need to forward X for this to work):

```
sudo sosetup
```

- Follow the prompts in the Setup wizard.
- Once Setup is complete, review alerts and logs using Sguil, Squert, and Kibana.
- Review the PostInstallation page.

3.13 Production Deployment

If you're going to be deploying Security Onion in production, please use the following steps.

3.13.1 Hardware Requirements

First, check the Hardware Requirements page.

3.13.2 Download and Verify

Download and verify the Security Onion ISO image
OR
download and verify the ISO image for your preferred flavor of Ubuntu 16.04 64-bit.

3.13.3 Distributed Deployments

If deploying a distributed environment, you'll need to perform the remaining steps on the server, as well as all forward and storage nodes, but make sure you install and configure the master server first. For best performance, the master server should be dedicated to just being a server for the other nodes (the master server should have no sniffing interfaces of its own). Please note that forward and heavy nodes need to connect to the master server on ports `22` and `7736`. If you choose to enable salt for node management, nodes will need to be able to connect to the master server on ports `4505` and `4506`.

3.13.4 Install

1. Using the downloaded ISO, install the operating system. If the boot menu has a `Boot and Install with the HWE kernel` option, select this option. If prompted with an `encrypt home folder` option, DO NOT enable this feature. If asked about `automatic updates`, DO NOT enable automatic updates. If prompted to install any additional packages, leave `standard system utilities` selected and also select `OpenSSH Server` (openssh-server). Do NOT choose `MySQL` at this point. All other required dependencies will be installed automatically.

2. When asked about partitioning, there are a few things to keep in mind:

    - If you have more than 2TB of disk space, you will probably want to create a dedicated `/boot` partition at the beginning of the disk to ensure that you don't have any Grub booting issues. Choosing the `LVM` option should do this automatically.

    - Check to see if the installer allocates a large amount of space to `/home`. If this is the case, you may want to shrink `/home` to give more space to `/`.

    - The Sguil database on the server (doesn't exist on other node types) can grow fairly large (100GB or more for decent-size networks). It's stored at `/var/lib/mysql/`, so you may want to put `/var` on a dedicated partition or disk and assign a good amount of disk space to it. Also see the `DAYSTOKEEP` instructions on the Post-Installation page.

    - Forward, Heavy, and Standalone nodes store full packet captures at `/nsm/sensor_data/`, so you may want to put `/nsm` on a dedicated partition/disk and assign as much disk space as possible (1TB or more). For larger volumes you might also consider using XFS for the `/nsm` partition.

    - For Heavy, Standalone, and Storage Nodes, it is highly recommended to place `/nsm/elasticsearch` and `/nsm/logstash` on SSD or fast spinning disk in a RAID 10 configuration. See Hardware Requirements for more details.

3. When installation completes, reboot into your new installation and login with the credentials you specified during installation.

4. If you're running a VM, now would be a good time to snapshot it so you can revert later if you need to.

3.13.5 Update

1. If this box is going to be a node (forward, heavy, or storage), make sure that your master server and all other nodes in your deployment are fully updated with `sudo soup` before adding a new node.

2. Verify that you have Internet connectivity. If necessary, configure your proxy settings.

3. If you installed from the Security Onion 16.04 ISO image, run `sudo soup` and reboot if prompted, then skip to the Setup section below (if you get any errors relating to MySQL, please see the MySQL-Upgrade-Errors section). Otherwise, if you're installing on Ubuntu, continue to the next step.

4. Install all Ubuntu updates and reboot:

```
sudo apt update && sudo apt dist-upgrade && sudo reboot
```

5. Log back in and configure MySQL not to prompt for root password (Setup will generate a random password later):

```
echo "debconf debconf/frontend select noninteractive" | sudo debconf-set-
↪selections
```

6. Install software-properties-common if it's not already installed:

```
sudo apt -y install software-properties-common
```

7. Add the Security Onion stable repository:

```
sudo add-apt-repository -y ppa:securityonion/stable
```

8. Update:

```
sudo apt update
```

9. Install the `securityonion-all` metapackage (or one of the more focused metapackages). This could take 15 minutes or more depending on the speed of your CPU and Internet connection.

```
sudo apt -y install securityonion-all syslog-ng-core
```

10. OPTIONAL: If you want to use Salt to manage your deployment, also install `securityonion-onionsalt`. You can do this before or after Setup, but it's much easier if you do it before Setup.

```
sudo apt -y install securityonion-onionsalt
```

11. Update all packages:

```
sudo soup
```

3.13.6 Setup

1. Run the Setup wizard. If you are locally on the box, you can run the GUI by double-clicking the Desktop shortcut or running the following from a terminal:

```
sudo sosetup
```

Otherwise, if you are remote and logged in over ssh, you can run CLI-only Setup using `sosetup.conf`. For more information, please see `/usr/share/securityonion/sosetup.conf`.

2. The Setup wizard will walk you through configuring `/etc/network/interfaces` and will then reboot.

3. When prompted whether you would like to configure `/etc/network/interfaces` now, choose `Yes, configure /etc/network/interfaces!`.

4. If you have more than one network interface, you'll be asked to specify which one should be the management interface.

5. You'll then be asked to choose DHCP or static addressing for the management interface. It is highly recommended you choose static.

6. Choosing static, you'll be prompted to enter a static IP address for your management interface, the network's subnet mask, gateway IP address, DNS server IP addresses (separated by spaces), and your local domain.

7. You'll then be prompted to select any additional interfaces that will be used for sniffing/monitoring network traffic.

8. When prompted, choose `Yes, make changes!`.

9. If you need to adjust any network settings manually (e.g. MTU), you may edit `/etc/network/interfaces` before rebooting.

10. When ready to reboot, click `Yes, reboot!`.

11. After rebooting, log back in and start the Setup wizard again (GUI if local, `sosetup.conf` CLI if remote). It will detect that you have already configured `/etc/network/interfaces` and will walk you through the rest of the configuration.

12. Select `Production Mode`.

13. Select `New` or `Existing` (`New` if this is a master or standalone, and `Existing` for forward, heavy, and storage nodes).

- New (Master Server or Standalone)

    1. Provide a username and password for the analyst user.

    2. Select `Best Practices`.

    3. Choose your IDS ruleset.

    4. Choose your IDS engine (Snort or Suricata).

    5. Choose whether or not to enable sensor services. If this is going to be a standalone box with no other nodes connected, you can enable sensor services. Otherwise, if this going to be a distributed deployment with multiple nodes connected, we recommend disabling sensor services on this master server.

    6. Choose whether or not to use storage nodes for log storage. Please note that, if you choose to use storage nodes, then until a storage node is configured and Logstash has intialized on the storage node, you will not be able to review log data for configured forward nodes.

    7. Select `Yes` to proceed with your changes.

- Existing (Forward Node, Heavy Node, or Storage Node)

    1. Provide the hostname or IP address of the master server (some folks may want to specify the IP/hostname of the master server in `/etc/hosts` and use the specified hostname during setup – this may help in the event the master server IP changes.)

    2. Provide a username to SSH to the master for the node (should have already been created on the master and added to the `sudo` group). Please make sure that your server has been set up and you have network connectivity and no firewall rules that would block this traffic. Additionally, consider creating a separate SSH account on the master server for each node so that if a node is ever compromised, its individual account can be disabled without affecting the other nodes. If you need to create a user account on the Master, you can do something like the following (where `$nodeuser` is your specified user): `sudo adduser $nodeuser && sudo adduser $nodeuser sudo` The new account must have a full home directory. If you do not create it when you create the account, copy `/etc/skel` to `/home/$nodeuser` and do `chown -R $nodeuser:$nodeuser /home/$nodeuser`. This is needed

so the .ssh directory may be created to manage the connection. *NOTE: This user should be removed from the sudo group on the master server after setup.*

3. Select Node Type:
   - Forward Node
     * Select `Best Practices`.
     * Keep the default for PF-RING `min_num_slots`, unless you would like to change it.
     * Modify the selected sniffing interfaces if necessary – otherwise, continue.
     * Modify `HOME_NET` as desired.
     * Select `Yes` to proceed with your changes.
     * *Please note: If you chose to use one or more storage nodes with your master server, you will be able to receive IDS alerts and pull PCAPs from the forward node once setup completes, however, you will not be able to review other logs (i.e. Bro logs in Kibana) from the node until a storage node has been configured for the master server and Logstash on the storage node has initialized.*
   - Heavy Node
     * Select `Best Practices`.
     * Keep the default for PF-RING `min_num_slots`, unless you would like to change it.
     * Modify the selected sniffing interfaces if necessary – otherwise, continue.
     * Modify `HOME_NET` as desired.
     * Provide amount of disk space to be used for Elasticsearch to store logs (default is half of available disk space).
     * Select `Yes` to proceed with your changes.
   - Storage Node
     * Provide amount of disk space to be used for Elasticsearch to store logs (default is half of available disk space).
     * Select `Yes` to proceed with your changes.

4. Remove `$nodeuser` from the `sudo` group on the master server:
   ```
   sudo deluser $nodeuser sudo
   ```

Proceed to PostInstallation.

3.14 After Installation

3.14.1 Resolution

If you need to change the screen resolution of your Security Onion installation:

- click the `Applications` menu in the upper left corner
- click `System Tools`
- click `Setttings`
- click `Displays`

- select your display
- choose your desired resolution
- click `Apply`

If you prefer a CLI method for changing screen resolution, you can use *xrandr*. For a list of available screen resolutions, simply execute `xrandr`. To set the screen resolution (replace `W` and `H` with the actual Width and Height desired):

```
xrandr -s WxH
```

If you have limited screen resolution options and are in a virtualized environment, you may need to install the Virtual Tools for your virtualization solution. For example, this can happen if you're running VirtualBox and you can install the VirtualBox Extensions to get more resolution options.

3.14.2 Services

- Verify services are running:

```
sudo so-status
```

- If any services are not running, try starting them:

```
sudo so-start
```

- If you have problems with Snort/Suricata/Bro/PF-RING and have UEFI Secure Boot enabled, please see the Secure Boot section.
- Log into Sguil, Squert, and Kibana and verify that you have events in the interfaces. If you don't have any IDS alerts, you can try to generate one by typing the following at a terminal (only works if you have Internet access):

```
curl http://testmyids.com
```

3.14.3 Other

- Full-time analysts may want to connect using a separate Analyst VM.
- Setup defaults to only opening port 22 in the firewall. If you want to connect analyst VMs, Wazuh agents, or syslog devices, you can run the so-allow utility which will walk you through creating firewall rules to allow these devices to connect.
- Run the following to see how your sensor is coping with the load. You should check this on a daily basis to make sure your sensor is not dropping packets. Consider adding it to a cronjob and having it emailed to you (see the "configure email" link below).

```
sudo sostat | less
```

- Any IDS/NSM system needs to be tuned for the network it's monitoring. Please see the tuning section.
- Review and categorize alerts in Sguil or Squert on a daily basis. Categorizing alerts and tuning rules should be an iterative process with the goal being to categorize *all* events every day. You should only run the IDS rules you really care about.

3.14.4 Optional

- Exclude unnecessary traffic from your monitoring using BPF.
- Configure Ubuntu to use your preferred NTP server.
- Add new Sguil user accounts with the following:

```
sudo so-user-add
```

- On the server running the Sguil database, set the `DAYSTOKEEP` variable in `/etc/nsm/securityonion.conf` to however many days you want to keep in your archive. The default is 30, but you may need to adjust it based on your organization's detection/response policy and your available disk space.
- If you're monitoring IP address ranges other than private RFC1918 address space (192.168.0.0/16, 10.0.0.0/8, 172.16.0.0/12), you may need to update your sensor configuration with the correct IP ranges. Modern versions of Setup should automatically ask you for `HOME_NET` and configure these for you, but if you need to update it later, you would do the following. Sensor configuration files can be found in `/etc/nsm/$HOSTNAME-$INTERFACE/`. Modify either `snort.conf` or `suricata.yaml` (depending on which IDS engine you chose during `sosetup`) and update the `HOME_NET` variable. You may also want to consider updating the `EXTERNAL_NET` variable. Then update Bro's network configuration in `/opt/bro/etc/networks.cfg`. Finally, restart the sensor processes:

```
sudo so-sensor-restart
```

- Configure Email for alerting and reporting.
- Place `/etc` under version control. If your organization doesn't already have a standard version control tool, you can use bazaar, git, etckeeper:

```
sudo apt install etckeeper
```

- Need "remote desktop" access to your Security Onion sensor or server? One option is SSH X-Forwarding, but if you want something more rdp-like, you can install xrdp:

```
sudo apt install xrdp
```

3.14.5 Learn More

- Read more about the tools contained in Security Onion: Tools

3.15 Secure Boot

Modern Linux kernels prevent the loading of unsigned third party modules (like PF-RING) if UEFI Secure Boot is enabled. An example of this can be found here:
https://groups.google.com/d/msg/security-onion/r64yl58KGJ4/uRedkKTBCAAJ

To avoid issues like this, modern versions of our Setup wizard now default to AF-PACKET instead of PF-RING for both Bro and Suricata:
https://blog.securityonion.net/2019/02/new-setup-and-nsm-packages-now.html

However, if you choose Snort as your NIDS engine, it will fall back to PF-RING (at least until Snort 3.0 is released). If you have problems with Snort / PF-RING and Secure Boot, then you can either switch from Snort to Suricata OR if you need to keep Snort you can disable Secure Boot:

https://wiki.ubuntu.com/UEFI/SecureBoot/DKMS

http://askubuntu.com/questions/762254/why-do-i-get-required-key-not-available-when-install-3rd-party-kernel-modules

CHAPTER 4

Analyst Tools

In this section, we'll look at different analyst tools that can be used for slicing and dicing data coming from your network and endpoints.

4.1 Kibana

From https://www.elastic.co/products/kibana :

> Kibana lets you visualize your Elasticsearch data and navigate the Elastic Stack, so you can do anything from learning why you're getting paged at 2:00 a.m. to understanding the impact rain might have on your quarterly numbers.

4.1.1 Screenshot

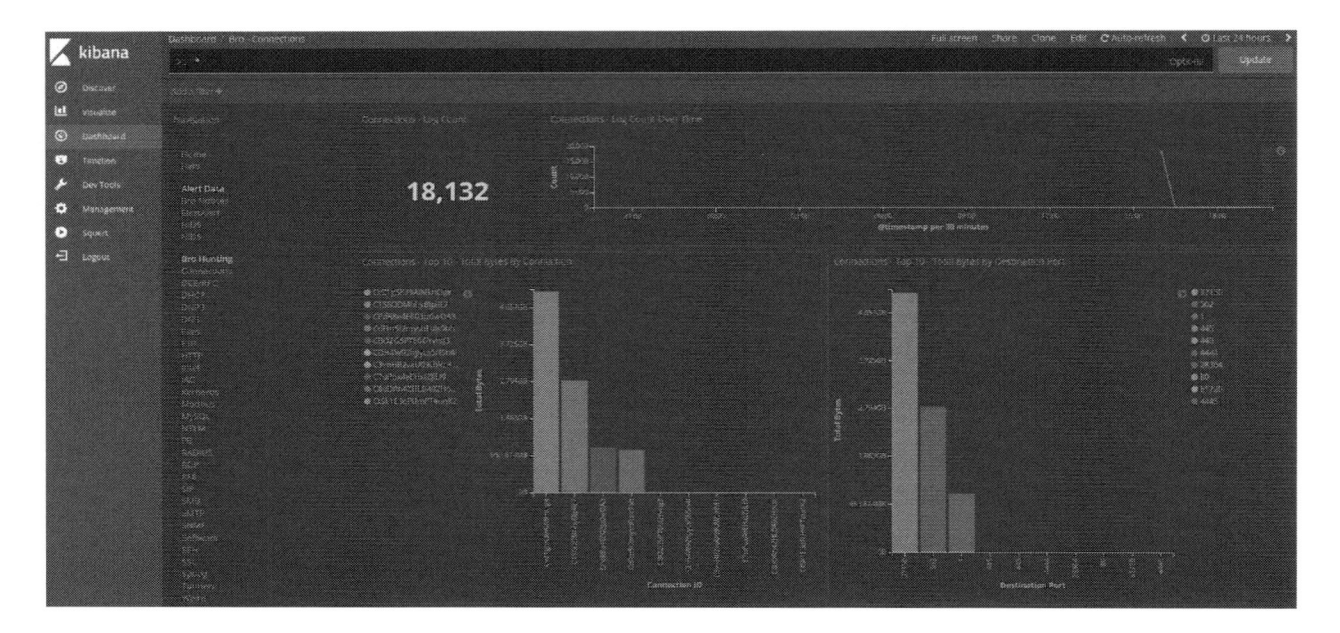

4.1.2 Authentication

If prompted for username and password, simply enter your normal Sguil/Squert/Kibana username and password.

4.1.3 Configuration

- Configuration files for Kibana can be found in `/etc/kibana/`.
- Other configuration options for Kibana can be found in `/etc/nsm/securityonion.conf`.
- Kibana logs can be found in `/var/log/kibana/`.

4.1.4 Pivoting

Kibana uses multiple hyperlinked fields to accelerate investigations and decision-making:

Transcript

When present, clicking the `_id` field allows an analyst to pivot to transcript via CapMe.

Indicator Dashboard

When present, clicking these fields allows an analyst to pivot to the Indicator dashboard, where a variety of information is presented relative to the term:value.

```
uid
source_ip
source_port
```

```
destination_ip
destination_port
```

4.1.5 Search Results

Search results in the dashboards and through Discover are limited to the first 10 results for a particular query. If you don't feel like this is adequate after narrowing your search, you can adjust the value for `discover:sampleSize` in Kibana by navigating to `Management -> Advanced Settings` and changing the value. It may be best to change this value incrementally to see how it affects performance.

4.1.6 Search Request Timeout

Sometimes searches can timeout in Kibana. To increase the timeout value to wait longer for results from Elasticsearch, we can adjust the value for `elasticsearch.requestTimeout` in `/etc/kibana/kibana.yml` and restart Kibana.

For example to increase the timeout from the default of 30 seconds to 90 seconds:

```
sudo vi /etc/kibana/kibana.yml
```

Add the following line:

```
elasticsearch.requestTimeout: 90000
```

Finally, restart Kibana:

```
sudo so-kibana-restart
```

4.1.7 Timestamps

By default, Kibana will display timestamps in the timezone of your local browser. If you would prefer timestamps in UTC, you can go to `Management -> Advanced Settings` and set `dateFormat:tz` to UTC.

4.1.8 Plugins

Please note that we do not officially support installing plugins. Do so at your own risk!

To add a plugin to Kibana, you can expose the plugins directory to the host filesystem and then copy your plugins to that directory. For example, to load the kbn_network plugin you can do something like the following.

Create a new directory in the host filesystem called `/nsm/kibana/plugins` to store plugins:

```
sudo mkdir -p /nsm/kibana/plugins
```

Download your desired plugin and decompress it to `/nsm/kibana/plugins`. For example:

```
wget -qO- https://github.com/dlumbrer/kbn_network/releases/download/6.5.X-1/network_
↪vis-6-5.tar.gz | sudo tar zxv -C /nsm/kibana/plugins
```

Kibana now requires `jquery.flot.log` when re-optimizing, so let's create that:

```
sudo touch /nsm/kibana/jquery.flot.log
```

Modify `KIBANA_OPTIONS` in `/etc/nsm/securityonion.conf` to mount `/nsm/kibana/plugins` directory and `jquery.flot.log` into the container:

```
sudo sed -i 's|^KIBANA_OPTIONS.*$|KIBANA_OPTIONS="--volume /nsm/kibana/plugins:/usr/
↪share/kibana/plugins:ro --volume /nsm/kibana/jquery.flot.log:/usr/share/kibana/src/
↪ui/public/flot-charts/jquery.flot.log"|g' /etc/nsm/securityonion.conf
```

Restart Kibana:

```
sudo so-kibana-restart
```

Monitor Kibana log file for errors:

```
tail -f /var/log/kibana/kibana.log
```

Kibana may take a few minutes to re-optimize. Once that's complete, you should be able to log into Kibana and test your new plugin.

4.2 CapME

CapME is a web interface that allows you to:

- view a pcap transcript rendered with tcpflow
- view a pcap transcript rendered with Bro (especially helpful for dealing with gzip encoding)
- download a pcap

4.2.1 Screenshot

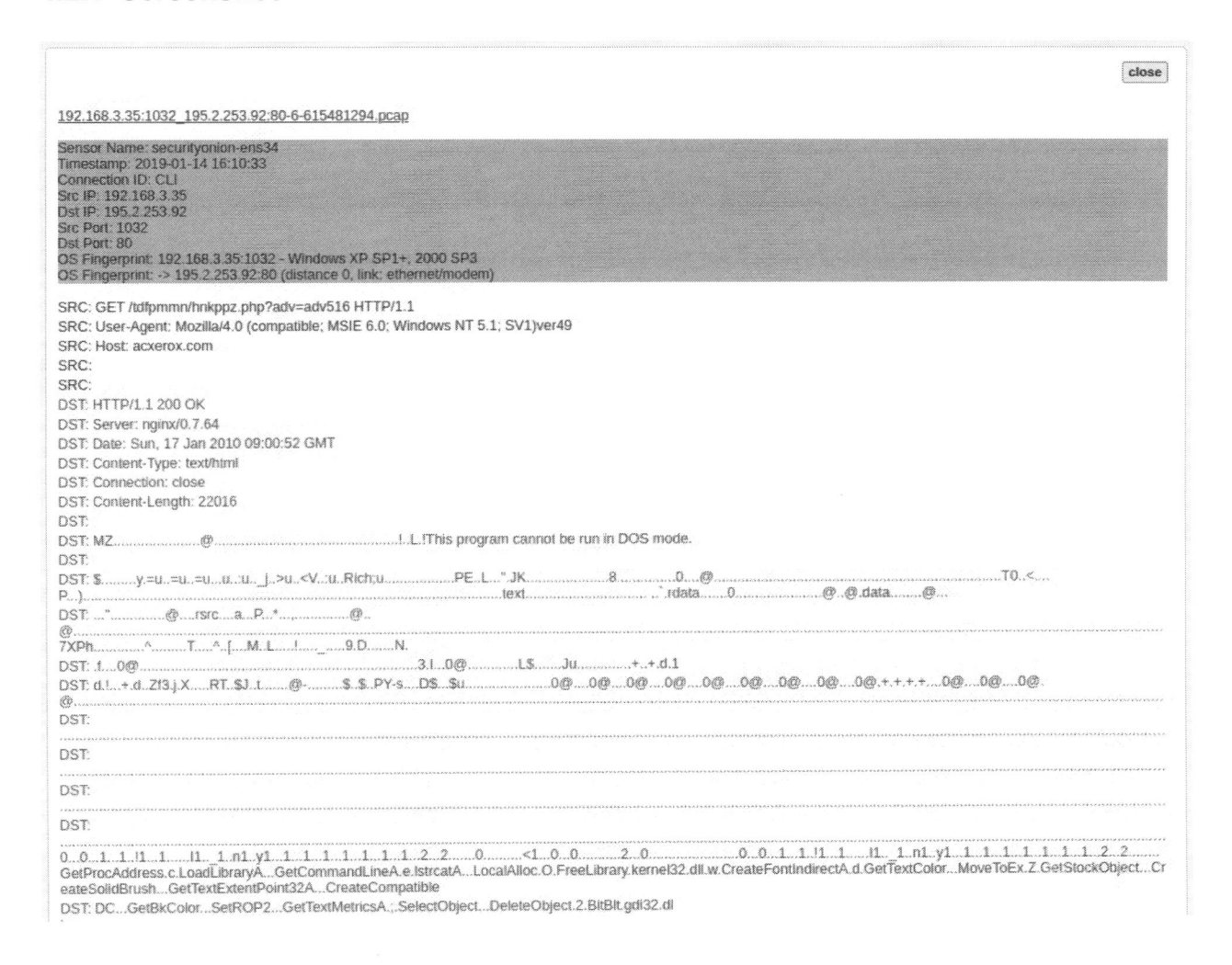

4.2.2 Accessing

You can pivot to CapME from a NIDS alert in Squert or from any log in Kibana that has timestamp, source IP, source port, destination IP, and destination port.

4.2.3 Authentication

If prompted for username and password, simply enter your normal Sguil/Squert/Kibana username and password.

4.3 CyberChef

From https://github.com/gchq/CyberChef :

> The Cyber Swiss Army Knife
>
> CyberChef is a simple, intuitive web app for carrying out all manner of "cyber" operations within a web browser. These operations include simple encoding like XOR or Base64, more complex encryption like

AES, DES and Blowfish, creating binary and hexdumps, compression and decompression of data, calculating hashes and checksums, IPv6 and X.509 parsing, changing character encodings, and much more.

The tool is designed to enable both technical and non-technical analysts to manipulate data in complex ways without having to deal with complex tools or algorithms. It was conceived, designed, built and incrementally improved by an analyst in their 10% innovation time over several years. Every effort has been made to structure the code in a readable and extendable format, however it should be noted that the analyst is not a professional developer.

4.3.1 Screenshot

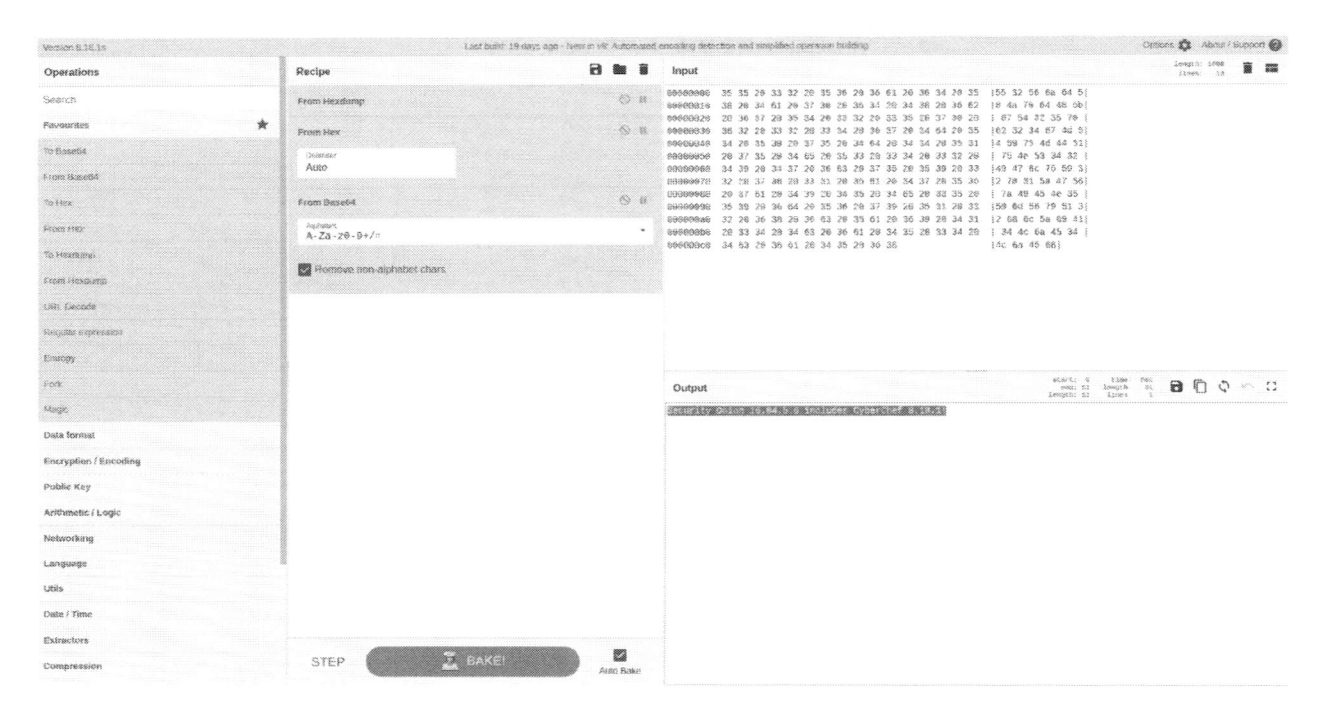

4.3.2 Accessing

To access CyberChef:

- go to the main web page of your Security Onion master server and click the CyberChef hyperlink

  OR

- go directly to the following URL (replacing `SecurityOnion` with the actual hostname or IP address of your Security Onion master server): https://SecurityOnion/cyberchef/cyberchef.htm

4.4 Squert

From http://www.squertproject.org/:

> Squert is a web application that is used to query and view event data stored in a Sguil database (typically IDS alert data). Squert is a visual tool that attempts to provide additional context to events through the use of metadata, time series representations and weighted and logically grouped result sets. The hope is that these views will prompt questions that otherwise may not have been asked.

Squert was originally developed by Paul Halliday:
http://www.squertproject.org/

Security Onion maintains its own fork of Squert:
https://blog.securityonion.net/2016/09/squert-development.html

Squert is a PHP web interface to the Sguil database and works best with Chromium/Chrome browsers.

4.4.1 Screenshot

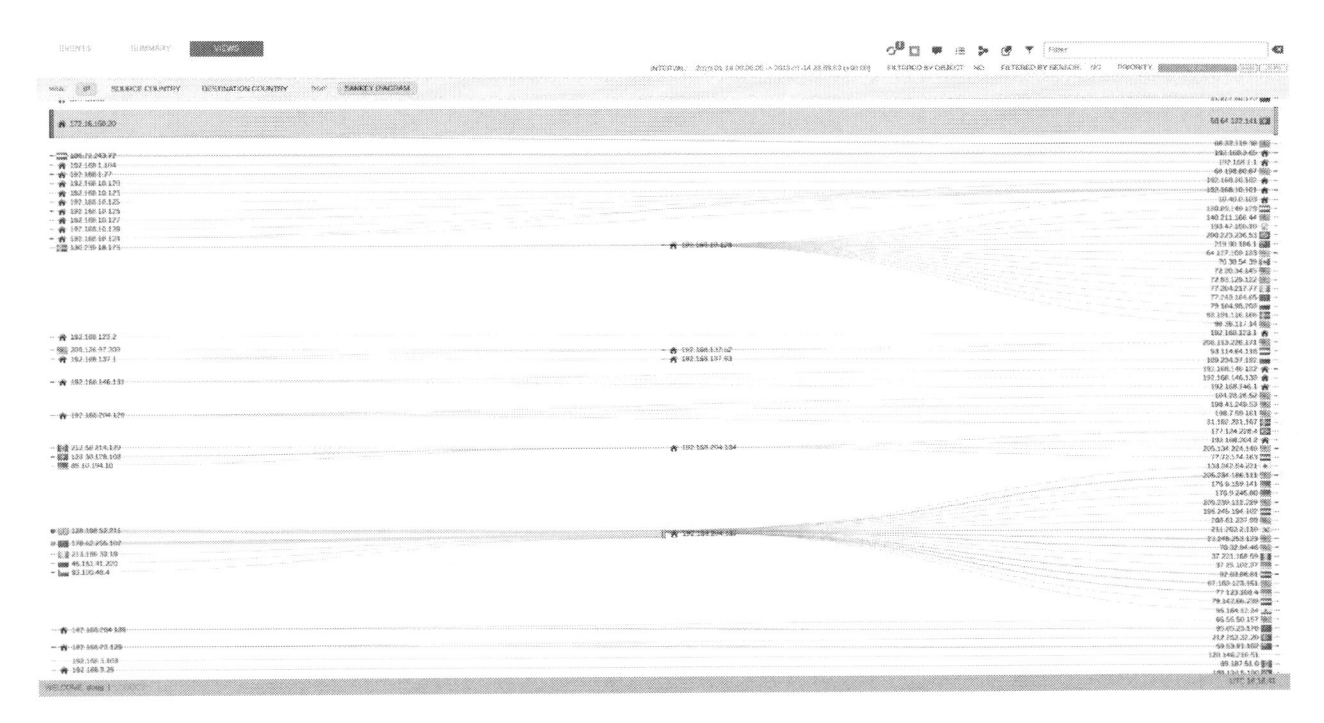

4.4.2 Authentication

If prompted for username and password, simply enter your normal Sguil/Squert/Kibana username and password.

4.4.3 Data Types

Squert gives you access to the following data types:

- NIDS alerts
- HIDS alerts

4.4.4 Time Interval

The default view shows alerts from today. To show older alerts, click `INTERVAL`, then click the 2 right arrows, set your custom date, and click Squert's refresh button (two circular arrows).

4.4.5 Time Zone

- click the time interval (labeled `INTERVAL`)
- on the right side, click the two arrows pointing right
- de-select `UTC`
- set your timezone offset (labeled `TZ OFFSET`)
- click the `save TZ` button

4.4.6 Timeplot

The timeplot at the top of the `EVENTS` page, represents events as they occur each day.
In summary, the timeplot:

- plots the raw number of events on a per minute basis.
- uses the X-axis as the hour of the day and the Y-axis is the number of events minute.
- treats each region equivalent to one hour.
- plots and underlines the number of events in each region for that hour.

4.4.7 Toggle Options

`queue only`
Default is `on`.

This option refers to only showing events that are of a status of 0, or uncategorized and still residing in the active queue. If you would like to see all events, change it to `off`.

`grouping`
Default is `on`.

This option refers to the grouping of the same type of event within a particular timeframe. If you would like to see the events as un-grouped, change this option to `off`.

4.4.8 Alerts

The alert pane consists of several columns, explained below:

`QUEUE` - refers to the number of grouped events in the queue
`SC` - number of distinct source IPs for the given alert
`DC` - number of distinct destination IPs for the given alert
`ACTIVITY` - number of events for a given alert on a per hour basis
`LAST EVENT` - time event last occurred
`SIGNATURE` - event IDS signature

`ID` - event signature ID
`PROTO` - protocol relative/recognized within/in regard to event
`% TOTAL` - percentage of event grouping vs. entire event count

4.4.9 Pivoting to Full Packet Capture

Squert can pivot to CapMe for full packet capture. To do this, drill into an event and click on the Event ID.

4.4.10 Pivoting to Kibana

Squert can pivot to Kibana to query Bro logs, Wazuh logs, syslog, etc. To do this, click an IP address, port, or signature, and then click `Kibana`.

4.4.11 Adding your own pivots

You can also add your own pivots as follows:

- In the upper right corner of Squert, click the Filters button.
- Set the type to URL.
- Click the + button.
- Click your New entry.
- Fill out the alias, name, notes, and URL fields as applicable.
- Click the Update button.
- Close the Filters and URLs window.
- To test, drill into an event and click an IP address. A context menu will appear and display your new link. Click the new link and verify that it opens a new browser tab going to the site you specified and passing the IP address that you clicked on.

4.4.12 Prepared Statements

Squert uses prepared statements. If you start seeing `Prepared statement needs to be re-prepared` in `/var/log/apache2/error.log`, please see the MySQLTuning#table_definition_cache section.

4.5 Sguil

From http://sguil.net:

> Sguil (pronounced sgweel) is built by network security analysts for network security analysts. Sguil's main component is an intuitive GUI that provides access to realtime events, session data, and raw packet captures. Sguil facilitates the practice of Network Security Monitoring and event driven analysis.

- Developed by Bamm Visscher:
  http://sguil.net
  http://nsmwiki.org/Sguil
  http://nsmwiki.org/Sguil_Client

Security Onion Documentation, Release 16.04.6.1

- tcl/tk (not web-based)
- Single central MySQL database

4.5.1 Screenshot

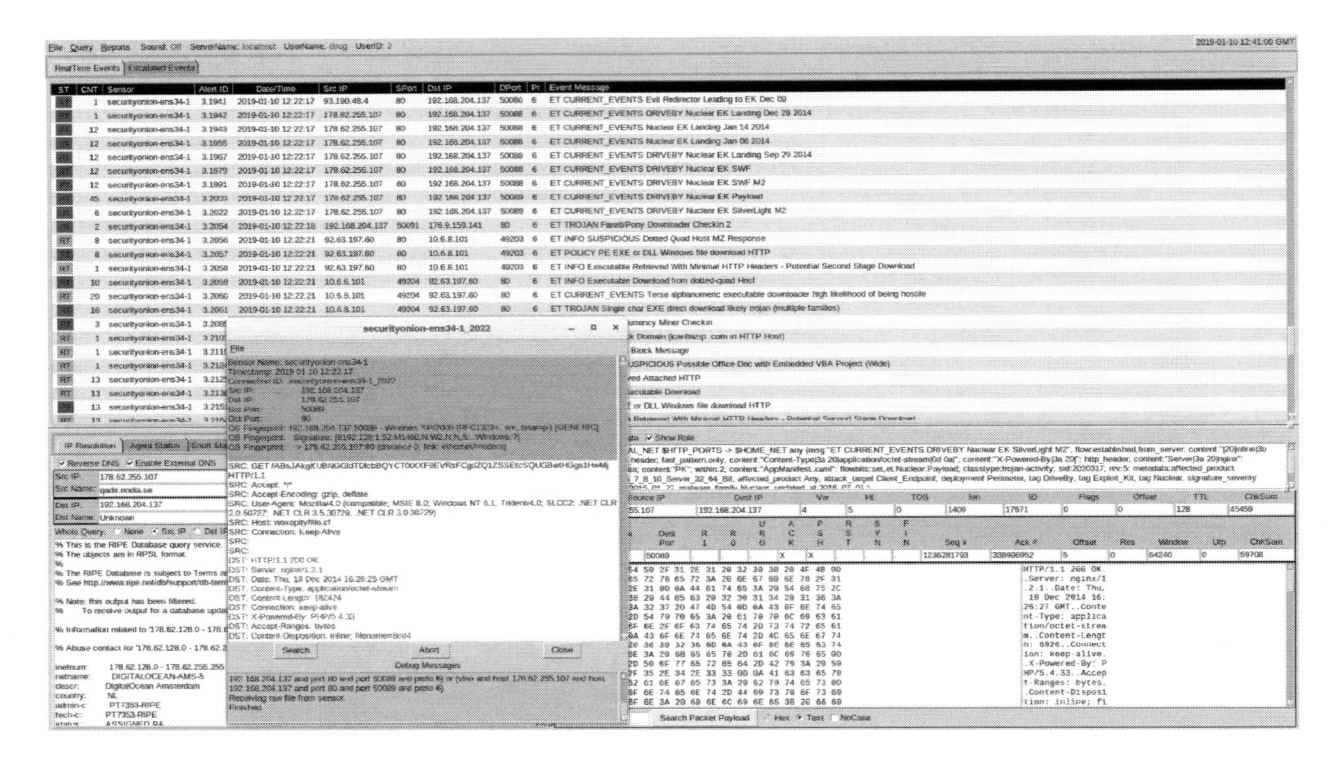

4.5.2 Authentication

For login information, please see the Passwords section.

For information on ways to connect to Sguil/sguild, please see the ConnectingtoSguil section.

4.5.3 Data Types

- NIDS alerts from Snort/Suricata (if snort_agent is enabled)
- HIDS alerts from OSSEC (if ossec_agent is enabled)

4.5.4 Pivot

- pivot to transcript/Wireshark/NetworkMiner by right-clicking the Alert ID.
- automatically pivot to ASCII transcript by middle-clicking the Alert ID.
- pivot to Kibana by right-clicking an IP address and choosing `Kibana IP Lookup`.

4.5.5 Agents

Sguil can only utilize `1024` sockets for receiving communication from various sensor agents (such as ossec_agent, pcap_agent, and snort_agent). Due to this restriction, you will want to keep in mind the number of sensors and sniffing interfaces you have connected to the master server/accessed by Sguil.

For more information, please see https://groups.google.com/d/msg/security-onion/DJ5NTLEu5MY/-tDQi_1eDQAJ.

4.5.6 Management

- It is important to ensure events displayed in Sguil are regularly classified, or else it could cause problems with the Sguil database. Consider creating an autocat rule to assist with this.
- Configure Sguil alert email notification(s)
- Configure retention for Sguil alerts

4.5.7 Customize

- resize columns by right-clicking on the column heading in the Sguil client.
- change fonts by clicking `File -> Change Font` from within the Sguil client.
- Sguil client settings are stored in `/etc/sguil/sguil.conf`:
- You can enable "Show Rule", "Show Packet Data", and "Display Detail" (respectively) by setting the following (also see https://groups.google.com/d/topic/security-onion/MJaAlxgpMvU/discussion):
  ```
  set SHOWRULE 1
  set PACKETINFO 1
  set DISPLAY_GENERIC 1
  ```
- You can separate realtime alerts into separate panes, based on severity level, by editing `/etc/sguil/sguil.conf` as follows:

```
#Number of RealTime Event Panes
#set RTPANES 1
set RTPANES 3

# Specify which priority events go into what pane
# According to the latest classification.config from snort,
# there are only 4 priorities. The sguil spp_portscan mod
# uses a priority of 5.
#set RTPANE_PRIORITY(0) "1 2 3 4 5"
set RTPANE_PRIORITY(0) "1"
set RTPANE_PRIORITY(1) "2 3"
set RTPANE_PRIORITY(2) "4 5"
```

4.5.8 DNS Lookups

Previously, when pivoting to transcript, the Sguil server would perform DNS lookups on the source and destination IP addresses. That default has since been changed to increase performance and avoid unnecessary information leakage. If you would like to re-enable DNS lookups, you can set the following in `/etc/nsm/securityonion/sguild.conf`:

```
set TRANSCRIPT_DNS_LOOKUP 1
```

4.6 NetworkMiner

From https://www.netresec.com/?page=networkminer:

> NetworkMiner is an open source Network Forensic Analysis Tool (NFAT) for Windows (but also works in Linux / Mac OS X / FreeBSD). NetworkMiner can be used as a passive network sniffer/packet capturing tool in order to detect operating systems, sessions, hostnames, open ports etc. without putting any traffic on the network. NetworkMiner can also parse PCAP files for off-line analysis and to regenerate/reassemble transmitted files and certificates from PCAP files.
>
> NetworkMiner makes it easy to perform advanced Network Traffic Analysis (NTA) by providing extracted artifacts in an intuitive user interface. The way data is presented not only makes the analysis simpler, it also saves valuable time for the analyst or forensic investigator.

4.6.1 Screenshot

4.6.2 Usage

You can launch NetworkMiner from the Applications menu and then open a pcap.

Alternatively, if you're using the Sguil client, you can pivot directly from an event in Sguil and send the pcap directly to NetworkMiner.

4.6.3 More Information

For more information about NetworkMiner, please see https://www.netresec.com/?page=networkminer.

4.7 Wireshark

From https://www.wireshark.org/:

> Wireshark is the world's foremost and widely-used network protocol analyzer. It lets you see what's happening on your network at a microscopic level and is the de facto (and often de jure) standard across many commercial and non-profit enterprises, government agencies, and educational institutions. Wireshark development thrives thanks to the volunteer contributions of networking experts around the globe and is the continuation of a project started by Gerald Combs in 1998.

4.7.1 Screenshot

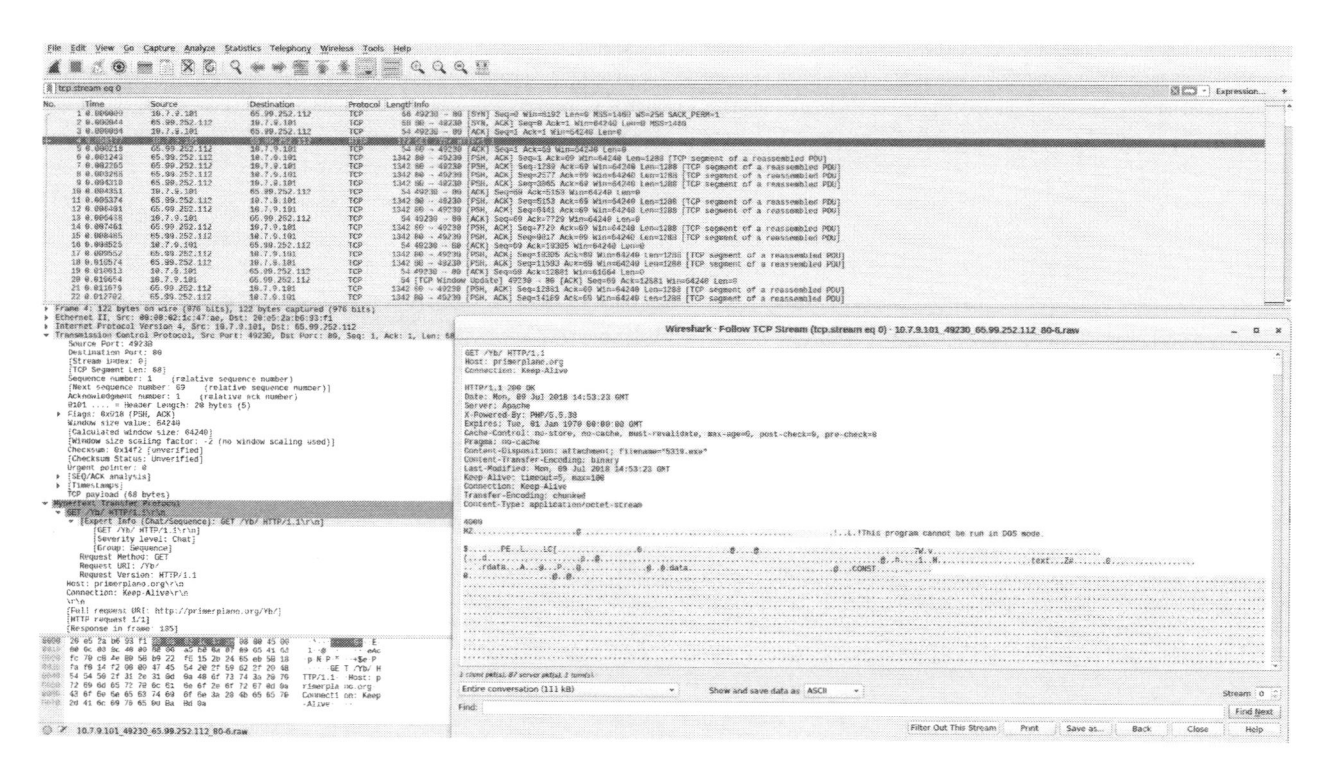

4.7.2 Usage

You can launch Wireshark from the Applications menu and then open a pcap.

Alternatively, if you're using the Sguil client, you can pivot directly from an event in Sguil and send the pcap directly to Wireshark.

4.7.3 More Information

For more information about Wireshark, please see https://www.wireshark.org/.

CHAPTER 5

Network Visibility

This section covers the various processes that Security Onion uses to analyze and log network traffic.

5.1 NIDS

NIDS stands for Network Intrusion Detection System. It is a means of monitoring network traffic, looking for specific activity, and generating alerts.

5.1.1 Usage

Security Onion can run either Snort or Suricata as its Network Intrusion Detection System (NIDS). When you run Setup and choose Evaluation Mode, it will automatically default to Snort. If you choose Production Mode, you will be asked to choose whether you want to run Snort or Suricata.

5.1.2 Performance

In Security Onion, we compile both Snort and Suricata to support PF-RING for higher performance. Suricata also supports AF-PACKET as an alternative. Modern versions of Setup default to running Suricata in AF-PACKET mode.

5.1.3 Analysis

You can analyze NIDS alerts from Snort/Suricata via:

- Squert
- Kibana
- Sguil

5.1.4 Switching from Snort to Suricata

Please note that, if you're running the Snort Talos ruleset, Snort Shared Object rules will not load in Suricata. Most folks who choose the Suricata engine choose to run the Emerging Threats ruleset.

```
sudo so-sensor-stop
sudo sed -i 's|ENGINE=snort|ENGINE=suricata|g' /etc/nsm/securityonion.conf
sudo rule-update
sudo so-sensor-start
```

5.1.5 Switching from Suricata to Snort

```
sudo so-sensor-stop
sudo sed -i 's|ENGINE=suricata|ENGINE=snort|g' /etc/nsm/securityonion.conf
sudo rule-update
sudo so-sensor-start
```

5.1.6 NIPS

Security Onion is designed to be passive and so Snort and Suricata run in NIDS mode rather than NIPS (inline) mode. Running in NIPS mode would require manual configuration and we do not recommend or support it.

5.1.7 More Information

- For more information about Snort, please see the Snort section.
- For more information about Suricata, please see the Suricata section.

5.2 Snort

Snort is a Network Intrusion Detection System (NIDS). It sniffs network traffic and generates IDS alerts.

5.2.1 Performance

In Security Onion, we compile Snort with PF-RING to allow you to spin up multiple instances to handle more traffic.

5.2.2 Configuration

You can configure Snort via `/etc/nsm/HOSTNAME-INTERFACE/snort.conf` (where HOSTNAME is your actual hostname and INTERFACE is your actual sniffing interface).

If you would like to configure/manage IDS rules, please see the Rules and ManagingAlerts sections.

5.2.3 Logging

If you need to troubleshoot Snort, check the Snort log file(s) `/var/log/nsm/HOSTNAME-INTERFACE/snortu-X.log` (where HOSTNAME is your actual hostname, INTERFACE is your actual sniffing interface, and X represents the number of PF-RING instances).

5.2.4 More Information

For more information about Snort, please see https://snort.org.

5.3 Suricata

From https://suricata-ids.org:

> Suricata is a free and open source, mature, fast and robust network threat detection engine. Suricata inspects the network traffic using a powerful and extensive rules and signature language, and has powerful Lua scripting support for detection of complex threats.

5.3.1 Performance

We compile Suricata to support both PF-RING and AF-PACKET to allow you to spin up multiple workers to handle more traffic. Modern versions of Setup default to AF-PACKET.

For high traffic levels, you may want to pin Suricata to specific CPU cores using the affinity settings in `suricata.yaml`:

https://suricata.readthedocs.io/en/latest/configuration/suricata-yaml.html#threading

5.3.2 Configuration

You can configure Suricata via `/etc/nsm/HOSTNAME-INTERFACE/suricata.yaml` (where `HOSTNAME` is your actual hostname and `INTERFACE` is your actual sniffing interface).

If you would like to configure/manage IDS rules, please see the Rules and ManagingAlerts sections.

5.3.3 Logging

If you need to troubleshoot Suricata, check `/var/log/nsm/HOSTNAME-INTERFACE/suricata.log` (where `HOSTNAME` is your actual hostname and `INTERFACE` is your actual sniffing interface).

5.3.4 Stats

For detailed Suricata statistics, check `/nsm/sensor_data/HOSTNAME-INTERFACE/stats.log` (where `HOSTNAME` is your actual hostname and `INTERFACE` is your actual sniffing interface).

If you want `stats.log` to show per-thread stats (for example, to verify that load balancing is working properly), you can set `threads: yes` under the `outputs: - stats:` section in `suricata.yaml` and then restart Suricata.

5.3.5 More Information

For more information about Suricata, please see https://suricata-ids.org.

5.4 Bro

From https://www.zeek.org/:

> Zeek is a powerful network analysis framework that is much different from the typical IDS you may know. (Zeek is the new name for the long-established Bro system. Note that parts of the system retain the "Bro" name, and it also often appears in the documentation and distributions.)

5.4.1 Logs

Bro logs are stored in `/nsm/bro/logs`. They are consumed by syslog-ng, parsed and augmented by Logstash, stored in Elasticsearch, and viewable in Kibana.

JSON

By default, we configure Bro to output in JSON for higher performance and better parsing. We recommend that most folks leave Bro configured for JSON output. If you need to parse those JSON logs from the command line, you can use jq.

TSV

If you really need the traditional Bro TSV (Tab Separated Values) format, you can disable JSON:

```
sudo sed -i 's|@load json-logs|#@load json-logs|g' /opt/bro/share/bro/site/local.bro
```

and then restart Bro:

```
sudo so-bro-restart
```

Bro monitors your network traffic and creates logs, such as:

conn.log

- TCP/UDP/ICMP connections
- For more information, see:

https://docs.zeek.org/en/latest/scripts/base/protocols/conn/main.bro.html#type-Conn::Info

dns.log

- DNS activity
- For more information ,see:

https://docs.zeek.org/en/latest/scripts/base/protocols/dns/main.bro.html#type-DNS::Info

ftp.log

- FTP activity
- For more information, see:

https://docs.zeek.org/en/latest/scripts/base/protocols/ftp/info.bro.html#type-FTP::Info

http.log

- HTTP requests and replies
- For more information, see:

https://docs.zeek.org/en/latest/scripts/base/protocols/http/main.bro.html#type-HTTP::Info

ssl.log

- SSL/TLS handshake info
- For more information, see:

https://docs.zeek.org/en/latest/scripts/base/protocols/ssl/main.bro.html#type-SSL::Info

notice.log

- Bro notices
- For more information, see:

https://docs.zeek.org/en/latest/scripts/base/frameworks/notice/main.bro.html#type-Notice::Info

...and others, which can be researched here:
https://docs.zeek.org/en/latest/script-reference/log-files.html

As you can see, Bro log data can provide a wealth of information to the analyst, all easily accessible through Kibana.

5.4.2 Email

`/opt/bro/etc/broctl.cfg`

- To configure email notifications, please see the email section.

5.4.3 Syslog

`/etc/syslog-ng/syslog-ng.conf`

- To forward Bro logs to an external syslog collector, please see the syslog-output section.

5.4.4 Intel

- You can add your own Intel to /opt/bro/share/bro/intel/intel.dat.
    - When editing /opt/bro/share/intel/intel.dat, ensure there are no leading/trailing spaces or lines, and that only (single) tabs are used as field delimiters.
    - If you experience an error, or do not notice /nsm/bro/logs/current/intel.log being generated, try having a look in /nsm/bro/logs/current/reporter.log for clues.
    - You may also want to restart Bro after making changes, by running the following command: sudo so-bro-restart.
- For more information, please see:

    https://www.bro.org/sphinx-git/frameworks/intel.html
    http://blog.bro.org/2014/01/intelligence-data-and-bro_4980.html
    https://github.com/weslambert/securityonion-misp

- To install and configure an Alienvault OTX Connector, please see the Alienvault-OTX section.

5.4.5 Bro * n

/opt/bro/etc/node.cfg

We compile Bro to support both PF-RING and AF-PACKET so that you can spin up multiple Bro workers to handle more traffic. Modern versions of Setup now default to AF-PACKET.

If you are monitoring high traffic levels, you may need to use the pin_cpus setting. For more information, please see https://docs.zeek.org/en/stable/configuration/#using-pf-ring.

5.4.6 Custom Scripts

/opt/bro/share/bro/site/local.bro

- You can add custom scripts in /opt/bro/share/bro/policy/ and then reference the scripts in /opt/bro/share/bro/site/local.bro.

Below is an example how to do so:

- Create a new directory under /opt/bro/share/bro/policy/. sudo mkdir /opt/bro/share/bro/policy/custom-scripts
- Add your custom script(s) and __load__.bro to this directory.
- Modify __load__.bro to reference the scripts in the custom-scripts directory:

    @load ./script1.bro
    @load ./script2.bro

- Edit /opt/bro/share/bro/site/local.bro so that it will load the new scripts in /opt/bro/share/bro/policy/custom-scripts, by adding @load custom-scripts at the bottom of the file and saving the file.

- Restart Bro. `sudo so-bro-restart`
- Check `/nsm/bro/logs/current/loaded_scripts.log` to see if your custom script(s) has/have been loaded.
- Check `/nsm/bro/logs/current/reporter.log` for clues if your custom script(s) is/are not working as desired.

To check and see if a Bro script has fired a Notice, go to Kibana and check our `Bro Notices` dashboard. Alternatively, you can check for entries in `/nsm/bro/logs/current/notice.log`.

PLEASE NOTE: In a distributed deployment, all custom scripts created under `/opt/bro/share/bro/policy/` on a master server will be replicated to sensors via Salt, however, they will not be enabled, as `/opt/bro/share/bro/site/local.bro` is not replicated. Therefore, you will either need to manually add a reference to the scripts in `/opt/bro/share/bro/site/local.bro`, or add additional configuration in `/opt/onionsalt/salt/sensor/init.sls` for Salt to replicate this information.

- Make a symlink to `local.bro`:

`sudo ln -s /opt/bro/share/bro/site/local.bro /opt/onionsalt/salt/sensor/bro/local.bro`

Then add the following to `/opt/onionsalt/salt/sensor/init.sls`:

```
localbro:
file.managed:
  - name: /opt/bro/share/bro/site/local.bro
  - source: salt://sensor/bro/local.bro
```

Then test, using:

`sudo salt "SENSOR" state.highstate`

You can then have Bro automatically restart upon a detected change in `local.bro` from the master by modifying `init.sls` similar to the following:

```
restart-bro
cmd.wait:
  - name: /usr/sbin/nsm_sensor_ps-restart --only-bro
  - cwd: /
  - watch:
    - file: /opt/bro/share/bro/site/local.bro
```

5.4.7 Top for Bro

- To view "top-like" information for Bro logs, consider using BroTop.
- "Brotop lets you stream your bro logs to the browser for easy debugging and a real-time glimpse into whats being processed".
- Written in Go, BroTop is a dependency-free binary that can be downloaded and run immediately, auto-detecting Bro log paths.
- For more information about BroTop, please see https://github.com/criticalstack/brotop.

5.4.8 /nsm/bro/spool/tmp

If you find that /nsm/bro/spool/tmp contains lots of old crash files, you can clean them up with:

```
sudo su sguil -c '/opt/bro/bin/broctl cleanup --all'
```

5.4.9 More Information

For more information about Bro, please see https://www.zeek.org/.

5.5 netsniff-ng

From http://netsniff-ng.org:

> netsniff-ng is a free Linux networking toolkit, a Swiss army knife for your daily Linux network plumbing if you will. Its gain of performance is reached by zero-copy mechanisms, so that on packet reception and transmission the kernel does not need to copy packets from kernel space to user space and vice versa.

5.5.1 Usage

Security Onion uses netsniff-ng to collect full packet capture in the form of pcap files.

5.5.2 Output

netsniff-ng writes full packet capture in the form of pcap files to:
`/nsm/sensor_data/HOSTNAME-INTERFACE/dailylogs/YYYY-MM-DD/`
where:

- `HOSTNAME` is your actual hostname
- `INTERFACE` is your actual sniffing interface
- `YYYY-MM-DD` is the year, month, and date the pcap was recorded

5.5.3 Analysis

Besides accessing the pcaps in the directory shown above, you can also pivot to full packet capture from Sguil and CapMe.

5.5.4 Troubleshooting

Check the netsniff-ng.log file in `/var/log/nsm/HOSTNAME-INTERFACE/netsniff-ng.log` (where `HOSTNAME` is your actual hostname and `INTERFACE` is your actual sniffing interface).

5.5.5 Tuning

If sostat report packet loss in netsniff-ng, you may want to consider one or more of the following options in `/etc/nsm/HOSTNAME-INTERFACE/sensor.conf`:

- increase `PCAP_RING_SIZE`
- set `PCAP_OPTIONS` to `--mmap` to enable memory-mapped IO

Please note that both of these options will cause netsniff-ng to consume more RAM.

5.5.6 Reducing Storage

Full packet capture obviously requires lots of disk space. Trimming your pcaps can allow you to store pcap for longer periods of time. For more information, please see the Trimming PCAPs section.

5.5.7 More Information

For more information about netsniff-ng, please see http://netsniff-ng.org/.

CHAPTER 6

Host Visibility

In this section, we'll review different ways that Security Onion can collect logs from endpoints.

6.1 Beats

We can use Elastic Beats to facilitate the shipping of endpoint logs to Security Onion's Elastic Stack. Currently, testing has only been performed with Filebeat (multiple log types) and Winlogbeat (Windows Event logs).

6.1.1 Download

To download a Beat, choose the correct version from the Past Releases page:

https://www.elastic.co/downloads/past-releases

PLEASE NOTE: Choosing a Beat version that is greater than the Elastic version is not supported and may not work as expected.

To check your current version of Elastic, navigate to the Management section in Kibana. The version should be displayed on the screen.

Alternatively, run the following command from your master server:

```
curl localhost:9200
```

6.1.2 Installation

To install a Beat, follow the instructions provided for the respective Beat, with the exception of loading the index template, as Security Onion uses its own template file to manage Beats fields.

Filebeat

https://www.elastic.co/guide/en/beats/filebeat/current/filebeat-installation.html

Winlogbeat

https://www.elastic.co/guide/en/beats/winlogbeat/current/winlogbeat-installation.html

*If installing Filebeat on a Linux distribution, you will want to ensure that the service is started after a reboot. We can ensure this by running the following commands after install:

```
sudo update-rc.d filebeat defaults
sudo update-rc.d filebeat enable
```

6.1.3 Firewall

To ensure a Beat is allowed to talk to Logstash on the Security Onion box, we need to run so-allow, and choose the b option for `Beats`. After choosing this option, simply provide the IP address of the machine on which the Beat is installed and press ENTER to confirm.

6.1.4 Log files

Filebeat

Windows: `C:\\Program Files\Filebeat\filebeat.log`

Linux: `/var/log/filebeat/filebeat`

Winlogbeat

`C:\\Program Files\Winlogbeat\winlogbeat.log`

Default fields: https://www.elastic.co/guide/en/beats/winlogbeat/master/exported-fields-eventlog.html

6.1.5 Data

Beats data can be viewed via the `Beats` dashboard, (or through the selection of the `*:logstash-beats-*` index pattern in `Discover`) in Kibana.

If you access the Beats dashboard and see logs but the visualizations have errors, you may need to refresh the `logstash-beats-*` field list as follows:

- On the sidebar on the left, click `Management`.
- Click `Index Patterns`.
- Click `logstash-beats-*`.
- Click the circular arrows in the upper right to refresh the field list.

6.1.6 Encryption

Beats communication with Elasticsearch/Logstash is `not encrypted` by default. If you require encryption, please consult the appropriate Elastic documentation to configure the use of TLS.

6.2 Wazuh

6.2.1 Description

From https://wazuh.com/:

> Wazuh is a free, open source and enterprise-ready security monitoring solution for threat detection, integrity monitoring, incident response and compliance.

6.2.2 Security Onion Usage

Security Onion uses Wazuh as a Host Intrusion Detection System (HIDS). Wazuh is monitoring and defending Security Onion itself and you can add Wazuh agents to monitor other hosts on your network as well.

Wazuh replaced OSSEC:
https://blog.securityonion.net/2018/10/wazuh-361-elastic-641-and-associated.html

6.2.3 Configuration

The main configuration file for Wazuh is `/var/ossec/etc/ossec.conf`.

6.2.4 Email

If you want to configure Wazuh to send email, please see the Email section.

6.2.5 Syslog

If you want to send Wazuh logs to an external syslog collector, please see the syslog-output section.

6.2.6 Active Response

Sometimes, Wazuh may recognize legitimate activity as potentially malicious, and engage in Active Response to block a connection. This may result in unintended consequences and/or blacklisting of trusted IPs. To prevent this from occurring, you can whitelist your IP address and change other settings in `/var/ossec/etc/ossec.conf`:

```
<global>
<white_list>desired_ip</white_list>
</global>
```

6.2.7 Tuning Rules

You can add new rules and modify existing rules in `/var/ossec/rules/local_rules.xml`.

Wazuh alerts of a level of 5 or greater will be populated in the Sguil database, and viewable via Sguil and/or Squert. If you would like to change the level for which alerts are sent to sguild, you can modify the value for `OSSEC_AGENT_LEVEL` in `/etc/nsm/securityonion.conf` and restart NSM services.

6.2.8 Adding Agents

The Wazuh agent is cross platform and you can download agents for Windows/Unix/Linux/FreeBSD from the Wazuh website:

https://documentation.wazuh.com/3.8/installation-guide/packages-list/index.html

Please note! It is important to ensure that you download the agent that matches the version of your Wazuh server. For example, if your Wazuh server is version 3.8.2, then you will want to deploy Wazuh agent version 3.8.2.

Once you've installed the Wazuh agent on the host(s) to be monitored, then perform the steps defined here:
https://documentation.wazuh.com/current/user-manual/agents/registering-agents/register-agent-manual.html

You may need to run so-allow to allow traffic from the IP address of your Wazuh agent(s).

6.2.9 Maximum Number of Agents

Security Onion is configured to support a maximum number of `14000` Wazuh agents reporting to a single Wazuh manager.

6.2.10 Automated Deployment

If you would like to automate the deployment of Wazuh agents, the Wazuh server includes `ossec-authd`:
https://documentation.wazuh.com/3.8/user-manual/reference/daemons/ossec-authd.html

When using `ossec-authd`, be sure to add a firewall exception for agents to access port `1515/tcp` on the Wazuh manager node:

```
sudo ufw allow proto tcp from agent_ip to any port 1515
```

6.2.11 Downloads

You can download Wazuh agents here:
https://documentation.wazuh.com/3.8/installation-guide/packages-list/index.html

6.2.12 More Information

For more information about Wazuh, please see https://documentation.wazuh.com/3.8/.

6.3 Sysmon

From https://technet.microsoft.com/en-us/sysinternals/sysmon:

System Monitor (Sysmon) is a Windows system service and device driver that, once installed on a system, remains resident across system reboots to monitor and log system activity to the Windows event log. It provides detailed information about process creations, network connections, and changes to file creation time. By collecting the events it generates using Windows Event Collection or SIEM agents and subsequently analyzing them, you can identify malicious or anomalous activity and understand how intruders and malware operate on your network.

6.3.1 Integration

Josh Brower wrote a great paper on integrating sysmon into Security Onion:

https://digital-forensics.sans.org/community/papers/gcfa/sysmon-enrich-security-onions-host-level-capabilities_10612

6.3.2 Configuration

SwiftOnSecurity has a great sysmon config file to use as a starting point:

https://github.com/SwiftOnSecurity/sysmon-config

6.3.3 Downloads

Download sysmon here:
https://download.sysinternals.com/files/Sysmon.zip

Download SwiftOnSecurity's example sysmon config here:
https://github.com/SwiftOnSecurity/sysmon-config/raw/master/sysmonconfig-export.xml

6.3.4 More Information

For more information about sysmon, please see https://technet.microsoft.com/en-us/sysinternals/sysmon.

Also see "How to Go from Responding to Hunting with Sysinternals Sysmon":
https://onedrive.live.com/view.aspx?resid=D026B4699190F1E6!2843&ithint=file%2cpptx

6.4 Autoruns

From https://technet.microsoft.com/en-us/sysinternals/bb963902.aspx:

> This utility, which has the most comprehensive knowledge of auto-starting locations of any startup monitor, shows you what programs are configured to run during system bootup or login, and when you start various built-in Windows applications like Internet Explorer, Explorer and media players. These programs and drivers include ones in your startup folder, Run, RunOnce, and other Registry keys. Autoruns reports Explorer shell extensions, toolbars, browser helper objects, Winlogon notifications, auto-start services, and much more. Autoruns goes way beyond other autostart utilities.

6.4.1 Integration

Wazuh

Currently, our Autoruns dashboard in Kibana works only with Autoruns logs shipped via Wazuh. If you are trying to ship Autoruns logs via Winlogbeat, you can create a custom dashboard and visualizations that reference the `logstash-beats-*` indices, or view Autoruns logs via the `Beats` dashboard.

Pertinax

Josh Brower developed a great project called Pertinax to normalize autoruns data and integrate it into Security Onion: https://github.com/defensivedepth/Pertinax/wiki/Introduction

Execute autoruns and ar-normalize.ps1 as shown here: https://github.com/defensivedepth/Pertinax/wiki/Reference%20Architecture

AutorunsToWinEventLog

Another method for integrating Autoruns into your logging infrastructure is AutorunsToWinEventLog: https://github.com/palantir/windows-event-forwarding/tree/master/AutorunsToWinEventLog

6.4.2 Downloads

Download Autoruns here: https://download.sysinternals.com/files/Autoruns.zip

Download ar-normalize.ps1 here: https://raw.githubusercontent.com/defensivedepth/Pertinax/master/normalize/ar-normalize.ps1

6.5 Syslog

From https://www.syslog-ng.com/products/open-source-log-management/:

> With syslog-ng, you can collect logs from any source, process them in real time and deliver them to a wide variety of destinations. syslog-ng allows you to flexibly collect, parse, classify, rewrite and correlate logs from across your infrastructure and store or route them to log analysis tools.

6.5.1 Usage

Security Onion uses syslog-ng as its primary syslog collector and to send logs to Logstash where they are parsed and augmented before being written to Elasticsearch.

6.5.2 Configuration

syslog-ng's configuration file is located at `/etc/syslog-ng/syslog-ng.conf`.

6.5.3 Forwarding

You can configure syslog-ng to forward Bro / Wazuh / IDS logs to external systems.

6.5.4 Collection

syslog-ng listens on port 514 (TCP and UDP) for incoming syslog from other devices. You may need to run so-allow to allow traffic from the IP address of your syslog sender.

6.5.5 Analysis

If you'd like to analyze logs collected from other devices, another option is to configure Wazuh to receive syslog directly on a port other than the syslog-ng port of 514. For more information, please see http://ossec-docs.readthedocs.org/en/latest/syntax/head_ossec_config.remote.html.

6.5.6 More Information

For more information about syslog-ng, please see https://www.syslog-ng.com/products/open-source-log-management/.

CHAPTER 7

Elastic Stack

Security Onion includes the Elastic Stack:

Elasticsearch
Logstash
Kibana

In addition, we've added the following:

Curator
DomainStats
ElastAlert
FreqServer

Each of the components above has its own Docker image.

You can get an idea of what this whole integration looks like at a high-level by viewing our architecture diagram.

7.1 Elasticsearch

From https://www.elastic.co/products/elasticsearch:

> Elasticsearch is a distributed, RESTful search and analytics engine capable of solving a growing number of use cases. As the heart of the Elastic Stack, it centrally stores your data so you can discover the expected and uncover the unexpected.

7.1.1 Configuration

Shards

Here are a few tips from https://www.elastic.co/blog/how-many-shards-should-i-have-in-my-elasticsearch-cluster:

> TIP: Avoid having very large shards as this can negatively affect the cluster's ability to recover from failure. There is no fixed limit on how large shards can be, but a shard size of 50GB is often quoted as a limit that has been seen to work for a variety of use-cases.

> TIP: Small shards result in small segments, which increases overhead. Aim to keep the average shard size between a few GB and a few tens of GB. For use-cases with time-based data, it is common to see shards between 20GB and 40GB in size.

> TIP: The number of shards you can hold on a node will be proportional to the amount of heap you have available, but there is no fixed limit enforced by Elasticsearch. A good rule-of-thumb is to ensure you keep the number of shards per node below 20 to 25 per GB heap it has configured. A node with a 30GB heap should therefore have a maximum of 600-750 shards, but the further below this limit you can keep it the better. This will generally help the cluster stay in good health.

To see your existing shards:

```
curl localhost:9200/_cat/indices
```

The number of shards will be shown in the fifth column.

If you want to view the detail for each of those shards:

```
curl localhost:9200/_cat/shards
```

Given the sizing tips above, if any of your indices are averaging more than 50GB per shard, then you should probably increase the shard count until you get below that recommended maximum of 50GB per shard.

The number of shards for an index is defined in the template file for that index. By default, there are three template files in `/etc/logstash/`:

- `beats-template.json` applies to `logstash-beats` indices
- `logstash-ossec-template.json` applies to `logstash-ossec` indices
- `logstash-template.json` applies to `logstash-ids`, `logstash-firewall`, `logstash-syslog`, `logstash-bro`, `logstash-import`, and `logstash-beats`.

Depending on which index you want to increase shards for, you have a few options.

If you want to increase shards for `logstash-beats` or `logstash-ossec`:

- First, copy the template to `/etc/logstash/custom/`. For example:

```
sudo cp /etc/logstash/logstash-ossec-template.json to /etc/logstash/custom/
```

- Then, update your new template in `/etc/logstash/custom/`.
- Finally, restart Logstash to push the new template to Elasticsearch:

```
sudo so-logstash-restart
```

If you want to increase shards for all indices defined in `logstash-template.json`, then you can follow a process similar to what was shown above. However, if you want to increase shard count for only one index type (example: bro), you can update the template as follows:

- First, copy `/etc/logstash/logstash-template.json` and give it a name based on the index (example: `logstash-bro-template.json`).
- Then, update your new template, changing the `index_patterns` line to only apply to the index you care about, increasing the value of the `order` field from 0 to 1, and setting your `number_of_shards`.
- Next, we need to tell Logstash to use this new template, so update the proper output file in `/etc/logstash/conf.d/` and update the template value.
- Then, we need to configure the Logstash container to be able to access the template by updating `LOGSTASH_OPTIONS` in `/etc/nsm/securityonion.conf` similar to the following:

```
LOGSTASH_OPTIONS="--volume /etc/logstash/logstash-bro-template.json:/logstash-bro-
↪template.json:ro"
```

- Finally, restart Logstash to push the new template to Elasticsearch:

```
sudo so-logstash-restart
```

Please keep in mind that old indices will retain previous shard settings and the above settings will only be applied to newly created indices.

Files

- Configuration files for Elasticsearch can be found in `/etc/elasticsearch/`.
- Other configuration options for Elasticsearch can be found in `/etc/nsm/securityonion.conf`.
- By default, if total available memory is 8GB or greater, the heap size in `/etc/elasticsearch/jvm.options` is configured (during Setup) to equal 25% of available memory, but no greater than 25GB.

For more information, please see:
https://www.elastic.co/guide/en/elasticsearch/guide/current/heap-sizing.html#compressed_oops
https://www.elastic.co/guide/en/elasticsearch/reference/current/heap-size.html

You may need to adjust the value for heap size depending on your system's performance (running `sudo so-elastic-restart` after).

Field limit

Security Onion currently utilizes the default field limit for Elasticsearch indices (`1000`). If you receive error messages from Logstash, or you would simply like to increase this, you can do so with one of the following options.

Temporary

If you only need to increase the field limit temporarily, you can do something like:

```
curl -XPUT -H'Content-Type: application/json' localhost:9200/logstash-syslog-*/_
↪settings -d'{ "index.mapping.total_fields.limit": 2000 }'
```

The above command would increase the field limit for the `logstash-syslog-*` indice(s) to `2000`. Keep in mind, this setting only applies to the current index, so when the index rolls over and a new one is created, your new settings will not apply.

Persistent

If you need this change to be persistent, you can modify the `settings` stanza for the matched indices in `/etc/logstash/logstash-template.json`.

```
"settings" : {
    "number_of_replicas": 0,
    "number_of_shards": 1,
    "index.refresh_interval" : "5s",
    "index.mapping.total_fields.limit": 2000
},
```

Then restart Logstash:

```
sudo so-logstash-restart
```

Please note that the change to the field limit will not occur immediately – only upon index creation. Therefore, it is recommended to run the previously mentioned temporary command and modify the template file.

Additional options

If you need to make additional directories accessible to Elasticsearch, or would like to specify additional options when starting Elasticsearch, you can do so by adding these items to `ELASTICSEARCH_OPTIONS` in `/etc/nsm/securityonion.conf`

7.1.2 Logs

- Elasticsearch logs can be found in `/var/log/elasticsearch/`.
- Logging configuration can be found in `/etc/elasticsearch/log4j2.properties`.

7.1.3 Distributed

7.1.4 Master

The `master server` runs it's own local copy of Elasticsearch, which manages cross-cluster search configuration for the deployment. This includes configuration for `heavy nodes` and `storage nodes` (where applicable), but not `forward nodes`, as they do not run Elastic Stack components.

7.1.5 Forward Nodes

When using a `forward node`, Elastic Stack components are not enabled. Syslog-NG forwards all logs to Logstash on the master server via an autossh tunnel, where they are stored in Elasticsearch on the master server or a storage node (if the master server has been configured to use storage nodes). From there, the data can be queried through the use of cross-cluster search.

7.1.6 Heavy Nodes

When using a `heavy node`, Security Onion implements distributed deployments using Elasticsearch's cross cluster search. When you run Setup and choose `Heavy Node`, it will create a local Elasticsearch instance and then configure the master server to query that instance (similar to ELSA distributed deployments). This is done by constructing an autossh tunnel from the heavy node to the master server, configuring reverse port forwarding to allow the master server to connect to the local Elasticsearch instance, and updating _cluster/settings on the master server so that it will query the local Elasticsearch instance.

7.1.7 Storage Nodes

`Storage nodes` extend the storage and processing capabilities of the master server, and run Elasticsearch, Logstash, and Curator. Just like heavy nodes, storage nodes are added to the master's cluster search configuration, so the data that resides on the nodes can be queried from the master.

7.1.8 Removing a node from the master

If you need to remove a node (such as a `heavy node` or a `storage node`) from your cross cluster search configuration, send the following to Elasticsearch on your master server (replacing "node1" with the actual node you'd like to remove and noting that null must be in square brackets):

```
PUT _cluster/settings
{
"persistent": {
"search": {
"remote": {
"node1": {
"seeds": null}}}}}
```

You can simply copy/paste the above code (modifying as necessary) into the Console, under "Dev Tools" in Kibana, and click the green triangle. Alternatively, you could submit it to Elasticsearch via a cURL command.

7.1.9 Storage

All of the data Elasticsearch collects is stored under `/nsm/elasticsearch/`.

7.1.10 Snapshots

Snapshots of the current indices can be taken and stored in a designated repository for archival purposes. Currently, you'll need to add something like the following to `/etc/elasticsearch/elasticsearch.yml`:

```
path.repo: <your file path here>
```

keeping in mind that the above file path is relative to the container's view of the filesystem.

So, if you decided to add a `path.repo` value of `/backups`, Elasticsearch would be looking for the file path `/backups` inside of the container. To achieve parity with what is present on the host's filesystem and make that directory accessible to the Elasticsearch Docker container, you'll want to add something like the following to ELASTICSEARCH_OPTIONS in `/etc/nsm/securityonion.conf`:

```
ELASTICSEARCH_OPTIONS="-v /backups:/backups"
```

(where `/backups` exists on the host file system and is writable by the Elasticsearch user – a directory named `/backups` will be created inside the container, and the container will be able to read/write from that location).

To automate the snapshotting process, you can use Curator, in conjunction with a cron job, much like what is done today with the close and delete jobs.

7.2 Logstash

From https://www.elastic.co/products/logstash :

> Logstash is an open source, server-side data processing pipeline that ingests data from a multitude of sources simultaneously, transforms it, and then sends it to your favorite "stash".

7.2.1 Configuration

pipeline.workers

> The number of workers that will, in parallel, execute the filter and output stages of the pipeline. If you find that events are backing up, or that the CPU is not saturated, consider increasing this number to better utilize machine processing power.

https://www.elastic.co/guide/en/logstash/current/logstash-settings-file.html

This setting can be adjusted in `/etc/logstash/logstash.yml`.

Logstash Heap

By default, if total available memory is 8GB or greater, the Logstash heap size in `/etc/logstash/jvm.options` is configured (during setup) to equal 25% of available memory, but no greater than 4GB.

See https://www.elastic.co/guide/en/elasticsearch/guide/current/heap-sizing.html#compressed_oops for more details.

You may need to adjust the value depending on your system's performance (running `sudo so-logstash-restart` after).

7.2.2 Adding New Logs or Modifying Existing Parsing

Syslog-NG

If you are parsing local log files, you may need to add these files to the Syslog-NG configuration in `/etc/syslog-ng/syslog-ng.conf` and restart the service.

Parsing

Configuration files for custom parsing can be placed in `/etc/logstash/custom`. These will automatically get copied over to `/etc/logstash/conf.d` during the starting of Logstash.

After adding your custom configuration file(s), restart Logstash and check the log(s) for errors:

```
sudo so-logstash-restart && sudo tail -f /var/log/logstash/logstash.log
```

Mapping Templates

Logstash loads default mapping templates for Elasticsearch to use from `/etc/logstash`.

The three templates currently being used include:

`logstash-template.json` - applies to `logstash-*` indices

`logstash-ossec-template.json` - applies to `logstash-ossec-*` indices

`beats-template.json` - applies to `logstash-beats-*` indices

Currently, new fields that do not match the template are stored in Elasticsearch, however, they are not indexed, unless provided in a mapping template.

If sending in custom logs to Security Onion that may not match existing fields for existing indices, it is recommended to create a dedicated index for the log source, as well as define a mapping template and output file for the custom log source.

To make sure Logstash can read the custom template:

1. Place the template in `/etc/logstash/custom`.
2. Make sure the template is added to `LOGSTASH_OPTIONS` in `/etc/nsm/securityonion.conf`: `LOGSTASH_OPTIONS="--volume /etc/logstash/testme-template.json:/testme-template.json:ro"`
3. Make sure the custom template is referenced in the appropriate output file (place the output file in `/etc/logstash/custom`, then modify it.).
4. Restart Logstash.

You can check to see if templates are loaded by typing something like the following at a command prompt:

```
sudo so-elasticsearch-template-list
```

You can also test the template before restarting Logstash, by using the following command:

```
sudo so-elasticsearch-template-add
```

If mappings defined in the template are different than in existing indices, you will receive mapping conflicts in Kibana.

To avoid this, either remove the existing indices, wiping all data, or re-index.

Logging

Log file settings can be adjusted in `/etc/logstash/log4j2.properties`. Currently, logs are set to rollover daily, and configured to be deleted after 7 days.

Options

You can specify your own custom options to be appended to the Logstash startup command, by editing `LOGSTASH_OPTIONS` in `/etc/nsm/securityonion.conf`.

7.2.3 Queue

Memory-backed

From: https://www.elastic.co/guide/en/logstash/current/persistent-queues.html

> By default, Logstash uses in-memory bounded queues between pipeline stages (inputs → pipeline workers) to buffer events. The size of these in-memory queues is fixed and not configurable.

Persistent

From: https://www.elastic.co/guide/en/logstash/current/persistent-queues.html

> In order to protect against data loss during abnormal termination, Logstash has a persistent queue feature which will store the message queue on disk. Persistent queues provide durability of data within Logstash.

If you experience adverse effects using the default memory-backed queue, you can configure a disk-based persistent queue by un-commenting the following lines in `/etc/logstash/logstash.yaml` and modifying the values as appropriate:

```
#queue.type: persisted
#queue.max_bytes: 1gb
```

Then restart Logstash:

```
sudo so-logstash-restart
```

More information:
https://www.elastic.co/guide/en/logstash/current/persistent-queues.html

Queue Max Bytes

> The total capacity of the queue in number of bytes. Make sure the capacity of your disk drive is greater than the value >you specify here. If both queue.max_events and queue.max_bytes are specified, Logstash uses whichever criteria is reached >first.

Dead Letter Queue

If you want to check for dropped events, you can enable the dead letter queue. This will write all records that are not able to make it into Elasticsearch into a sequentially-numbered file (for each start/restart of Logstash).

This can be achieved by adding the following to `/etc/logstash/logstash.yml`:

dead_letter_queue.enable: true

and restarting Logstash:

```
sudo so-logstash-restart
```

The dead letter queue files are located in `/nsm/logstash/dead_letter_queue/main/`.

More information:
https://www.elastic.co/guide/en/logstash/current/dead-letter-queues.html

Redis

When using storage nodes, Logstash on the master server outputs to Redis (on the master server). Redis queues events from the Logstash output (on the master) and the Logstash input on the storage node(s) pull(s) from Redis. If you notice new events aren't making it into Kibana, you may want to first check Logstash on the master, then the redis queue.

7.2.4 Data Fields

Logstash process Bro logs, syslog, IDS alerts, etc., formatting said data into many different data fields, as described in the Data Fields section.

7.2.5 Log

The Logstash log is located at `/var/log/logstash/logstash.log`.

7.2.6 Errors

Read-Only

```
[INFO ][logstash.outputs.elasticsearch] retrying failed action with response code:
↪403 ({"type"=>"cluster_block_exception", "reason"=>"blocked by: [FORBIDDEN/12/index
↪read-only / allow delete (api)];"})
```

This error is usually caused by the `cluster.routing.allocation.disk.watermark` (`low`,`high`) being exceeded.

You may want to check `/var/log/elasticsearch/<hostname>.log` to see specifically which indices have been marked as read-only.

Additionally, you can run the following command to allow writing to the affected indices:

```
curl -XPUT -H 'Content-Type: application/json' localhost:9200/<your_index>/_settings -
↪d'{ "index.blocks.read_only": false }'
```

7.3 ElastAlert

From http://elastalert.readthedocs.io/en/latest/elastalert.html#overview:

> ElastAlert is a simple framework for alerting on anomalies, spikes, or other patterns of interest from data in Elasticsearch.
>
> At Yelp, we use Elasticsearch, Logstash and Kibana for managing our ever increasing amount of data and logs. Kibana is great for visualizing and querying data, but we quickly realized that it needed a companion tool for alerting on inconsistencies in our data. Out of this need, ElastAlert was created. If you have data being when that data matches certain patterns, ElastAlert is the tool for you.

ElastAlert runs as a Docker container within Security Onion, queries ElasticSearch, and provides an alerting mechanism with multiple output types, such as Slack, Email, JIRA, OpsGenie, and many more.

7.3.1 Configuration

ElastAlert rules are stored in `/etc/elastalert/rules/`.

Security Onion's default ElastAlert rules are configured with an output type of "debug", which simply outputs all matches queries to a log file, found in `/var/log/elastalert/elastalert_stderr.log`.

Slack

To have ElastAlert send alerts to something like Slack, we can simply change the alert type and details for a rule like so:

```
alert:
- "slack":
    slack_webhook_url: "https://hooks.slack.com/services/YOUR_WEBHOOK_URI"
```

Email - Internal

To have ElastAlert send to email, we could do something like the following:

```
alert:
- "email"
email:
- "youremail@yourcompany.com"
smtp_host: "your_company_smtp_server"
smtp_port: 25
from_addr: "elastalert@yourcompany.com"
```

Email - External

If we need to use an external email provider like Gmail, we can add something like the following:

```
alert:
- "email"
email:
- "youremail@gmail.com"
smtp_host: "smtp.gmail.com"
smtp_port: 465
smtp_ssl: true
from_addr: "youremail@gmail.com"
smtp_auth_file: '/etc/elastalert/rules/smtp_auth_file.txt'
```

In the `smtp_auth_file.txt`, add:

```
user: youremail@gmail.com
password: yourpassword
```

MISP

See MISP

TheHive

See TheHive

so-elastalert-create

`so-elastalert-create` is a tool created by Bryant Treacle that can be used to help ease the pain of ensuring correct syntax and creating Elastalert rules from scratch. It will walk you through various questions, and eventually output an Elastalert rule file that you can deploy in your environment to start alerting quickly and easily.

so-elastalert-test

`so-elastalert-test` is a wrapper script originally written by Bryant Treacle for ElastAlert's `elastalert-test-rule` tool. The script allows you to test an ElastAlert rule and get results immediately. Simply run `so-elastalert-test`, and follow the prompt(s).

Please note, all options available to `elastalert-test-rule` are not yet included with `so-elastalert-test`.

Defaults

With Security Onion's example rules, Elastalert is configured by default to only count the number of hits for a particular match, and will not return the actual log entry for which an alert was generated.

This is governed by the use of `use_count_query:   true` in each rule file.

If you would like to view the data for the match, you can simply remark this line in the rule file(s). Keep in mind, this may impact performance negatively, so testing the change in a single file at a time may be the best approach.

Timeframe

Keep in mind, for queries that span greater than a minute back in time, you may want to add the following fields to your rule to ensure searching occurs as planned (for example, for 10 minutes):

```
buffer_time:
    minutes: 10
```

```
allow_buffer_time_overlap:   true
```

https://elastalert.readthedocs.io/en/latest/ruletypes.html#buffer-time
https://github.com/Yelp/elastalert/issues/805

7.3.2 More Information

You can learn more about ElastAlert and its output types here:
http://elastalert.readthedocs.io/en/latest/

7.4 Curator

From: https://www.elastic.co/guide/en/elasticsearch/client/curator/current/about.html#about

> Elasticsearch Curator helps you curate, or manage, your Elasticsearch indices and snapshots by:
>
> 1. Obtaining the full list of indices (or snapshots) from the cluster, as the actionable list

2. Iterate through a list of user-defined filters to progressively remove indices (or snapshots) from this actionable list as needed.

3. Perform various actions on the items which remain in the actionable list.

Curator runs as a Docker container within Security Onion. It runs every minute and is controlled by cron jobs defined in `/etc/cron.d/`. When Curator completes an action, it logs such activity in a log file found in `/var/log/curator/curator.log`.

Curator defaults to closing indices older than 30 days. To modify this, change CURATOR_CLOSE_DAYS in `/etc/nsm/securityonion.conf`.

As your disk reaches capacity, Curator starts deleting old indices to prevent your disk from filling up. To change the limit, modify LOG_SIZE_LIMIT in `/etc/nsm/securityonion.conf`.

7.4.1 Actions

Curator `actions` are stored in `/etc/curator/actions`. These actions are run every minute from the cron jobs located in `/etc/cron.d/curator-*`.

If you would like to add a new action, you can certainly do so, and add another cron job in `/etc/cron.d` to automate the process.

For example, a new process for snapshotting would require a new action file, Elasticsearch configuration, and a cron job to automate it all:

- Elasticsearch#snapshots
- https://www.elastic.co/guide/en/elasticsearch/client/curator/current/snapshot.html

7.5 FreqServer

FreqServer is based on freq.py and freq_server.py (originally created by Mark Baggett).
Thanks to Justin Henderson for all his work with the FreqServer docker image!

From https://github.com/sans-blue-team/freq.py:

> Mark Baggett's (@MarkBaggett - GSE #15, SANS SEC573 Author) Awesome-Sauce tool for detecting randomness using NLP techniques rather than pure entropy calculations. Uses character pair frequency analysis to determine the likelihood of tested strings of characters occurring based upon the chosen frequency tables (some prebuilt English text freq tables provided). Extremely useful for detecting high entropy where it shouldn't be. Especially powerful for discovering DNS based DGAs commonly used for malware C2 and exfiltration. Think bigger than DGAs though. Random file names, script names, process names, service names, workstation names, TLS certificate subjects and issuer subjects, etc.

From https://isc.sans.edu/forums/diary/Continuous+Monitoring+for+Random+Strings/20451/

> Freq_server.py is a multithreaded web based API that will allow you to quickly query your frequency tables. The server isn't intended to replace freq.py. Instead, after building a frequency table of normal strings in your environment with freq.py, you start a server up to allow services to measure various strings against that table. You can run multiple servers to provide access to different frequency tables.

7.5.1 Configuration

For information how to modify configuration for FreqServer, consult the following:
https://github.com/SMAPPER/docker_freq_server

FreqServer is disabled by default when running `Production Mode` with `Best Practices`.
You can enable it by doing the following:

```
sudo sed -i 's/FREQ_SERVER_ENABLED="no"/FREQ_SERVER_ENABLED="yes"/' /etc/nsm/
↪securityonion.conf
sudo so-elastic-start
sudo so-logstash-restart
```

FreqServer's logs can be found in `/var/log/freq_server/`.

7.5.2 Kibana

You can find FreqServer data on the Frequency Analysis dashboard.

7.5.3 DNS Highest Registered Domain Frequency Analysis

Domain	Frequency Score
bbc.net.uk	2.092
tahmqkmvzg.com	2.337
yahoodns.net	3.132
2o7.net	3.227
olugixyixy.com	3.286
yfksjfsunyiypu.com	3.414
iphaeba.eu	3.447
fwhynaxzwkv.com	3.648
npkxghmoru.biz	3.779
dsms0mj1bbhn4.cloudfront.net	3.795

7.5.4 DNS Parent Domain Frequency Analysis

Domain	Frequency Score
tahmqkmvzg.com	0.434
dsms0mj1bbhn4.cloudfront.net	1.085
oiugixyixy.com	1.683
yfksjfsunyiypu.com	2.053
fwhynaxzwkv.com	2.329
yahoodns.net	2.697
muihoc.com	2.914
qfrwozmoaqc.com	3.153
aemmiphbweeuef59.com	3.345
brovztkzbl.com	3.391

7.5.5 HTTP Frequency Analysis

Virtual Host	Frequency Score
www.w3.org	1.687
nrkuktxvn.myftp.org	2.332
epzqy.iphaeba.eu	2.374
cs.gmu.edu	2.469
jigsaw.w3.org	2.541
eytmxgnqlm.nirval.eu	2.743
tags.w55c.net	3.095
l.w55c.net	3.233
www.msftncsi.com	3.514
www.osu.edu	3.596

7.5.6 SSL Certificate Common Name Frequency Analysis

Common Name	Frequency Score
d3fr3g4tgwf	2.781
www.spidh.org	3.425
imap.gmx.net	3.96
www.lilawelt.net	4.538
www.paypal.com	5.324
www.google.com	5.454
www.jeffbryner.com	6.144
*.s3.amazonaws.com	6.185
s3.amazonaws.com	6.185
plesk3.gigaspark.com	6.458

7.5.7 SSL Certificate Server Name Frequency Analysis

SSL - Certificate Server Name Frequency Analysis	
Server Name	Frequency Score
aemmiphbweeuef59.com	4.128
www.lilawelt.net	4.538
fbstatic-a.akamaihd.net	4.934
www.google.at	5.231
www.facebook.com	5.368
www.google.com	5.454
www.lamas.si	5.519
tls13.crypto.mozilla.org	5.622
www.gstatic.com	5.72
ssl.gstatic.com	6.236

7.5.8 SSL Certificate Issuer Name Frequency Analysis

Issuer Common Name	Frequency Score
d3fr3g4tgwf	2.781
RapidSSL CA	7.664
web	7.752
Apple IST CA 2 - G1	7.991
bro	8.218
Go Daddy Secure Certification Authority	8.6
Globus Simple CA	8.603
VeriSign Class 3 Extended Validation SSL SGC CA	8.731
Google Internet Authority G2	8.76
EssentialSSL CA	8.998

7.5.9 X.509 Certificate Common Name Frequency Analysis

Common Name	Frequency Score
a	0
d3fr3g4tgwf	2.781
www.spidh.org	3.425
imap.gmx.net	3.96
vladg.net	4.101
www.cviis.org	4.457
www.lilawelt.net	4.538
www.lilawelt.de	4.964
www.paypal.com	5.324
www.google.com	5.454

7.5.10 X.509 Certificate Issuer Organization Frequency Analysis

X.509 - Certificate Issuer Organization Frequency Analysis

Issuer Organization	Frequency Score
ggfbfghdfh	1.802
fe3f44tgrfdsdf	3.608
Tokbox	4.688
StartCom Ltd.	5.999
Grid	6.624
Starfield Technologies| Inc.	6.785
Root CA	7.112
T-Systems International GmbH	7.148
Company Ltd	7.269
GoDaddy.com| Inc.	7.428

7.5.11 X.509 Certificate Issuer Frequency Analysis

X.509 - Certificate Issuer Frequency Analysis

Issuer	Frequency Score
a	0
d3fr3g4tgwf	2.781
vladg.net	4.101
RapidSSL CA	7.664
web	7.752
Apple IST CA 2 - G1	7.991
bro	8.218
Starfield Secure Certificate Authority - G2	8.547
Go Daddy Secure Certification Authority	8.6
Globus Simple CA	8.603

7.6 DomainStats

DomainStats is based on Mark Baggett's domain_stats.py, found at https://github.com/MarkBaggett/domain_stats. Thanks to Justin Henderson for all his work with the DomainStats docker image!

From https://github.com/SMAPPER/docker_domain_stats:

> This docker image runs domain_stats.py. This is a python service that is designed to perform mass domain analysis. It can do things such as find the creation_date of a domain and identify if a domain is a member of the Alexa/Cisco Umbrella top 1 million sites.
>
> It was developed to be used in conjunction with a SIEM and is in production environments. Specifically, it has been used in conjunction with the Elastic Stack, such as queried by Logstash, with large success.

7.6.1 Configuration

Internet Access

DomainStats does whois lookups so it needs to connect outbound on port 43 to whois servers on the Internet. If this traffic is not allowed through your firewall, then whois lookups will hang causing DomainStats to hang. This results in the logstash pipeline backing up and Kibana showing no data. In the current release, Setup will automatically disable DomainStats if whois lookups fail.

Enabling DomainStats

DomainStats is disabled by default when running `Production Mode` with `Best Practices`.
You can enable it by doing the following:

```
sudo sed -i 's/DOMAIN_STATS_ENABLED="no"/DOMAIN_STATS_ENABLED="yes"/' /etc/nsm/
↪securityonion.conf
sudo so-elastic-start
sudo so-logstash-restart
```

Updating Top-1m file

From https://github.com/SMAPPER/docker_domain_stats#updating-top-1m-file:

> The docker image does not currently automatically update the top-1m.csv. The below example shows how to download a new top 1 million site list and have a domain_stats container use it. This could be scheduled as a cron job on your host to keep a current Alexa/Cisco Umbrella top-1m.csv in use.

(Slightly modified for Security Onion)

```
#/etc/cron.d/domainstats
#
#crontab entry to grab new Top 1m CSV for DomainStats Docker image
SHELL=/bin/sh
PATH=/usr/local/sbin:/usr/localbin:/sbin:/bin/usr/sbin:/usr/bin
1 07 * * *    root ( wget -q http://s3.amazonaws.com/alexa-static/top-1m.csv.zip -O /
↪tmp/top-1m.csv.zip && unzip -o
```

(continues on next page)

(continued from previous page)
```
/tmp/top-1m.csv.zip -d /tmp && docker cp /tmp/top-1m.csv so-domainstats:/opt/domain_
↪stats/top-1m.csv && docker restart
so-domainstats && rm -f /tmp/top-1m.csv* ) > /dev/null 2>&1
```

For information how to modify configuration for DomainStats, consult the following: https://github.com/SMAPPER/docker_domain_stats

DomainStats logs can be found in `/var/log/domain_stats/`.

7.6.2 Kibana

You can find DomainStats data by going to the Domain Stats dashboard in Kibana:

Domain	creation_date: Descending	Count
adminaoffline.com	August 25th 2017, 12:41:24.000	3

DNS - Baby Domain Requests

7.7 Docker

From https://www.docker.com/what-docker:

> Docker is the world's leading software container platform. Developers use Docker to eliminate "works on my machine" problems when collaborating on code with co-workers. Operators use Docker to run and manage apps side-by-side in isolated containers to get better compute density. Enterprises use Docker to build agile software delivery pipelines to ship new features faster, more securely and with confidence for both Linux, Windows Server, and Linux-on-mainframe apps.

7.7.1 Images

To maintain a high level of stability, reliability, and support, our Elastic Docker images are based on the Docker images provided by Elastic.co. Their Docker images are built on CentOS 7: https://www.elastic.co/blog/docker-base-centos7

To leverage a common core OS layer, all of our Docker images are then built on CentOS 7.

7.7.2 Registry

From https://docs.docker.com/registry/recipes/mirror/:

> If you have multiple instances of Docker running in your environment (e.g., multiple physical or virtual machines, all running the Docker daemon), each time one of them requires an image that it doesn't have it will go out to the internet and fetch it from the public Docker registry. By running a local registry mirror, you can keep most of the redundant image fetch traffic on your local network.

We can leverage the Docker registry (as a pull-through cache) with our Security Onion Docker images. As mentioned above, this will allow us to cut down on external requests and bandwidth, cache the images on a local server, and only pull new images when they are available.

We can easily configure our Security Onion master server and sensor by running the following script on each machine (watch out for line-wrapping) :

```
wget https://raw.githubusercontent.com/weslambert/securityonion-docker-registry/
↪master/so-docker-registry
sudo bash so-docker-registry
```

The above script:

- Sets up a Docker container named `docker-registry` on the master server - this container exposes port 5000 for 127.0.0.1 (only locally).
- Configures the master server to use the `docker-registry` container as its proxy to pull images (`registry-mirror` in `/etc/default/docker`).
- Configures a sensor to use to `docker-registry` on the master server as a proxy to pull images – this is done through the addition of a local port forward (5000) through the existing autossh tunnel (`/root/.ssh/securityonion_ssh.conf`), and setting the `registry-mirror` value for the docker client on the sensor (`/etc/default/docker`)
- Restarts Security Onion Docker containers so the latest images are cached on the master and pulled to the sensor.

After the script has completed (after running on both machines), the newest images from the `securityonionsolutions` repo should be locally cached on the master, and already pulled to the sensor.

We can check this by running the following from the master (or sensor):

```
curl localhost:5000/v2/_catalog
```

From here on, whenever `soup` checks for new images, it will pull them from the master server instead of Docker Hub.

7.7.3 Sneakernet Updates

If we need to perform offline updates of Docker images, we can do so by cloning the `security-onion-docker-airgap` script(s) at https://github.com/weslambert/securityonion-docker-airgap:

```
git clone https://github.com/weslambert/securityonion-docker-airgap
cd securityonion-docker-airgap
```

The script(s) should be run first on a machine with internet access – Docker images will be downloaded and saved to a single `images.tar` file.

```
sudo ./so-elastic-airgap
```

Choose the `Save` option.

From there, the `securityonion-docker-airgap` directory (including the `images.tar` file) should be copied to the destination machine.

Once there, change into the `securityonion-docker-airgap` directory:

```
cd securityonion-docker-airgap
```

Run the `so-elastic-airgap` script, and choose the `Load` option.

The Docker images should now be loaded. We can verify this by running:

```
sudo docker images
```

7.7.4 Networking

7.7.5 Bridge

By default, Docker configures it's bridge with an IP of `172.17.0.1`.

https://docs.docker.com/engine/userguide/networking/#default-networks

For many folks this is fine, but what if we actually use the the `172.17.0.0/16` range within our internal network(s)? This results in a **conflict** when trying to assign IP addresses to interfaces and trying to route outside of the host.

A simple solution to this is to do the following:

Create the following file - `/etc/docker/daemon.json`.
Inside of the file, place the following:

```
{
  "bip": "your_docker_bridge_ip/netmask"
}
```

Restart Docker:

```
sudo service docker restart
```

Running `netstat -rn` should show that the range for the `docker0` bridge has changed.

For more information/options, see:
https://docs.docker.com/engine/userguide/networking/default_network/custom-docker0/

7.7.6 Containers

Our Docker containers all belong to a common Docker bridge network, called `so-elastic-net`. Each container is also aliased, so that communication can occur between the different docker containers using said alias. For example, communication to the `so-elasticsearch` container would occur through an alias of `elasticsearch`.

You may come across interfaces in `ifconfig` with the format `veth*`. These are the external interfaces for each of the Docker containers. These interfaces correspond to internal Docker container interfaces (within the Docker container itself).

To identify which external interface belongs to which container, we can do something like the following:

From the host, type:

```
sudo docker exec so-elasticsearch cat /sys/class/net/eth0/iflink
```

This should provide you with a value with which you can grep the host `net` class `ifindex(es)`:

Example:

```
grep 25 /sys/class/net/veth*/ifindex | cut -d'/' -f5
```

You should then receive some output similar to the following:

```
vethc5ff027
```

where `vethc5ff027` is the external interface of `eth0` within the `so-elasticsearch` container.

7.7.7 Download

Our Docker images are stored on Docker Hub:
https://hub.docker.com/u/securityonionsolutions/

If you download our Security Onion ISO image, the Docker engine and these Docker images are baked right into the ISO image.

If you instead use another ISO image, you will install the securityonion-elastic package and will then run `sudo so-elastic-download` which will install the Docker engine and then download the Docker images from Docker Hub.

7.7.8 Update

Our `soup` utility for installing updates now includes support for updating Docker images.

7.7.9 Security

To prevent tampering, our Docker images are signed using Docker Notary:
https://docs.docker.com/notary/getting_started/

Any time we push an image to Docker Hub, we explicitly set `--disable-content-trust=false` to sign the image using Docker Notary.

Any time we download an image from Docker Hub, we also explicitly set `--disable-content-trust=false` to verify that signature using Docker Notary.

7.7.10 VMware Tools

If you have VMware Tools installed and you suspend and then resume, the Docker interfaces will no longer have IP addresses and the Elastic stack will no longer be able to communicate. One workaround is to remove `/etc/vmware-tools/scripts/vmware/network` to prevent VMware suspend/resume from modifying your network configuration.

7.8 Redis

From: https://redis.io/

Redis is an open source (BSD licensed), in-memory data structure store, used as a database, cache and message broker. It supports data structures such as strings, hashes, lists, sets, sorted sets with range queries, bitmaps, hyperloglogs and geospatial indexes with radius queries. Redis has built-in replication, Lua scripting, LRU eviction, transactions and different levels of on-disk persistence, and provides high availability via Redis Sentinel and automatic partitioning with Redis Cluster.

During setup, you can choose to extend your master server storage using separate storage nodes. When you choose this option, Logstash on the master server outputs to redis. Storage nodes then consume from redis.

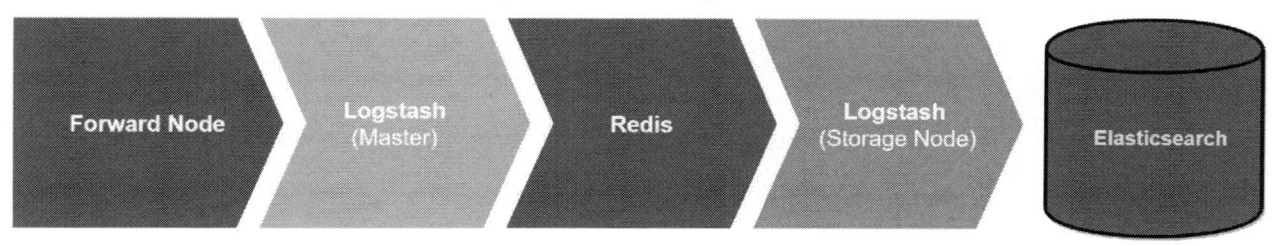

7.8.1 Queue

To see how many logs are in the redis queue:

```
redis-cli LLEN logstash:redis
```

If the queue is backed up and doesn't seem to be draining, try stopping Logstash on the master server:

```
sudo docker stop so-logstash
```

Then monitor the queue to see if it drains:

```
watch 'redis-cli llen logstash:redis'
```

If the Redis queue looks okay, but you are still having issues with logs getting indexed into Elasticsearch, you will want to check the Logstash statistics on the storage node(s).

7.9 Data Fields

This page references the various types of data fields utilized by Security Onion on the Elastic Stack.

The various fields types are described below.

7.9.1 Fields

Alert Data
Bro
Elastalert

7.9.2 Template files

Fields are mapped to their proper type using template files, found in `/etc/logstash/`. The current template files include:

`logstash-template.json` - mapping information for logs going into `logstash-*` indices

`beats-template.json` - mapping information for logs going into `logstash-beats-*` indices.

`logstash-ossec-template.json` - mapping information for logs going into `logstash-ossec-*` indices.

7.10 Alert Data Fields

Below are the fields derived from IDS alerts (Snort/Suricata), after being processed by Logstash:

```
type:snort
/etc/logstash/conf.d/1033_preprocess_snort.conf
```

alert
category
classification
source_ip
source_port
destination_ip
destination_port
gid
host
priority
protocol
rev
rule (*added through augmentation*)
rule_type
severity
sid
Signature_Info (*added through augmentation*)

7.11 Bro Fields

The following lists field names as they are formatted in Bro logs, then processed by Logstash and ingested into Elasticsearch.

The original field name (from Bro) appears on the left, and if changed, the updated name or formatting of the field (Elasticsearch) will appear on the right.

(Bro => Elastic)

7.11.1 conn.log

```
type:bro_conn
/etc/logstash/conf.d/1100_preprocess_bro_conn.conf
```

ts => timestamp
uid
id.orig_h => source_ip
id.orig_p => source_port
id.resp_h => destination_ip
id.resp_p => destination_port
proto => protocol
service
duration
orig_bytes => original_bytes
resp_bytes => respond_bytes
conn_state => connection_state => connection_state_description

```
Dictionary
S0 "Connection attempt seen, no reply"
S1 "Connection established, not terminated"
S2 "Connection established and close attempt by originator seen (but no reply from
↪responder)"
S3 "Connection established and close attempt by responder seen (but no reply from
↪originator)"
SF "Normal SYN/FIN completion"
REJ "Connection attempt rejected"
RSTO "Connection established, originator aborted (sent a RST)"
RSTR "Established, responder aborted"
```

local_orig
local_resp => local_respond
missed_bytes
history
orig_pkts => original_packets
orig_ip_bytes => original_ipbytes
resp_pkts => respond_packets
resp_ip_bytes => respond_ipbytes
tunnel_parents
original_country_code
respond_country_code
sensor_name

7.11.2 dhcp.log

type:bro_dhcp
/etc/logstash/conf.d/1101_preprocess_bro_dhcp.conf

ts => timestamp
uid
id.orig_h => source_ip

id.orig_p => source_port
id.resp_h => destination_ip
id.resp_p => destination_port
mac
assigned_ip
lease_time
trans_id => transaction_id

7.11.3 dns.log

```
type:bro_dns
/etc/logstash/conf.d/1102_preprocess_bro_dns.conf
```

ts = > timestamp
uid
id.orig_h => source_ip
id.orig_p => source_port
id.resp_h => destination_ip
id.resp_p => destination_port
proto => protocol
trans_id => transaction_id
rtt
query
qclass => query_class
qclass_name => query_class_name
qtype => query_type
qtype_name => query_type_name
rcode
rcode_name
AA => aa
TC => tc
RD => rd
RA => ra
Z => z
answers
TTLS => ttls (removed if not available)
rejected

7.11.4 dpd.log

```
type:bro_dpd
/etc/logstash/conf.d/1103_preprocess_bro_dpd.conf
```

ts => timestamp
uid

id.orig_h => source_ip
id.orig_p => source_port
id.resp_h => destination_ip
id.resp_p => destination_port
proto => protocol
analyzer
failure_reason

7.11.5 files.log

```
type:bro_files
/etc/logstash/conf.d/1104_preprocess_bro_files.conf
```

ts => timestamp
fuid
tx_hosts => file_ip
rx_hosts => destination_ip
conn_uids => connection_uids
source
depth
analyzers => analyzer
mime_type => mimetype
filename => file_name
duration
local_orig
is_orig
seen_bytes
total_bytes
missing_bytes
overflow_bytes
timedout => timed_out
parent_fuid
md5
sha1
sha256
extracted
extracted_cutoff
extracted_size

7.11.6 ftp.log

```
type:bro_ftp
/etc/logstash/conf.d/1105_preprocess_bro_ftp.conf
```

ts => timestamp

uid
id.orig_h => source_ip
id.orig_p => source_port
id.resp_h => destination_ip
id.resp_p => destination_port
user => ftp_username
password
command => ftp_command
arg => ftp_argument
mime_type => mimetype
file_size
reply_code
reply_msg => reply_message
data_channel.passive => data_channel_passive
data_channel.orig_h => data_channel_source_ip
data_channel.resp_h => data_channel_destination_ip
data_channel.resp_h => data_channel_destination_port
fuid

7.11.7 http.log

```
type:bro_http
/etc/logstash/conf.d/1106_preprocess_bro_http.conf
```

ts => timestamp
uid
id.orig_h => source_ip
id.orig_p => source_port
id.resp_h => destination_ip
id.resp_p => destination_port
trans_depth
method
host => virtual_host
uri
referrer
version
user_agent => useragent
request_body_len => request_body_length
response_body_len => response_body_length
status_code
status_message
info_code
info_msg => info_message
tags (removed)
username => user
password

proxied
orig_fuids
orig_filenames
orig_mime_types
resp_fuids
resp_filenames
resp_mime_types

7.11.8 intel.log

```
type:bro_intel
/etc/logstash/conf.d/1124_preprocess_bro_intel.conf
```

ts => timestamp
uid
id.orig_h => source_ip
id.orig_p => source_port
id.resp_h => destination_ip
id.resp_p => destination_port
seen.indicator => indicator
seen.indicator_type => indicator_type
seen.where => seen_where
seen.node => seen_node
matched
sources
fuid
file_mime_type => mimetype
file_desc => file_description

7.11.9 irc.log

```
type:bro_irc
/etc/logstash/conf.d/1107_preprocess_bro_irc.conf
```

ts => timestamp
uid
id.orig_h => source_ip
id.orig_p => source_port
id.resp_h => destination_ip
id.resp_p => destination_port
nick
user => irc_username
command => irc_command
value
addl => additional_info

dcc_file_name
dcc_file_size
dcc_mime_type
fuid

7.11.10 kerberos.log

```
type:bro_kerberos
/etc/logstash/conf.d/1108_preprocess_bro_kerberos.conf
```

timestamp
uid
id.orig_h => source_ip
id.orig_p => source_port
id.resp_h => destination_ip
id.resp_p => destination_port
request_type
client
service
success => kerberos_success
error_msg => error_message
from => email_from
till => valid_till
cipher
forwardable
renewable
client_cert => client_certificate_subject
client_cert_fuid => client_certificate_uid
server_cert_subject => server_certificate_subject
server_cert_fuid => server_certificate_fuid

7.11.11 modbus.log

```
type:bro_modbus
/etc/logstash/conf.d/1125_preprocess_bro_modbus.conf
```

ts => timestamp
uid
id.orig_h => source_ip
id.orig_p => source_port
id.resp_h => destination_ip
id.resp_p => destination_port
func => function
exception

7.11.12 mysql.log

type:bro_mysql
/etc/logstash/conf.d/1121_preprocess_bro_mysql.conf

ts => timestamp
uid
id.orig_h => source_ip
id.orig_p => source_port
id.resp_h => destination_ip
id.resp_p => destination_port
cmd => mysql_command
arg => mysql_argument
success => mysql_success
rows
response

7.11.13 notice.log

type:bro_notice
/etc/logstash/conf.d/1109_preprocess_bro_notice.conf

ts => timestamp
uid
id.orig_h => source_ip
id.orig_p => source_port
id.resp_h => destination_ip
id.resp_p => destination_port
fuid
mime => file_mime_type
desc => file_description
proto => protocol
note => note
msg => msg
sub => sub_msg
src => source_ip
dst => destination_ip
p
n
peer_descr => peer_description
actions => action
suppress_for
dropped
destination_country_code
destination_region

destination_city
destination_latitude
destination_longitude

7.11.14 pe.log

```
type:bro_pe
/etc/logstash/conf.d/1128_preprocess_bro_pe.conf
```

ts => timestamp
fuid
machine
compile_ts
os
subsystem
is_exe
is_64bit
uses_aslr
uses_dep
uses_code_integrity
uses_seh
has_import_table
has_export_table
has_cert_table
has_debug_data
section_names

7.11.15 radius.log

```
type:bro_radius
/etc/logstash/conf.d/1127_preprocess_bro_radius.conf
```

ts => timestamp
uid
id.orig_h => source_ip
id.orig_p => source_port
id.resp_h => destination_ip
id.resp_p => destination_port
username => radius_username
mac
remote_ip
connect_info
result
logged

7.11.16 rdp.log

type:bro_rdp
/etc/logstash/conf.d/1110_preprocess_bro_rdp.conf

ts => timestamp
uid
id.orig_h => source_ip
id.orig_p => source_port
id.resp_h => destination_ip
id.resp_p => destination_port
cookie
result
security_protocol
keyboard_layout
client_build
client_name
client_dig_product_id => client_digital_product_id
desktop_width
desktop_height
requested_color_depth
cert_type => certificate_type
cert_count => certificate_count
cert_permanent => certificate_permanent
encryption_level
encryption_method

7.11.17 rfb.log

type:bro_rfb
/etc/logstash/conf.d/1129_preprocess_bro_rfb.conf

ts => timestamp
uid
id.orig_h => source_ip
id.orig_p => source_port
id.resp_h => destination_ip
id.resp_p => destination_port
client_major_version
client_minor_version
server_major_version
server_minor_version
authentication_method
auth
share_flag

desktop_name
width
height

7.11.18 signatures.log

```
type:bro_ssl
/etc/logstash/conf.d/1111_preprocess_bro_signatures.conf
```

ts => timestamp
uid
id.orig_h => source_ip
id.orig_p => source_port
id.resp_h => destination_ip
id.resp_p => destination_port
note
sig_id => signature_id
event_msg => event_message
sub_msg => sub_message
sig_count => signature_count
host_count

7.11.19 sip.log

```
type:bro_sip
/etc/logstash/conf.d/1126_preprocess_bro_sip.conf
```

ts => timestamp
uid
id.orig_h => source_ip
id.orig_p => source_port
id.resp_h => destination_ip
id.resp_p => destination_port
trans_depth
method
uri
date
request_from
request_to
response_from
response_to
reply_to
call_id
seq
subject

request_path
response_path
user_agent
status_code
status_msg
warning
request_body_len
response_body_len
content_type

7.11.20 smtp.log

```
type:bro_smtp
/etc/logstash/conf.d/1112_preprocess_bro_smtp.conf
```

ts => timestamp
uid
id.orig_h => source_ip
id.orig_p => source_port
id.resp_h => destination_ip
id.resp_p => destination_port
trans_depth
helo
mailfrom => mail_from
rcptto => recipient_to
date => mail_date
from
to
cc
reply_to
msg_id => message_id
in_reply_to
subject
x_originating_ip
first_received
second_received
last_reply
path
useragent => user_agent
tls
fuids
is_webmail

7.11.21 snmp.log

```
type:bro_snmp
/etc/logstash/conf.d/1113_preprocess_bro_snmp.conf
```

ts => timestamp
uid
id.orig_h => source_ip
id.orig_p => source_port
id.resp_h => destination_ip
id.resp_p => destination_port
duration
version
community
get_requests
get_bulk_requests
get_responses
set_requests => set_responses
display_string
up_since

7.11.22 socks.log

```
type:bro_socks
/etc/logstash/conf.d/1122_preprocess_bro_socks.conf
```

timestamp
uid
id.orig_h => source_ip
id.orig_p => source_port
id.resp_h => destination_ip
id.resp_p => destination_port
version
user
password
status => server_status
request

- => request_host
- => request_name

request_p => request_port
bound

- => bound_host
- => bound_name

bound_p => bound_port

7.11.23 software.log

```
type:bro_software
/etc/logstash/conf.d/1114_preprocess_bro_software.conf
```

ts => timestamp
host => source_ip
host_p => source_port
software_type
name
major => version_major
minor => version_minor
minor2 => version_minor2
minor3 => version_minor3
addl => version_additional_info
unparsed_version

7.11.24 ssh.log

```
type:bro_ssh
/etc/logstash/conf.d/1115_preprocess_bro_ssh.conf
```

ts => timestamp
uid
id.orig_h => source_ip
id.orig_p => source_port
id.resp_h => destination_ip
id.resp_p => destination_port
version
auth_success => authentication_success
auth_attempts => authentication_attempts
direction
client
server
cipher_alg => cipher_algorithm
mac_alg => mac_algorithm
compression_alg => compression_algorithm
kex_alg => kex_algorithm
host_key_alg => host_key_algorithm
host_key
destination_country_code
destination_region
destination_city

destination_latitude

destination_longitude

7.11.25 ssl.log

```
type:bro_ssl
/etc/logstash/conf.d/1116_preprocess_bro_ssl.conf
```

ts => timestamp

uid

id.orig_h => source_ip

id.orig_p => source_port

id.resp_h => destination_ip

id.resp_p => destination_port

version

cipher

curve

server_name

resumed

last_alert

next_protocol

established

cert_chain_fuids => certificate_chain_fuids

client_cert_chain_fuids => client_certificate_chain_fuids

subject => certificate_subject

```
CN => "certificate_common_name"
C => "certificate_country_code"
O => "certificate_organization"
OU => "certificate_organization_unit"
ST => "certificate_state"
SN => "certificate_surname"
L => "certificate_locality"
GN => "certificate_given_name"
pseudonym => "certificate_pseudonym"
serialNumber => "certificate_serial_number"
title => "certificate_title"
initials" => "certificate_initials"
```

certificate_issuer

```
CN => "issuer_common_name"
C => "issuer_country_code"
O => "issuer_organization"
OU => "issuer_organization_unit"
ST => "issuer_state"
SN => "issuer_surname"
L => "issuer_locality"
DC => "issuer_distinguished_name"
```

(continues on next page)

(continued from previous page)
```
GN => "issuer_given_name"
pseudonym => "issuer_pseudonym"
serialNumber => "issuer_serial_number"
title => "issuer_title"
initials => "issuer_initials"
```

client_subject
client_issuer
validation_status
ja3 (if JA3 enabled)

7.11.26 syslog.log

`type:bro_syslog`
`/etc/logstash/conf.d/1117_preprocess_bro_syslog.conf`

ts => timestamp
uid
id.orig_h => source_ip
id.orig_p => source_port
id.resp_h => destination_ip
id.resp_p => destination_port
proto => protocol
facility
severity
message

7.11.27 tunnel.log

`type:bro_tunnel`
`/etc/logstash/conf.d/1118_preprocess_bro_tunnel.conf`

ts => timestamp
uid
id.orig_h => source_ip
id.orig_p => source_port
id.resp_h => destination_ip
id.resp_p => destination_port
tunnel_type
action

7.11.28 weird.log

```
type:bro_weird
/etc/logstash/conf.d/1119_preprocess_bro_weird.conf
```

ts => timestamp
uid
name
addl => additional_info
notice
peer

7.11.29 x509.log

```
type:bro_x509
/etc/logstash/conf.d/1123_preprocess_bro_x509.conf
```

ts => timestamp
id
certificate =>

- certificate_version
- certificate_serial
- certificate_subject
- certificate_issuer
- certificate_not_valid_before
- certificate_not_valid_after
- certificate_key_algorithm
- certificate_signing_algorithm
- certificate_key_type
- certificate_key_length
- certificate_exponent
- certificate_curve

san =>

- san_dns
- san_uri
- san_email
- san_ip

basic_constraints =>

- basic_constraints_ca

- basic_constraints_path_length

7.11.30 Pivot Fields

The following fields are formatted as a URL within Kibana, so we can easily pivot from them to the Indicator dashboard by clicking on them:

destination_ip
destination_port
file_ip
indicator
orig_fuids
query
resp_fuids
server_name
source_ip
source_port
uid
virtual_host

7.12 Elastalert Fields

The following lists field names as they are formatted in Elasticsearch. Elastalert provides its own template to use for mapping into Elastalert, so we do not current utilize a config file to parse data from Elastalert.

```
index:*:elastalert_status
```

alert_info.type
alert_sent
alert_time
endtime
hist
matches
match_body.@timestamp
match_body.num_hits
match_body.num_matches
rule_name
starttime
time_taken

7.13 Re-Indexing

When changing mappings or index settings, we may need to re-index the existing indices to ensure there are no mapping conflicts.

One way to do this by using the following **experimental** example script:

https://raw.githubusercontent.com/weslambert/securityonion-elastic-misc/master/so-elastic-reindex

Pull down the script to your Security Onion box:

```
wget https://raw.githubusercontent.com/weslambert/securityonion-elastic-misc/master/
↪so-elastic-reindex
```

Make the script executable:

```
sudo chmod +x so-elastic-reindex
```

Re-index all indices matching `logstash-*`, pulling the appropriate `refresh_interval` from the template named `logstash` in Elasticsearch:

```
sudo ./so-elastic-reindex -i "logstash-*" -t "logstash"
```

The script should then progress to re-index the matching indices, and inform you when it has completed.

Please note, abnormal execution of this script may result in data loss– there are **NO GUARANTEES** this process will work perfectly for you.

CHAPTER 8

Updating

In this section, we'll review how to keep Security Onion up-to-date.

8.1 Updating

8.1.1 soup

We recommend using our `soup` script to update. Soup will automatically install **all** available package updates (from both Ubuntu and Security Onion) and **all** updated Docker images.

```
sudo soup
```

Please pay attention to the output of this command as it may request that you take specific action, such as manually restarting services. Also refer to the relevant blog entry for the update at https://blog.securityonion.net as there may be additional information there.

8.1.2 Snort/Suricata

Snort package upgrades will back up each of your existing `snort.conf` files to `snort.conf.bak` and migrate your HOME_NET and EXTERNAL_NET variables.

Suricata package upgrades will back up each of your existing `suricata.yaml` files to `suricata.yaml.bak` and migrate your HOME_NET and EXTERNAL_NET variables.

You'll then need to do the following:

- re-apply any other local customizations to your `snort.conf/suricata.yaml` file(s)
- update ruleset and restart Snort/Suricata as follows:

```
sudo rule-update
```

8.1.3 Bro

Bro package upgrades will attempt to migrate your Bro config. You should double-check your config and see if there are any local customizations that you need to manually re-apply. Then restart Bro as follows:

```
sudo so-bro-restart
```

8.1.4 Wazuh

Wazuh package upgrades will back up your `ossec.conf` and put the new `ossec.conf` in place. You'll then need to do the following:

- re-apply any other local customizations to your `ossec.conf` file
- restart Wazuh as follows:

```
sudo so-ossec-restart
```

8.1.5 MySQL

If you get any errors relating to MySQL, please see the MySQL-Upgrade-Errors section.

8.1.6 Initiating an update over SSH

If you're updating your Security Onion box over an SSH connection and your connection drops, then your update process may be left in an inconsistent state. It is therefore recommended to run `byobu` so that your session will continue to run on the Security Onion box even if your connection drops. Byobu is very handy and we recommend running it all the time to avoid forgetting about it before an update.

```
# install byobu
sudo apt-get install byobu

# enable byobu
byobu-enable

# you're now ready to update
```

For more information about `byobu`, please see https://help.ubuntu.com/community/Byobu.

8.1.7 Distributed deployments

If you have a distributed deployment with a master server and separate sensor boxes and/or storage nodes, always update the master server first before updating other boxes. Then make sure to update the remaining boxes shortly thereafter. This will help to ensure that all boxes in your deployment are running the same code versions and help to avoid any incompatibilities.

8.1.8 Using salt and soup to update your entire deployment

salt and soup

8.1.9 Content Inspection

If your Security Onion box(es) go through a firewall, proxy, or other network security device that does content inspection, you may need to add an exception for `ppa.launchpad.net`.

8.1.10 Standard Ubuntu package management tools

The `soup` command described above is the recommended method to install updates. If you instead choose to use standard Ubuntu package management tools to install updates, there are some caveats to be aware of:

- Docker - Ubuntu package management tools don't update our Docker images (used for the Elastic Stack currently)
- MySQL - if you've already run Setup, please see the recommended procedure for updating the MySQL packages.
- PF-RING and new kernel packages

    You may be prompted to update your kernel packages and PF-RING at the same time. If you do so, the PF-RING kernel module may get built for your current kernel and not for the newly installed kernel and upon reboot services will fail. To avoid this, you should install just the PF-RING kernel module by itself and then install the kernel and any other remaining package updates. Here's a one-liner that will do that:

```
sudo apt-get update ; sudo apt-get install securityonion-pfring-module ; sudo apt-get dist-upgrade
```

If you accidentally install both the kernel and PF-RING packages at the same time and then reboot and find out that PF-RING services (Snort and Suricata) are failing, you can reinstall the `securityonion-pfring-module` package:

```
sudo apt-get install --reinstall securityonion-pfring-module
```

Security Onion 14.04

Please note: If you're still running the old Security Onion 14.04, `soup` will continue to install Ubuntu updates until Ubuntu stops releasing updates for 14.04. However, there won't be any more Security Onion updates for version 14.04 as all development will be on version 16.04 moving forward.

8.1.11 Upgrades

To upgrade from Security Onion 14.04 to Security Onion 16.04, please see the Upgrading-from-14.04-to-16.04 section.

8.2 MySQL Upgrade Errors

Ubuntu releases new MySQL packages periodically as needed. If you have a Security Onion 16.04 installation and run `soup` to install these new MySQL packages, you may see a few error messages as described below.

8.2.1 Error messages regarding MySQL upgrade process

If your installation has MySQL disabled (because you haven't yet run Setup or you've run Setup and chosen Forward Node or Storage Node), then you may also see error messages like the following:

```
mysql_upgrade: Got error: 2002: Can't connect to local MySQL server through socket '/
↪var/run/mysqld/mysqld.sock' (2) while connecting to the MySQL server
Upgrade process encountered error and will not continue.
mysql_upgrade failed with exit status 11
dpkg: error processing package mysql-server-5.7 (--configure):
 subprocess installed post-installation script returned error exit status 1

No apport report written because the error message indicates its a followup error␣
↪from a previous failure.

                        dpkg: dependency problems prevent configuration of mysql-server:
 mysql-server depends on mysql-server-5.7; however:
  Package mysql-server-5.7 is not configured yet.

dpkg: error processing package mysql-server (--configure):
 dependency problems - leaving unconfigured

Errors were encountered while processing:
 mysql-server-5.7
 mysql-server
E: Sub-process /usr/bin/dpkg returned an error code (1)
```

You can resolve this issue using the following one-liner:

```
sudo systemctl enable mysql.service && sudo apt -f install && sudo systemctl stop␣
↪mysql.service && sudo systemctl disable mysql.service
```

8.2.2 Error message regarding MySQL 5.5

Older versions of soup may result in error messages regarding MySQL 5.5. Newer versions of soup have been updated to correct this. If you are running an older version of soup and see error messages like this, they can be ignored as Security Onion 16.04 uses MySQL 5.7:

```
Package mysql-server-5.5 is not available, but is referred to by another package.
This may mean that the package is missing, has been obsoleted, or
is only available from another source
However the following packages replace it:
  mysql-server-5.7 mysql-common percona-xtradb-cluster-server-5.6:i386 percona-server-
↪server-5.6:i386 mysql-testsuite-5.7:i386 mariadb-server-10.0:i386 percona-xtradb-
↪cluster-server-5.6
  percona-server-server-5.6 mysql-testsuite-5.7 mariadb-server-10.0 mysql-server-5.
↪7:i386

Package mysql-server-core-5.5 is not available, but is referred to by another package.
This may mean that the package is missing, has been obsoleted, or
is only available from another source
However the following packages replace it:
  mysql-server-core-5.7 percona-server-server-5.6:i386 mariadb-server-core-10.0:i386␣
↪percona-server-server-5.6 mariadb-server-core-10.0 mysql-server-core-5.7:i386

E: Package 'mysql-server-core-5.5' has no installation candidate
E: Package 'mysql-server-5.5' has no installation candidate
```

8.3 apt-cacher-ng

If you have multiple Security Onion boxes in your environment and want to cache the package updates to save time and bandwidth, you can use apt-cacher-ng as a caching proxy.

For more information, please see:

https://www.unix-ag.uni-kl.de/~bloch/acng/

https://wiki.debian.org/AptCacherNg

https://help.ubuntu.com/community/Apt-Cacher-Server

8.4 End Of Life

This page lists End Of Life (EOL) dates for older versions of Security Onion and older components.

Security Onion 14.04 reached EOL on November 30, 2018:
https://blog.securityonion.net/2018/06/6-month-eol-notice-for-security-onion.html

ELSA reached EOL on October 9, 2018:
https://blog.securityonion.net/2018/04/6-month-eol-notice-for-elsa.html

Xplico reached EOL on June 5, 2018:
https://blog.securityonion.net/2017/12/6-month-eol-notice-for-security-onion.html

CHAPTER 9

Customizing for Your Environment

This section covers how to customize Security Onion for your environment.

9.1 Network Configuration

All of this configuration will happen automatically if you choose `Yes, configure /etc/network/interfaces` in the Setup wizard. If for some reason you need to configure `/etc/network/interfaces` manually, you can do the following.

NOTE! You may lose network connectivity during this process! Have a backup plan if attempting over SSH!

Stop Network Manager:

```
sudo /etc/init.d/network-manager stop
```

Prevent Network Manager from starting at next boot:

```
sudo mv /etc/init/network-manager.conf /etc/init/network-manager.conf.DISABLED
```

Next, configure your network interfaces in `/etc/network/interfaces`.

9.1.1 Management interface

You'll want a management interface (preferably connected to a dedicated management network) using either DHCP OR preferably static IP.

9.1.2 Sniffing interface(s)

You'll want one or more interfaces dedicated to sniffing (no IP address). NIC offloading functions such as `tso`, `gso`, and `gro` should be disabled to ensure that Snort/Suricata/Bro get an accurate view of the traffic (see https://blog.securityonion.net/2011/10/when-is-full-packet-capture-not-full.html).

9.1.3 Sample /etc/network/interfaces

```
auto lo
iface lo inet loopback

# Management interface using DHCP
auto eth0
iface eth0 inet dhcp

# OR

# Management interface using STATIC IP (instead of DHCP)
auto eth0
iface eth0 inet static
  address 192.168.1.14
  gateway 192.168.1.1
  netmask 255.255.255.0
  network 192.168.1.0
  broadcast 192.168.1.255
  dns-nameservers 192.168.1.1 192.168.1.2

# AND one or more of the following

# Connected to TAP or SPAN port for traffic monitoring
auto eth1
iface eth1 inet manual
  up ifconfig $IFACE -arp up
  up ip link set $IFACE promisc on
  down ip link set $IFACE promisc off
  down ifconfig $IFACE down
  post-up for i in rx tx sg tso ufo gso gro lro; do ethtool -K $IFACE $i off; done
  post-up echo 1 > /proc/sys/net/ipv6/conf/$IFACE/disable_ipv6
  # You probably don't need to enable or edit the following setting,
  # but it is included for completeness.
  # Note that 4096 is just an example and your NIC may have a different maximum rx␣
↪size.
  # To determine the maximum rx setting for your NIC: ethtool -g ethX
  # Also note that increasing beyond the default may result in inconsistent traffic:
  # https://taosecurity.blogspot.com/2019/04/troubleshooting-nsm-virtualization.html
  # post-up ethtool -G $IFACE rx 4096
```

If necessary, configure DNS in `/etc/resolv.conf`:

http://en.wikipedia.org/wiki/Resolv.conf

http://www.cyberciti.biz/tips/howto-ubuntu-linux-convert-dhcp-network-configuration-to-static-ip-configuration.html

http://manpages.ubuntu.com/manpages/lucid/man5/resolver.5.html

Restart networking:

```
sudo /etc/init.d/networking restart
```

If you already had sensors running on these interfaces, you should restart them:

```
sudo so-sensor-restart
```

For more information on network configuration in Ubuntu, please see https://help.ubuntu.com/community/NetworkConfigurationCommandLine/Automatic.

9.2 Proxy Configuration

If you need to force your Internet traffic through a proxy server, you can put your proxy server settings in `/etc/environment` like this:

```
export http_proxy=http://server:port
export https_proxy=https://server:port
export ftp_proxy=https://server:port
export PERL_LWP_ENV_PROXY=https://server:port
export no_proxy="localhost,127.0.0.1"
```

9.2.1 Docker

To configure Docker proxy settings, perform the following steps:

```
sudo -i
mkdir /etc/systemd/system/docker.service.d
cat <<EOT >> /etc/systemd/system/docker.service.d/proxy.conf
[Service]
Environment="HTTP_PROXY=http://proxy.someplace.com:8080/" "HTTPS_PROXY=http://proxy.
↪someplace.com:8080/" "NO_PROXY=127.0.0.1,localhost,.someplace.com"
EOT
systemctl daemon-reload && systemctl restart docker && exit
sudo soup
```

For older versions of Security Onion on the Elastic Stack, if the above did not work, you may want to try the following:

Modify `/etc/default/docker` and add the appropriate proxy information, like so:

```
export http_proxy="http://server:port/"
export https_proxy="https://server:port/"
```

Then restart Docker with:

```
sudo so-elastic-stop
sudo service docker restart
sudo so-elastic-start
```

9.2.2 sudo

If you're going to run something using sudo, remember to use the `-i` option to force it to process the environment variables. For example:

```
sudo -i rule-update
```

Alternatively, see the `env_keep` option under the `sudo caveat` section of https://help.ubuntu.com/community/EnvironmentVariables.

9.2.3 PulledPork

As of PulledPork 0.7.2, you may need to pass the `-W` option to Pulledpork:

```
-W Where you want to work around the issue where some implementations of LWP do not
↪work with pulledpork's proxy configuration.
```

If you find that you need this option, you can add the following to `/etc/nsm/securityonion.conf`:

```
PULLEDPORK_OPTIONS="-W"
```

For older versions of PulledPork and certain proxies (Bluecoat in particular), you may need to change from `https` to `http` in `/etc/nsm/pulledpork/pulledpork.conf`. For more information, please see:

PulledPork Issue 154

https://groups.google.com/d/topic/security-onion/NQ-dLLPxR6A/discussion

https://groups.google.com/d/topic/security-onion-testing/piRYj-7Ar8M/discussion

9.3 Firewall

9.3.1 Setup defaults to only allowing port 22 (ssh)

When you run Setup, it defaults to locking down the local `ufw` firewall to only allowing port 22 (ssh). There is a note at the end of Setup that tells you this and lets you know that, if you need to allow connections on other ports, you can run the so-allow utility.

9.3.2 Sensors automatically add their own firewall rules to the master server

When you run Setup on a sensor-only installation, it will ssh to the master server and add new firewall rules to the master server to allow the sensor to connect on the following ports:

- 22/tcp (ssh)
- 4505/tcp (salt)
- 4506/tcp (salt)
- 7736/tcp (sguil)

9.3.3 UFW

For more information about `ufw`, please see https://help.ubuntu.com/community/UFW.

9.4 Email Configuration

9.4.1 so-email

If you want to configure email, you can run `so-email` and it will automatically configure automated server-side email for you as described below. Simply run the following command and follow the prompts:

```
sudo so-email
```

To automate email setup, copy and modify the example file located at `/usr/share/securityonion/so-email.conf`, then run `so-email` with the `-f` flag:

```
sudo so-email -f ~/so-email.conf
```

9.4.2 Sguil client

Please note that the Sguil client has its own email configuration (separate from the Sguil server) which can be modified in `/etc/sguil/sguil.conf`.

9.4.3 Manual Configuration

If you don't want to run `so-email` as described above, you can configure email manually as described in the following sections. Applications such as Sguil and Wazuh have their own mail configuration and don't rely on a mail server in the OS itself. However, you may still want to install a mail server in the OS so that you can get daily emails from the sostat script and from Bro.

9.4.4 Operating System

Install and configure your favorite mail server. Depending on your needs, this could be something simple like `nullmailer` (recommended) or something more complex like `exim4`.

Here are some `nullmailer` instructions provided by Michael Iverson:

```
sudo apt-get install nullmailer

# edit /etc/mailname to hold your "from" domain name. (If you were google, you'd use
↪"gmail.com".)

# edit /etc/nullmailer/adminaddr to contain the address you want mail to root to be
↪routed to.

# edit /etc/nullmailer/remotes to contain the mail server to forward email to.
```

Alternatively, here are some instructions for the more complex `exim4`:

```
sudo apt-get -y install mailutils
sudo dpkg-reconfigure exim4-config
```

Once you've configured your mail server and verified that it can send email properly, you might want to create a daily cronjob to execute `/usr/sbin/sostat` and email you the output:

```
# /etc/cron.d/sostat
crontab entry to run sostat and email its output
------------------------------------------------
SHELL=/bin/sh
PATH=/usr/local/sbin:/usr/local/bin:/sbin:/bin:/usr/sbin:/usr/bin
EMAIL=YourUsername@YourDomain.com\
01 12 * * * root HOSTNAME=$(hostname); /usr/sbin/sostat 2>&1 | mail -s "$HOSTNAME
↪stats" $EMAIL
```

If you don't already have the `mail` utility, you can try installing:

```
sudo apt-get install mailutils
```

9.4.5 Sguild

Modify `/etc/nsm/securityonion/sguild.email` (on the master server) as needed and restart sguild:

```
sudo so-sguild-restart
```

You can then verify the email configuration by looking at the top of sguild's log file:

```
head -20 /var/log/nsm/securityonion/sguild.log
```

For more information, please see http://nsmwiki.org/Sguil_FAQ#Can_sguil_page_me_when_it_sees_a_particular_alert.3F.

You may want to install a local mail relay on your master server, configure it to relay mail to your corporate mail server, and then configure Sguil to send email to the local mail relay.

Please note: Sguil will only send email alerts for what is considers *new* events. Ensure you classify events within the Sguil console, or consider creating an Autocat rule to automatically classify them if you prefer to receive emails for all instances of an alert. Otherwise, you may not receive alerts as intended.

9.4.6 Wazuh

Modify `/var/ossec/etc/ossec.conf` as follows:

```
<global>
<email_notification>yes</email_notification>
<email_to>YourUsername@YourDomain.com</email_to>
<smtp_server>YourMailRelay.YourDomain.com</smtp_server>
<email_from>ossec@YourDomain.com</email_from>
<email_maxperhour>100</email_maxperhour>
</global>
```

Then restart Wazuh:

```
sudo so-ossec-restart
```

You can specify the severity of an event for which Wazuh will send email alerts by specifying an appropriate value for `email_alert_level` in `/var/ossec/etc/ossec.conf`. If you notice `email_alert_level` is not being respected for a certain rule, it may be that the option is overridden by `<options>alert_by_email</options>` being set for a rule. You can modify this behavior in `/var/ossec/rules/local.rules`.

You can also find an explanation of the alert levels at http://ossec-docs.readthedocs.io/en/latest/manual/rules-decoders/rule-levels.html.

9.4.7 Bro

Edit `/opt/bro/etc/broctl.cfg` and set the following:

```
MailTo = YourUsername@YourDomain.com
sendmail = /usr/sbin/sendmail
```

Then update and restart Bro:

```
sudo so-bro-restart
```

You should then start receiving hourly connection summary emails. If you don't want the connection summary emails, you can add the following to `broctl.cfg` and update and restart Bro as shown above:

```
tracesummary=
```

You may want to receive emails for Bro notices. To do that, add the following to `/opt/bro/share/bro/site/local.bro` and update/restart Bro as shown above:

```
hook Notice::policy(n: Notice::Info)
{
add n$actions[Notice::ACTION\_ALARM];
}
```

Also see http://mailman.icsi.berkeley.edu/pipermail/bro/2013-December/006418.html.

9.4.8 Elastalert

Follow the steps on the Elastalert page.

9.4.9 Lack of network traffic

If you configured Wazuh or Bro as shown above, they should automatically email you if your network sensors stop seeing traffic.

9.5 Changing IP Addresses

If you need to update the IP address of your server/sensor to move it to a different area of your network, you need to do a few things:

- update the actual IP address of the management interface
- update NSM config files to reflect the new IP address

9.5.1 Update the actual IP address of the management interface

To update the actual IP address of the management interface, you have two options:

- manually update `/etc/network/interfaces`

    OR

- re-run the `FIRST` phase of Setup (select `Yes, configure /etc/network/interfaces`)

9.5.2 Update NSM config files to reflect the new IP address

To update NSM config files to reflect the new IP address, you have two options:

- re-run the `SECOND` phase of Setup on all server/sensors (**wiping all data and config**)

    OR

- manually update the IP address as shown below

9.5.3 Files to update when changing the IP address

Changing Server IP

- /etc/nsm/HOSTNAME-INTERFACE/http_agent.conf:

```
set SERVER_HOST [SERVER-IP]
```

- /etc/nsm/HOSTNAME-INTERFACE/pads_agent.conf:

```
set SERVER_HOST [SERVER-IP]
```

- /etc/nsm/HOSTNAME-INTERFACE/pcap_agent.conf:

```
set SERVER_HOST [SERVER-IP]
```

- /etc/nsm/HOSTNAME-INTERFACE/sancp_agent.conf:

```
set SERVER_HOST [SERVER-IP]
```

- /etc/nsm/HOSTNAME-INTERFACE/sensor.conf:

```
SENSOR_SERVER_HOST="[SERVER-IP]"
```

- /etc/nsm/HOSTNAME-INTERFACE/snort_agent-N.conf:

```
set SERVER_HOST [SERVER-IP]
```

- /etc/nsm/ossec/ossec_agent.conf:

```
set SERVER_HOST [SERVER-IP]
```

- /root/.ssh/securityonion_ssh.conf

```
SERVERNAME=[SERVER-IP]
```

- /etc/salt/minion.d/onionsalt.conf

```
master: [SERVER-IP]
```

Automating the change of the server IP

You may be able to use sed to update all files at once using something like this:

```
sudo so-stop
sudo sed -i 's|OLD.SERVER.IP.ADDR|NEW.SERVER.IP.ADDR|g' /etc/nsm/*/*agent* /etc/nsm/*/
↪sensor.conf /root/.ssh/securityonion_ssh.conf /etc/salt/minion.d/onionsalt.conf
sudo so-start
```

9.6 NTP

Ubuntu configures its NTP service to pull time updates from the NTP Pool Project and from ntp.ubuntu.com. From `/etc/ntp.conf`:

```
# Use servers from the NTP Pool Project. Approved by Ubuntu Technical Board
# on 2011-02-08 (LP: #104525). See http://www.pool.ntp.org/join.html for
# more information.
server 0.ubuntu.pool.ntp.org
server 1.ubuntu.pool.ntp.org
server 2.ubuntu.pool.ntp.org
server 3.ubuntu.pool.ntp.org

# Use Ubuntu's ntp server as a fallback.
server ntp.ubuntu.com
```

9.6.1 Modifying

You may want to change this default NTP config to use your preferred NTP provider. For more information, please see https://help.ubuntu.com/lts/serverguide/NTP.html.

9.6.2 IDS Alerts

Anybody can join the NTP Pool Project and provide NTP service. Occasionally, somebody provides NTP service from a residential DHCP address that at some point in time may have also been used for TOR. This results in IDS alerts for TOR nodes where the port is 123 (NTP). This is another good reason to modify the NTP configuration to pull time updates from your preferred NTP provider.

CHAPTER 10

Tuning

To get the best performance out of Security Onion, you'll want to tune it for your environment. Start by creating Berkeley Packet Filters (BPFs) to ignore any traffic that you don't want your network sensors to process. Then tune your rulesets using PulledPork's `disablesid.conf` and `modifysid.conf`. There may be entire categories of rules that you want to disable first and then look at the remaining enabled rules to see if there are individual rules that can be disabled. Once your ruleset is a manageable size, then look at tuning your alerts via Sguil's autocat feature. Once your rules and alerts are under control, then look at sostat to see if you have packet loss. If so, then tune using PF-RING or AF-PACKET. If you are on a large network, you may need to do additional tuning like pinning processes to CPU cores. More information on each of these topics can be found in this section.

10.1 BPF

BPF stands for Berkeley Packet Filter:
https://en.wikipedia.org/wiki/Berkeley_Packet_Filter
http://biot.com/capstats/bpf.html

10.1.1 Configuration

Global bpf.conf

You can specify your BPF in `/etc/nsm/rules/bpf.conf` on your master server and, by default, it will apply to Snort/Suricata/Bro/netsniff-ng/prads on all interfaces in your entire deployment. If you have separate sensors reporting to that master server, they will copy `/etc/nsm/rules/bpf.conf` as part of the daily rule-update cron job (or you can run it manually) which will also restart Snort/Suricata so that the BPF change will take effect. Bro automatically monitors `bpf.conf` for changes and will update itself as needed. Other services (such as prads and netsniff-ng) will need to be restarted manually for the change to take effect.

Granular bpf.conf

Each process on each interface has its own bpf file, but by default the per-process bpf files are symlinked to the interface bpf and the interface bpf is then symlinked to the global `bpf.conf`:

```
lrwxrwxrwx 1 root    root         8 Jan 13 21:47 bpf-bro.conf -> bpf.conf
lrwxrwxrwx 1 root    root        23 Jan 13 21:47 bpf.conf -> /etc/nsm/rules/bpf.conf
lrwxrwxrwx 1 root    root         8 Jan 13 21:47 bpf-ids.conf -> bpf.conf
lrwxrwxrwx 1 root    root         8 Jan 13 21:47 bpf-pcap.conf -> bpf.conf
lrwxrwxrwx 1 root    root         8 Jan 13 21:47 bpf-prads.conf -> bpf.conf
```

If you don't want your sensors to inherit `bpf.conf` from the master server and/or you need to specify a bpf per-interface or per-process, you can simply replace the default symlink(s) with the desired bpf file(s) and restart service(s) as necessary. For example, suppose you want to apply a BPF to NIDS (Snort/Suricata) only:

```
# Remove the default NIDS BPF symlink
sudo rm bpf-ids.conf
# Create a new NIDS BPF file and add your custom BPF
sudo vi bpf-ids.conf
# Restart NIDS
sudo so-nids-restart
```

BPF Examples

Exclude traffic to/from a host:

```
!(host xxx.xxx.xxx.xxx)
```

Exclude traffic from a source host to a destination port:

```
!(src host xxx.xxx.xxx.xxx && dst port 161)
```

Combine multiple BPFs together using `&&`, but note that the last entry has no final `&&`:

```
#Nothing from src host to dst port
!(src host xxx.xxx.xxx.xxx && dst port 161) &&

#Nothing from src host to dst host and dst port
!(src host xxx.xxx.xxx.xxx && dst host xxx.xxx.xxx.xxx && dst port 80) &&

#Nothing to or from:
!(host xxx.xxx.xxx.xxx) &&

#Last entry has no final &&
!(host xxx.xxx.xxx.xxx)
```

VLAN

From Seth Hall regarding VLAN tags:

```
(not (host 192.168.53.254 or host 192.168.53.60 or host 192.168.53.69 or host 192.168.
↪53.234)) or (vlan and (not (host 192.168.53.254 or host 192.168.53.60 or host 192.
↪168.53.69 or host 192.168.53.234)))
```

This amazingly works if you are only using it to restrict the traffic passing through the filter. The basic template is. . .

```
<your filter> and (vlan and <your filter>)
```

Once the `vlan` tag is included in the filter, all subsequent expressions to the right are shifted by four bytes so you need to duplicate the filter on both sides of the vlan keyword. There are edge cases where this will no longer work and probably edge cases where a few undesired packets will make it though, but it should work in the example case that you've given.

Also, I'm assuming that any tools you are running will support vlan tags and no tags simultaneously. Bro 2.0 should work fine at least.

Troubleshooting BPF using tcpdump

If you need to troubleshoot BPF, you can use `tcpdump` as shown in the following articles.

http://taosecurity.blogspot.com/2004/09/understanding-tcpdumps-d-option-have.html

http://taosecurity.blogspot.com/2004/12/understanding-tcpdumps-d-option-part-2.html

http://taosecurity.blogspot.com/2008/12/bpf-for-ip-or-vlan-traffic.html

10.2 Managing Rules

NIDS rulesets are chosen during setup and are specified in `/etc/nsm/pulledpork/pulledpork.conf`. If you change any of the configuration in `/etc/nsm/pulledpork/`, then you will need to update your rules as shown in the following section.

10.2.1 Updating Rules

To update your rules, run `rule-update` on your master server:

```
sudo rule-update
```

If you have a distributed deployment with salt enabled and you run `rule-update` on your master server, then those new rules will automatically replicate from the master to your sensors within 15 minutes. If you don't want to wait 15 minutes, you can force the sensors to update immediately by running the following command on your master server:

```
sudo salt '*' state.highstate
```

If you have a distributed deployment with salt disabled and you run `rule-update` on your master server, then those new rules will replicate from the master to your sensors during the daily cron job. If you don't want to wait for that daily cron job, you can force an immediate update on the sensor by logging into the sensor and running:

```
sudo rule-update
```

10.2.2 Rulesets

Security Onion offers the following choices for rulesets to be used by Snort/Suricata.

10.2.3 ET Open

- optimized for Suricata, but available for Snort as well
- **free**

For more information, see:
https://rules.emergingthreats.net/open/

10.2.4 ET Pro (Proofpoint)

- optimized for Suricata, but available for Snort as well
- rules retrievable as released
- license fee per sensor

For more information, see:
https://www.proofpoint.com/us/threat-insight/et-pro-ruleset

10.2.5 Snort Community

- optimized for Snort
- community-contributed rules
- **free**

For more information, see:
https://www.snort.org/downloads/#rule-downloads
https://www.snort.org/faq/what-are-community-rules

10.2.6 Snort Registered

- optimized for Snort
- Snort SO (Shared Object) rules will only work with Snort
- same rules as Snort Subscriber ruleset, except rules only retrievable after 30 days past release
- **free**

For more information, see:
https://www.snort.org/downloads/#rule-downloads
https://snort.org/documents/registered-vs-subscriber

10.2.7 Snort Subscriber (Talos)

- optimized for Snort
- Snort SO (Shared Object) rules will only work with Snort
- rules retrievable as released
- license fee per sensor

For more information, see:
https://www.snort.org/downloads/#rule-downloads
https://snort.org/documents/registered-vs-subscriber

10.3 Adding Local Rules

Adding local rules in Security Onion is a rather straightforward process. However, generating custom traffic to test the alert can sometimes be a challenge. Here, we will show you how to add the local rule and then use the python library scapy to trigger the alert.

- Open `/etc/nsm/rules/local.rules` using your favorite text editor. If this is a distributed deployment, edit local.rules on your master server and it will replicate to your sensors.
- Let's add a simple rule that will alert on the detection of a string in a tcp session:

```
alert tcp any any -> $HOME_NET 7789 (msg: "Vote for Security Onion Toolsmith Tool
of 2011!"; reference: url,http://holisticinfosec.blogspot.com/2011/12/choose-
2011-toolsmith-tool-of-year.html; content: "toolsmith"; flow:to_server; nocase;
sid:9000547; rev:1)
```

- Run `rule-update` (this will merge `local.rules` into `downloaded.rules`, update `sid-msg.map`, and restart processes as necessary):

```
sudo rule-update
```

- If you built the rule correctly, then Snort/Suricata should be back up and running.

10.3.1 Testing Local Rules

- Generate some traffic to trigger the alert. To generate traffic we are going to use the python library `scapy` to craft packets with specific information to ensure we trigger the alert with the information we want:

```
sudo scapy
```

- Craft the layer 2 information. The ip addresses can be random, but I would suggest sticking to RFC1918:

```
ip = IP()
ip.dst = "192.168.200.4"
ip.src = "192.168.100.3"
```

- Craft the layer 3 information Since we specified port 7789 in our snort rule:

```
tcp = TCP()
tcp.dport = 7789
tcp.sport = 1234
```

- Set the playload:

```
payload = "Toolsmith"
```

- Use the / operator to compose our packet and transfer it with the send() method:

```
send(ip/tcp/payload)
```

- Check Sguil/Squert/Kibana for the corresponding alert.
- You can see that we have an alert with the IP addresses we specified and the TCP ports we specified. If you pivot from that alert to the corresponding pcap you can verify the payload we sent.
- You can learn more about snort and writing snort signatures from the Snort Manual.
- You can learn more about scapy at secdev.org and itgeekchronicles.co.uk.

10.3.2 IPS Policy

Please note if you are using a ruleset that enables an IPS policy in `/etc/nsm/pulledpork/pulledpork.conf`, your local rules will be disabled. To enabled them, either revert the policy by remarking the `ips_policy` line (and run `rule-update`), or add the policy type to the rules in local.rules.

For example, if `ips_policy` was set to `security`, you would add the following to each rule:

`metadata:policy security-ips`

The whole rule would then look something like:

```
alert tcp any any -> $HOME_NET 7789 (msg: "Vote for Security Onion Toolsmith Tool of
↪2011!"; reference: url,http://holisticinfosec.blogspot.com/2011/12/choose-2011-
↪toolsmith-tool-of-year.html; content: "toolsmith"; flow:to_server; nocase;
↪sid:9000547; metadata:policy security-ips; rev:1)
```

These policy types can be found in `/etc/nsm/rules/downloaded.rules`.

10.3.3 MISP

If you would like to pull in NIDS rules from a MISP instance, please see the MISP Rules section.

10.4 Managing Alerts

Security Onion generates a lot of valuable information for you the second you plug it into a TAP or SPAN port. Between Bro logs, alert data from Snort/Suricata, and full packet capture from netsniff-ng, you have, in a very short amount of time, enough information to begin making identifying areas of interest and making positive changes to your security stance.

However, Network Security Monitoring, as a practice, is not a solution you can plug into your network, make sure you see blinking lights and tell people you are "secure." It requires active intervention from an analyst to qualify the quantity of information presented. One of those regular interventions is to ensure that you are tuning properly and proactively attempting to reach an acceptable level of signal to noise.

10.4.1 Testing to make sure the IDS is working

Below, we'll provide a few ways we can test our IDS (Snort/Suricata) to make sure it is working as expected.

1. The easiest way to test might be simply accessing `testmyids.com` from a machine who's traffic is being monitored:

   ```
   curl testmyids.com
   ```

   We should see a corresponding alert (`GPL ATTACK_RESPONSE id check returned root`) pop up in Sguil if everything is configured correctly. If you do not see this alert, try checking to see if the rule is enabled in `/etc/nsm/rules/downloaded.rules`. If it is not enabled, try enabling it via `/etc/nsm/pulledpork/enablesid.conf` and run `rule-update` (if this is a distributed deployment, update the master first, run `rule-update`, then push the changes out to the other sensor(s)).

2. If running a test or evaluation version of Security Onion, consider replaying some of the example PCAP files present in `/opt/samples/`:

   ```
   sudo so-test
   ```

   Alerts for various signatures should appear in Sguil.

3. If in a production environment where you might not want to replay the example PCAPs, another way to test would be to use Scapy to craft a test PCAP file, in conjunction with a custom Snort rule added to `/etc/nsm/rules/local.rules`:

   - **Snort Rule**

     ```
     alert tcp any any -> any any (msg: "Security Onion - testing"; content:
     ↪"SecurityOnion"; nocase; sid:1234567;)
     ```

     Now update your ruleset:

     ```
     sudo rule-update
     ```

   - **Scapy**

     ```
     sudo scapy
     pkt = Ether()/IP(dst="192.168.1.30")/TCP()/"SecurityOnion"
     wrpcap("so-testing.pcap", pkt)
     ```

     Press `CTRL+D` to exit scapy. Then use tcpreplay to replay the pcap to your sniffing interface:

     ```
     sudo tcpreplay -i ens34 -M10 so-testing.pcap
     ```

     If everything went as planned, an alert should pop up in Sguil with the message `Security Onion - testing`.

10.4.2 Identifying overly active signatures

Given the large number of analyst tools available in Security Onion by default there are multiple ways to see signatures that are producing too many alerts. We'll take a look at identifying the alerts using Squert, Sguil, and the command line.

10.4.3 From Squert

You can access the Squert interface from a web browser using the URL: https://IP_ADDRESS/squert/. You will need to log in using the username and password you set for Sguil. Click the Summary tab and then look at the TOP SIGNATURES section.

10.4.4 From Sguil

Sguil is a powerhouse of an interface for alerts and we since it allows us a more direct interaction with the database holding our alerts, we can gain a little bit more insight into the alerts, the associated IPs, and the rules in general.

Here, I have logged into the sguil interface and clicked on the "CNT" column to sort the alerts by the number of correlated alerts.

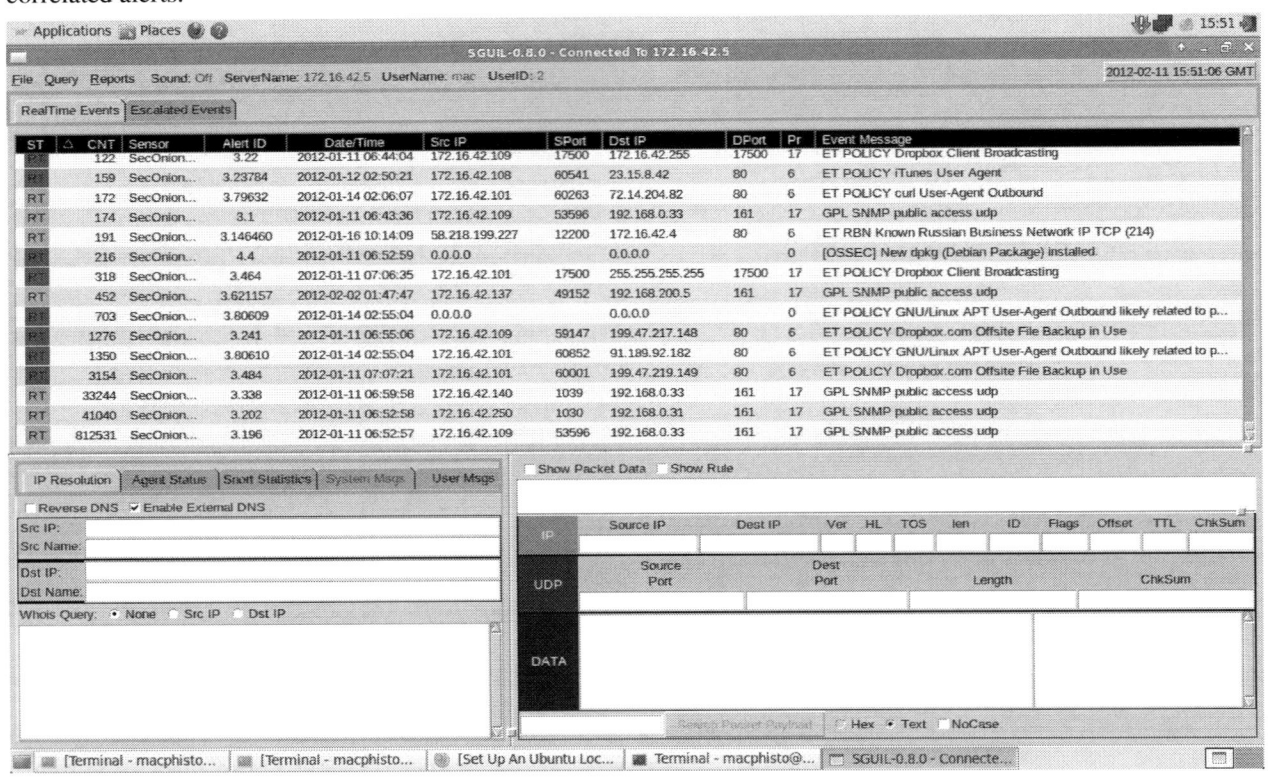

10.4.5 From the Command Line

If there are a large number of uncategorized events in the securityonion_db database, sguil can have a hard time of managing the vast amount of data it needs to process to present a comprehensive overview of the alerts.

At those times, it can be useful to query the database from the commandline. Interacting with the mysql database directly demands caution. Issuing SELECT queries should not have any adverse effect on your database, but if you attempt to UPDATE while the various NSM framework tools are also accessing the database it has the potential to introduce corruption.

You can enter the mysql shell or issue mysql one-liner's from the command line.

To enter the mysql shell, issue the following command:

```
sudo mysql --defaults-file=/etc/mysql/debian.cnf -Dsecurityonion_db
```

To issue commandline one-liners use the following template:

```
sudo mysql --defaults-file=/etc/mysql/debian.cnf -Dsecurityonion_db -e "QUERY"
```

10.4.6 Listing the top twenty signatures

Giving the following query to mysql will return a table much like you see below. Here, we are asking mysql to return the columns "signature and signature_id" as well as a count of each row returned. We also want the output grouped by the signature message and ordered by the count (cnt) in descending order.

```
SELECT COUNT(*) AS cnt, signature, signature_id FROM event WHERE status=0 GROUP BY
↪signature ORDER BY cnt DESC LIMIT 20;
```

```
+--------+----------------------------------------------------------------------
↪------+--------------+
| cnt    | signature
↪       | signature_id |
+--------+----------------------------------------------------------------------
↪------+--------------+
| 900286 | GPL SNMP public access udp
↪       |      2101411 |
|   4709 | ET POLICY Dropbox.com Offsite File Backup in Use
↪       |      2012647 |
|   2334 | ET POLICY GNU/Linux APT User-Agent Outbound likely related to package
↪management |      2013504 |
|   1169 | GPL SHELLCODE x86 inc ebx NOOP
↪       |         1390 |
|    464 | ET POLICY Dropbox Client Broadcasting
↪       |      2012648 |
|    343 | ET POLICY iTunes User Agent
↪       |      2002878 |
|    270 | ET POLICY Executable served from Amazon S3
↪       |      2013437 |
|    216 | [OSSEC] New dpkg (Debian Package) installed.
↪       |         2902 |
|    191 | ET RBN Known Russian Business Network IP TCP (214)
↪       |      2406426 |
|    188 | ET POLICY curl User-Agent Outbound
↪       |      2013028 |
|    119 | [OSSEC] Integrity checksum changed.
↪       |          550 |
|    106 | ET GAMES STEAM Connection (v2)
↪       |      2003089 |
|     84 | GPL ICMP_INFO PING *NIX
↪       |      2100366 |
|     69 | GPL CHAT MISC Jabber/Google Talk Outgoing Traffic
↪       |    100000230 |
|     65 | ET CHAT Google IM traffic Jabber client sign-on
↪       |      2002334 |
|     59 | ET CHAT Google Talk (Jabber) Client Login
↪       |      2002327 |
|     56 | [OSSEC] Attempt to login using a non-existent user
↪       |         5710 |
```

(continues on next page)

```
|     47 | ET SCAN Potential SSH Scan OUTBOUND                                      ␣
↪       |    2003068 |
|     44 | ET SCAN Potential SSH Scan                                               ␣
↪       |    2001219 |
|     38 | GPL ICMP_INFO PING BSDtype                                               ␣
↪       |    2100368 |
+--------+-------------------------------------------------------------------------
↪------+--------------+
20 rows in set (32.65 sec)
```

Again we can see that the top signature is the "GPL SNMP public access udp" alert and here we can see there are over 900,000 uncategorized events. Not only will the processing of these uncategorized events slow our use of tools they will cost the analyst time which could be better used in responding to alerts of greater significance.

If we're going to take action on this alert, it's best to ensure that these alerts are benign as part of our tuning process. See which machines generated these alerts can be helpful in making that decision.

```
SELECT COUNT(*) AS ip_cnt, INET_NTOA(src_ip) FROM event WHERE status=0 AND signature_
↪id=2101411 GROUP BY src_ip ORDER BY ip_cnt DESC;
```

```
+--------+-------------------+
| ip_cnt | INET_NTOA(src_ip) |
+--------+-------------------+
| 824459 | 172.16.42.109     |
|  41643 | 172.16.42.250     |
|  33732 | 172.16.42.140     |
|    452 | 172.16.42.137     |
+--------+-------------------+
4 rows in set (9.60 sec)
```

We can gather a little more information by using a query that also returns the destination IP address as well.

```
SELECT COUNT(*) as ip_cnt, INET_NTOA(src_ip), INET_NTOA(dst_ip) FROM event WHERE␣
↪status=0 and signature_id=2101411 GROUP BY dst_ip ORDER BY ip_cnt DESC;
```

```
+--------+-------------------+-------------------+
| ip_cnt | INET_NTOA(src_ip) | INET_NTOA(dst_ip) |
+--------+-------------------+-------------------+
| 858191 | 172.16.42.109     | 192.168.0.33      |
|  41643 | 172.16.42.250     | 192.168.0.31      |
|    226 | 172.16.42.137     | 192.168.200.5     |
|    226 | 172.16.42.137     | 192.168.200.51    |
+--------+-------------------+-------------------+
4 rows in set (9.65 sec)
```

10.4.7 Identifying rule categories

Both the Snort Subscriber (Talos) and the Emerging Threats rulesets come with a large number of rules enabled (over 15,000 by default). You should only run the rules necessary for your environment. So you may want to disable entire categories of rules that don't apply to you. Run the following command to get a listing of categories and the number of rules in each:

```
cut -d\" -f2 /etc/nsm/rules/downloaded.rules | grep -v "^$" | grep -v "^#" | awk '
↪{print $1, $2}'|sort |uniq -c |sort -nr
```

Also see:

https://github.com/shirkdog/pulledpork/blob/master/doc/README.CATEGORIES

10.4.8 Recovering from too many alerts

Sometimes we may get flooded with a barrage of alerts that make it difficult or not possible to categorize within Sguil or Squert. When this happens, we can perform mass categorization of alerts using MySQL on the master server, where sguild (the Sguil server) runs. The steps below outline an example of this:

- Stop the Sguil server:

```
sudo so-sguild-stop
```

- List the top twenty signatures (descending) pertaining to uncategorized alerts (with a status of 0):

```
sudo mysql --defaults-file=/etc/mysql/debian.cnf -Dsecurityonion_db -e 'SELECT
↪COUNT(signature)as count, signature FROM event WHERE status=0 GROUP BY
↪signature ORDER BY count DESC LIMIT 20;'
```

- Update any records (to have a status value of 1) with a signature that contains the text ET INFO:

```
sudo mysql --defaults-file=/etc/mysql/debian.cnf -Dsecurityonion_db -e "UPDATE
↪event SET status=1, last_modified='2018-06-27 01:00:00', last_uid='sguil' WHERE
↪event.status='0' and event.signature LIKE '%ET INFO%';"
```

- **Check again to see if our alerts have been categorized as `acknowledged` (these should no longer be visible in the output):**

```
sudo mysql --defaults-file=/etc/mysql/debian.cnf -Dsecurityonion_db -e 'SELECT
↪COUNT(signature)as count, signature FROM event WHERE status=0 GROUP BY
↪signature ORDER BY count DESC LIMIT 20;'
```

- Bring the Sguil server back up:

```
sudo so-sguild-start
```

Adapted from https://taosecurity.blogspot.com/2013/02/recovering-from-suricata-gone-wild.html.

10.4.9 So what's next?

Firstly, in tuning your sensor, you must understand whether or not taking corrective actions on this signature will lower your overall security stance. For some alerts, your understanding of your own network and the business being transacted across it will be the deciding factor. If you don't care that users are accessing facebook, you can silence the policy-based signatures that will generate alerts.

This signature, sid:1411, /is/ a useful signature to have on hand. Attackers will often search for SNMP enabled devices with default community strings in their attempts to pivot to other parts of the network. In this case, I know the alerts are being generated by benign traffic but I cannot guarantee that further alerts will be.

Another consideration to take into mind is determine whether or not the traffic is being generated by a misconfigured piece of equipment. If so, the most expedient measure is to correctly configure said equipment and then reinvestigate tuning.

There are multiple ways to handle overly productive signatures and we'll try to cover as many as we can without producing a full novel on the subject.

10.4.10 Disable the sid

Security Onion uses PulledPork to download new signatures every night and process them against a set list of user generated configurations.

In a distributed Security Onion environment, you only need to change the configuration file on the server and the rule-update script will sync with the signatures from the Server.

As mentioned before, take care in disabling signatures as it can be likely that a more appropriate response is warranted.

- Edit the disablesid.conf configuration file:

```
sudo vi /etc/nsm/pulledpork/disablesid.conf
```

- Append the signature you wish to disable in the format gid:sid. The generator ID is most likely going to be a "1" in most cases. You can check the generator ID by checking the exact signature. If a gid is not listed, it is assumed to be "1".

```
# Disable the GPL SNMP public access udp signature
1:2101411
```

- Update rules as shown in the Updating Rules section.

10.4.11 Disable the category

In `/etc/nsm/pulledpork/disablesid.conf`, instead of providing a sid, we can use a PCRE (Perl-compatible regular expression) or refer to the rule category (found in the header above the rule grouping in `/etc/nsm/rules/downloaded.rules`).

For example, if we wanted to disable the entire ET-emerging-misc category, we could do so by putting the following in `/etc/nsm/pulledpork/disablesid.conf`:

```
ET-emerging-misc
```

If we wanted to disable all rules with `ET MISC` in the rule description, we could put the following in `/etc/nsm/pulledpork/disablesid.conf`:

```
pcre:ET MISC
```

After making changes to the file, update your rules as shown in the Updating Rules section.

10.4.12 modifysid.conf

PulledPork's modifysid.conf will allow you to write modifications to rules that are applied every time PulledPork downloads the latest ruleset. There are several examples in the modifysid.conf file, so we won't repeat them here. Edit the modifysid.conf configuration file:

```
sudo vi /etc/nsm/pulledpork/modifysid.conf
```

Update rules as shown in the Updating Rules section.

10.4.13 Rewrite the signature

In some cases, you may not want to use Pulledpork's modifysid.conf, but instead create a copy of the rule and disable the original. In Security Onion, locally created rules are stored in /etc/nsm/rules/local.rules

- Edit the /etc/nsm/rules/local.rules file:

```
sudo vi /etc/nsm/rules/local.rules
```

- Snort rules are incredibly flexible, this is a bird's eye view of the rule format:

```
Action Protocol SrcIP SrcPort Direction DestIP DestPort (rule options)
```

- Here is the rule that has been generating so many alerts on our sensor(s)

```
macphisto@SecOnion-Dev:~$ grep -i "GPL SNMP public access udp" /etc/nsm/rules/
↪downloaded.rules
 alert udp $EXTERNAL_NET any -> $HOME_NET 161 (msg:"GPL SNMP public access udp";␣
↪content:"public"; fast_pattern:only; reference:bugtraq,2112; reference:bugtraq,
↪4088; reference:bugtraq,4089; reference:cve,1999-0517; reference:cve,2002-0012;␣
↪reference:cve,2002-0013; classtype:attempted-recon; sid:2101411; rev:11;)
```

- We can rewrite the rule so it's a little less active. We will rewrite the rule to ignore this kind of alert if the destination is any of the hosts we've identified.

- For starters let's create some variables in /etc/nsm/rules/local.rules to define the traffic. First we're going to define a variable for our called overactive hosts called OVERACTIVE

```
var OVERACTIVE [192.168.0.31,192.168.0.33,192.168.0.5,192.168.0.51]
```

- We can plug this information into our snort rule format,

```
alert udp $HOME_NET any -> !$OVERACTIVE any (msg:"GPL SNMP public access udp";␣
↪content:"public"; fast_pattern:only; reference:bugtraq,2112; reference:bugtraq,
↪4088; reference:bugtraq,4089; reference:cve,1999-0517; reference:cve,2002-0012;␣
↪reference:cve,2002-0013; classtype:attempted-recon; sid:9001411; rev:1;)
```

- We also gave the alert a unique signature id (sid) by bumping it into the 90,000,000 range and set the revision to 1.

- Now that we have a signature that will generate alerts a little more selectively, we need to disable the original signature. Like above, we edit the disablesid.conf file and add:

```
1:2101411
```

- Update rules as shown in the Updating Rules section.

10.4.14 Threshold

See `/etc/nsm/rules/threshold.conf` for more information and examples.

10.4.15 Suppressions

A suppression rule allows you to make some finer grained decisions about certain rules without the onus of rewriting them. With this functionality we can suppress rules based on their signature, the source or destination address and even the IP or full CIDR network block. This way, you still have the basic ruleset, but the situations in which they fire are altered. It's important to note that with this functionality, care should be given to the suppressions being written to make sure they do not suppress legitimate alerts.

Sticking with our current example of disabling the `GPL SNMP public access udp` alert we can build a suppression rule that limits this signature from firing for machines in which this behavior is deemed acceptable. For example, you would often see this rule firing rapidly for any service that queries SNMP on a regular basic. Services like Nagios produce a great many of these alerts. In this example, we will operate on the following known information:

Source IP Address	172.16.42.109
Generator ID	1
Signature ID	2101411

The format for a suppression is very straight forward. Below is the basic format for a suppression with the configurable areas marked in bold text.

suppress gen_id **gen-id**, sig_id **sid-id**, track **[by_src|by_dst]**, ip **IP/MASK-BITS**

We can simply transplant the known information for the bold text above and place the following in `/etc/nsm/rules/threshold.conf`:

```
suppress gen_id 1, sig_id 2101411, track by_src, ip 172.16.42.109
```

Once the correct suppression has been placed in `threshold.conf`, restart the alert engine:

```
sudo so-nids-restart
```

10.4.16 Autocategorize events

The sguild server can be set to autocategorize events as it processes them. This is a great way to have sguil process the events for us as it sees them, saving us from any laborious categorization. In the Sguil console, you can create an autocat by right-clicking the event status or by clicking File -> Autocat. In Squert, you can click the Autocat icon in the upper right corner.

10.4.17 Why is pulledpork ignoring disabled rules in downloaded.rules

If your syntax is correct, you are likely trying to disable a rule that has flowbits set. For a quick primer on flowbits see http://blog.snort.org/2011/05/resolving-flowbit-dependancies.html and section 3.6.10 of the Snort Manual (http://www.snort.org/docs).

Let's look at the following rules using:

```
alert tcp $HOME_NET any -> $EXTERNAL_NET !1433 (msg:"ET POLICY Outbound MSSQL
→Connection to Non-Standard Port - Likely Malware"; flow:to_server,established;
→content:"|12 01 00|"; depth:3; content:"|00 00 00 00 00 00 15 00 06 01 00 1b 00 01
→02 00 1c 00|"; distance:1; within:18; content:"|03 00|"; distance:1; within:2;
→content:"|00 04 ff 08 00 01 55 00 00 00|"; distance:1; within:10; flowbits:set,ET.
→MSSQL; classtype:bad-unknown; sid:2013409; rev:3;)

alert tcp $HOME_NET any -> $EXTERNAL_NET 1433 (msg:"ET POLICY Outbound MSSQL
→Connection to Standard port (1433)"; flow:to_server,established; content:"|12 01 00|
→"; depth:3; content:"|00 00 00 00 00 00 15 00 06 01 00 1b 00 01 02 00 1c 00|";
→distance:1; within:18; content:"|03 00|"; distance:1; within:2; content:"|00 04 ff
→08 00 01 55 00 00 00|"; distance:1; within:10; flowbits:set,ET.MSSQL; classtype:bad-
→unknown; sid:2013410; rev:4;)

alert tcp $HOME_NET any -> $EXTERNAL_NET !1433 (msg:"ET TROJAN Bancos.DV MSSQL CnC
→Connection Outbound"; flow:to_server,established; flowbits:isset,ET.MSSQL; content:
→"|49 00 B4 00 4D 00 20 00 54 00 48 00 45 00 20 00 4D 00 41 00 53 00 54 00 45 00 52
→00|"; classtype:trojan-activity; sid:2013411; rev:1;)
```

If you try to disable the first two rules without disabling the third rule (which has "flowbits:isset...") the third rule could never fire due to one of the first two rules needing to fire first. Pulled Pork (helpfully) resolves all of your flowbit dependencies, and in this case, is "re-enabling" that rule for you on the fly. Disabling all three of those rules by adding the following to disablesid.conf has the obvious negative effect of disabling all three of the rules:

```
1:2013409
1:2013410
1:2013411
```

When you run `sudo rule-update`, watch the "Setting Flowbit State..." section and you can see that if you disable all three (or however many rules share that flowbit) that the "Enabled XX flowbits" line is decrimented and all three rules should then be disabled in your `downloaded.rules`.

10.4.18 Sguil Days To Keep

You can configure Sguil's database retention by editing securityonion.conf and changing the `DAYSTOKEEP` setting (the default is 30 days):

```
/etc/nsm/securityonion.conf
```

You can also use this setting to perform a Sguil database purge by lowering the `DAYSTOKEEP` variable to a small number (like 7 or 1) and manually running:

```
sudo sguil-db-purge
```

10.5 PF-RING

PF-RING acts as a flow-based load balancer to allow us to spin up multiple instances of Snort/Suricata/Bro to handle more traffic than a single instance.

Starting in `securityonion-setup - 20120912-0ubuntu0securityonion285`, running Setup will configure Suricata and Bro to use AF-PACKET instead of PF-RING.

10.5.1 Tuning

If you want to change the number of PF-RING instances after running Setup, you can do the following.

10.5.2 Snort/Suricata

To change the number of PF-RING instances for Snort or Suricata:

- Stop sensor processes:

```
sudo so-sensor-stop
```

- Edit `/etc/nsm/$HOSTNAME-$INTERFACE/sensor.conf` and change the `IDS_LB_PROCS` variable to desired number of cores.

- Start sensor processes:

```
sudo so-sensor-start
```

If running Snort, `so-sensor-start` automatically spawns `$IDS_LB_PROCS` instances of Snort (using PF-RING), barnyard2, and snort_agent.

If running Suricata, `so-sensor-start` automatically copies `$IDS_LB_PROCS` into `suricata.yaml` and then Suricata spins up the PF-RING instances itself.

10.5.3 Bro

To change the number of PF-RING instances for Bro:

- Stop bro:

```
sudo so-bro-stop
```

- Edit `/opt/bro/etc/node.cfg` and change the `lb_procs` variable to the desired number of cores.

- Start bro:

```
sudo so-bro-start
```

10.5.4 Slots

If you've already run Setup and want to modify `min_num_slots`, you can manually create/edit `/etc/modprobe.d/pf_ring.conf`.

For example, to increase `min_num_slots` to `65534`, do the following:

```
echo "options pf_ring transparent_mode=0 min_num_slots=65534" | sudo tee /etc/
↪modprobe.d/pf_ring.conf
```

After creating/editing `/etc/modprobe.d/pf_ring.conf`, you'll need to reload the PF-RING module as follows (or just reboot):

```
sudo so-sensor-stop
sudo rmmod pf_ring
sudo so-sensor-start
```

10.5.5 Updating

Please see the Upgrade section for notes on updating the PF-RING kernel module.

10.6 AF-PACKET

Modern versions of Setup will configure Suricata and Bro to use AF-PACKET instead of PF-RING. (Snort will continue to use PF-RING for load balancing until Snort 3.0 is released.)

If you want to change the number of AF-PACKET workers after running Setup, you can do the following.

10.6.1 Suricata

To change the number of AF-PACKET workers for Suricata:

- Stop sensor processes:

```
sudo so-suricata-stop
```

- Edit `/etc/nsm/$HOSTNAME-$INTERFACE/sensor.conf` and change the `IDS_LB_PROCS` variable to the desired number of workers.

- Start sensor processes:

```
sudo so-suricata-start
```

- `so-suricata-start` automatically copies `$IDS_LB_PROCS` into `suricata.yaml` and then Suricata creates the appropriate number of AF-PACKET workers.

10.6.2 Bro

To change the number of AF-PACKET workers for Bro:

- Stop Bro:

```
sudo so-bro-stop
```

- Edit `/opt/bro/etc/node.cfg` and change the `lb_procs` variable to the desired number of cores.
- Start Bro:

```
sudo so-bro-start
```

10.6.3 tcpreplay

If you try to test AF-PACKET load balancing using tcpreplay locally, please note that load balancing will not work properly and all (or most) traffic will be handled by the first worker in the AF-PACKET cluster. If you need to test AF-PACKET load balancing properly, you can run tcpreplay on another machine connected to your AF-PACKET machine.

10.7 High Performance Tuning

10.7.1 Ubuntu Server

For best performance, we recommend starting with Ubuntu Server (no GUI) and adding our Security Onion packages as described in our ProductionDeployment guide.

10.7.2 Best Practices

When you run Setup, make sure you choose Best Practices.

10.7.3 Disable GUI

If you're unable to start with Ubuntu Server (no GUI) as recommended above, you can disable the GUI after the system is fully configured.

10.7.4 Disable Unnecessary Services

Disable any other unnecessary services. For example, to disable bluetooth:

```
sudo systemctl stop bluetooth.service
sudo systemctl disable bluetooth.service
```

10.7.5 CPU Affinity/Pinning

For best performance, CPU intensive processes like Bro and Suricata should be pinned to specific CPUs.

For Bro, use the `pin_cpus` setting in `/opt/bro/etc/node.cfg`:
https://docs.zeek.org/en/stable/configuration/#using-pf-ring

For Suricata, use the affinity settings in `suricata.yaml`:
https://suricata.readthedocs.io/en/latest/configuration/suricata-yaml.html#threading

10.7.6 RSS

Check your sniffing interfaces to see if they have Receive Side Scaling (RSS) queues. If so, you may need to reduce to 1:
https://suricata.readthedocs.io/en/latest/performance/packet-capture.html#rss

10.7.7 Disk/Memory

If you have plenty of RAM, disable swap altogether.

Use `hdparm` to gather drive statistics and alter settings, as described here:
http://www.linux-magazine.com/Online/Features/Tune-Your-Hard-Disk-with-hdparm

`vm.dirty_ratio` is the maximum amount of system memory that can be filled with dirty pages before everything must get committed to disk.

`vm.dirty_background_ratio` is the percentage of system memory that can be filled with "dirty" pages, or memory pages that still need to be written to disk – before the pdflush/flush/kdmflush background processes kick in to write it to disk.

More information:
https://lonesysadmin.net/2013/12/22/better-linux-disk-caching-performance-vm-dirty_ratio/

10.7.8 Other

Consider adopting some of the suggestions from here:
https://suricata.readthedocs.io/en/latest/performance/packet-capture.html
https://github.com/pevma/SEPTun
https://github.com/pevma/SEPTun-Mark-II

10.8 MySQL Tuning

As of Security Onion 16.04.4.1 MySQL (on the master server) should have a randomized root password set by default. You can still access MySQL using the following as an example of the syntax to run a command against security-onion_db (Sguil DB):

```
sudo mysql --defaults-file=/etc/mysql/debian.cnf -Dsecurityonion_db -e 'select * from
↪event limit 10';
```

10.8.1 mysqltuner

You can install and run `mysqltuner` to get some initial recommendations.

Install `mysqltuner` if you haven't already:

```
sudo apt update && sudo apt install mysqltuner
```

Run `mysqltuner` with privileges:

```
sudo mysqltuner
```

You may also want to install `mysqltuner` via the following manner, given that Security Onion now uses `defaults-file` to handle MySQL database credentials:

```
wget http://mysqltuner.pl/ -O mysqltuner.pl && chmod +x mysqltuner.pl
sudo ./mysqltuner.pl
```

10.8.2 /etc/mysql/my.cnf vs /etc/mysql/conf.d/

Implement mysqltuner's recommendations in `/etc/mysql/my.cnf` or create a new file in `/etc/mysql/conf.d/` with the changes. We recommend `/etc/mysql/conf.d/` so that your changes don't get overwritten during MySQL package upgrades.

10.8.3 Restart MySQL

Changes don't take effect until MySQL is restarted and you should ensure that Sguil and other services aren't using MySQL before shutting it down.

10.8.4 Variables

Here are some common variables that may need to be tuned for your system:

- `open-files-limit`
- `table_cache`
- `key_buffer`
- `max_connections`

10.8.5 MySQL slow to start on boot

At boot time, MySQL checks all tables, which can take a long time. If you wish to disable this check, comment out `check_for_crashed_tables` in `/etc/mysql/debian-start`.

10.8.6 table_definition_cache

MySQL defaults `table_definition_cache` to `400`. You may want to increase this value if one or more of the following conditions applies to you:

- you have more than 400 MySQL `.frm` files
- you've increased `DAYSTOKEEP` in `/etc/nsm/securityonion.conf` above its default value of 30 (each day requires 5 `.frm` files for OSSEC and 5 `.frm` files for each sniffing interface)
- you're running prepared statements

Check mysql `table_definition cache` (defaults to `400`):

```
mysql -uroot -e "show global variables like 'table_definition_cache'"
```

Check current `open_table_definitions` (probably maxed out at `table_definition_cache`):

```
mysql -uroot -e "show global status like 'open_table_definitions'"
```

Check number of `.frm` files:

```
sudo find /var/lib/mysql/ -name "*.frm" |wc -l
```

Increase table_definition_cache above number of `.frm` files by creating a file called `/etc/mysql/conf.d/securityonion-table_definition_cache.cnf` (please note `.cnf` extension NOT `.conf`) and adding the following (replacing `4000` with your desired setting):

```
[mysqld]
table_definition_cache = 4000
```

Reboot and then verify that `open_table_definitions` never gets limited by `table_definition_cache`.

For more information, please see:

https://bugs.mysql.com/bug.php?id=42041

https://dev.mysql.com/doc/refman/5.7/en/server-system-variables.html#sysvar_table_definition_cache

10.9 Trimming PCAPs

PCAPs (as a data type) typically take up the most disk space on a Security Onion sensor, and usually aren't able to be kept for extended periods of time. We can lessen the space consumed by PCAPs and extend our retention time by trimming them, using a special tool called TrimPCAP from NETRESEC. Using this tool, we can trim the flows within PCAPs to a desired size.

Please be aware that it may take a while to process a large amount of PCAPs. With this in mind, you'll want to consider running TrimPCAP at non-peak times (without high PCAP write volume, etc.).

One retention schedule that could be used is as follows:

(http://www.netresec.com/?page=Blog&month=2017-12&post=Don%27t-Delete-PCAP-Files—Trim-Them)

Age	Size (per flow)
Older than 3 days	1MB
Older than 6 days	102KB
Older than 30 days	10KB

10.9.1 Trimming

We can install TrimPCAP using the following commands:

```
sudo apt-get install python-pip
sudo pip install dpkt
sudo pip install repoze.lru
sudo wget -O /opt/trimpcap.py https://www.netresec.com/?download=trimpcap
```

Then we can run TrimPCAP, as follows (specifying a size of `102KB` per flow, iterating over all PCAPs of all ages, in all directories):

```
sudo /usr/bin/find /nsm/sensor_data/ -name "snort.log.??????????" -type f -exec sudo
↪python /opt/trimpcap.py 102400 {} \;
```

If we want to this for PCAPs older than 3 days, we can do something like the following:

```
sudo /usr/bin/find /nsm/sensor_data/ -name "snort.log.??????????" -mmin +$((60*72)) -
↪type f -exec sudo python /opt/trimpcap.py 102400 {} \;
```

We can then automate this using a cron job, so our PCAPs are checked daily.

```
#/etc/cron.d/trimpcap
#
#crontab entry for TrimPCAP

TRIMPCAP="/opt/trimpcap.py"
LOG="/var/log/trimpcap.log"
SHELL=/bin/sh
PATH=/usr/local/sbin:/usr/local/bin:/sbin:/bin:/usr/sbin:/usr/bin

# Trim after 3 days
0 1 * * * root echo $(date) >> $LOG; /usr/bin/find /nsm/sensor_data/ -name "snort.log.
↪??????????" -mmin +$((60*72)) -type f -exec /usr/bin/python
$TRIMPCAP 1000000 {} \; >> $LOG 2>&1;
```

To automatically configure PCAPs to be trimmed at the above recommended intervals, we can do the following:

```
sudo wget https://raw.githubusercontent.com/weslambert/misc/master/trimpcap_install &&
↪ sudo chmod +x ./trimpcap_install && sudo ./trimpcap_install
```

10.10 Disabling Processes

If you've already run Setup and want to disable a certain sensor service, you can simply stop the running service and then change the corresponding config value from `yes` to `no` to prevent it from restarting the next time the NSM scripts are run.

For example, suppose you access Bro's HTTP logs via Kibana, so you want to disable `http_agent` to prevent those HTTP logs from being duplicated into the `Sguil` database. You would first stop the running `http_agent` service:

```
sudo nsm_sensor_ps-stop --only-http-agent
```

You would then edit `/etc/nsm/$HOSTNAME-$INTERFACE/sensor.conf` and change:

```
HTTP_AGENT_ENABLED="yes"
```

to:

```
HTTP_AGENT_ENABLED="no"
```

to prevent `http_agent` from restarting the next time the NSM scripts are run. A quick way to do this for all `/etc/nsm/*/sensor.conf` files on one box is to use the `sed` command as follows:

```
sudo sed -i 's|HTTP_AGENT_ENABLED="yes"|HTTP_AGENT_ENABLED="no"|g' /etc/nsm/*/sensor.
↪conf
```

10.10.1 Sguil Agent

If you use the Sguil client and want to remove the disabled agent from Sguil's `Agent Status` tab, then stop `sguild`, set the sensor's `active` field to `N` in the database, and then restart `sguild`:

```
# Stop sguild
sudo so-sguild-stop

# Set active="N", replacing HOSTNAME-INTERFACE-INSTANCE with your actual HOSTNAME,
↪INTERFACE, and INSTANCE
sudo mysql --defaults-file=/etc/mysql/debian.cnf -Dsecurityonion_db -e 'update sensor
↪set active="N" where hostname="HOSTNAME-INTERFACE-INSTANCE";'

# Restart sguild
sudo so-sguild-start
```

10.10.2 Wazuh

Occasionally, folks ask about disabling Wazuh. Please keep in mind that in addition to providing endpoint visibility from Wazuh agents, the Wazuh server also monitors and protects the Security Onion box itself. For example, suppose that you have an active adversary who is trying to compromise your Security Onion box. Wazuh may see those attempts and engage `Active Response` to block the attacker's IP address in the host-based firewall.

If you understand all of this and still want to disable Wazuh, you can do so as follows:

```
# Stop the running Wazuh processes
sudo so-ossec-stop

# Disable Wazuh
sudo update-rc.d -f ossec-hids-server disable
```

CHAPTER 11

Tricks and Tips

This section is a collection of miscellaneous tricks and tips for Security Onion.

11.1 Airgapped Networks

Some organizations have airgapped networks with no connection to the Internet. Security Onion works fine on these airgapped networks, although it may be missing some updates due to lack of Internet connection.

11.1.1 Updating

You can transfer updates to airgapped networks via DVD, USB, or other media.

@SkiTheSlicer has created a set of scripts to assist in updating airgapped Security Onion installations: https://github.com/SkiTheSlicer/securityonion-airgap

11.1.2 Docker

For Docker containers, sneakernet updates can be performed by doing something like the following: Docker#sneakernet-updates

11.2 Analyst VM

Full-time analysts should install Security Onion in a VM on their workstation. Run through the Ubuntu installer, but you do not need to run our Setup wizard since the analyst VM won't be sniffing any live traffic. This gives you a local copy of Wireshark, NetworkMiner, and our customized Sguil client.

To connect from the Analyst VM to your production master server, you will need to run so-allow on the master server and choose the `analyst` option to allow the traffic through the host-based firewall.

Once you've allowed the traffic using so-allow, you can launch the Sguil client and connect to the IP address or hostname of your production master server and/or launch the web browser and connect to Squert or Kibana on your production master server.

This allows you to investigate pcaps without fear of impacting your production server/sensors.

11.2.1 Ultimate Forensics VM

Want an analyst VM that also includes forensics and reverse engineering tools from SANS SIFT and Remnux? See Brian Kellogg's Ultimate Forensics VM:

https://github.com/theflakes/Ultimate-Forensics-VM

11.3 Best Practices

Security Onion comes with the option to implement what is considered a set of `Best Practices` during Setup. For many users, this is a quick and easy way to ensure you are configuring your deployment to disable any services that you may not need, and that would otherwise duplicate work and data. The `Best Practices` option not only disables these unnecessary services, but (assuming the appropriate packages are installed) enables Salt by default, to allow for ease of sensor management.

The below sections assume that you already have these services installed, and provide advice on how to disable them in your deployment.

Most folks will want to disable the following services:

- prads (prads creates session data and asset data, already provided by Bro)
- pads_agent (not needed if prads is disabled)
- sancp_agent (not needed if prads is disabled)
- argus (argus creates session data, which is already provided by Bro)
- http_agent (duplicates Bro http.log into Sguil database, which may cause performance issues)

To do so, stop the required service/s:

```
sudo nsm_sensor_ps-stop --only-prads
sudo nsm_sensor_ps-stop --only-pads-agent
sudo nsm_sensor_ps-stop --only-sancp-agent
sudo nsm_sensor_ps-stop --only-argus
sudo nsm_sensor_ps-stop --only-http-agent
```

And then disable them so they don't start on reboot:

```
sudo sed -i 's|PRADS_ENABLED="yes"|PRADS_ENABLED="no"|g' /etc/nsm/*/sensor.conf
sudo sed -i 's|PADS_AGENT_ENABLED="yes"|PADS_AGENT_ENABLED="no"|g' /etc/nsm/*/sensor.
↪conf
sudo sed -i 's|SANCP_AGENT_ENABLED="yes"|SANCP_AGENT_ENABLED="no"|g' /etc/nsm/*/
↪sensor.conf
sudo sed -i 's|ARGUS_ENABLED="yes"|ARGUS_ENABLED="no"|g' /etc/nsm/*/sensor.conf
sudo sed -i 's|HTTP_AGENT_ENABLED="yes"|HTTP_AGENT_ENABLED="no"|g' /etc/nsm/*/sensor.
↪conf
```

For more information, please see the Disabling Processes section.

11.4 Cloud Client

Many folks ask how they can use Security Onion to monitor and defend their cloud environments. Most cloud environments don't provide anything like a tap or span port, but we can use daemonlogger or netsniff-ng as a virtual tap. This virtual tap will copy all traffic from our production cloud box to an OpenVPN bridge that transports the traffic to our Security Onion sensor where it is then analyzed.

Warning! This cloud client is considered experimental! USE AT YOUR OWN RISK!

This guide was originally written for Security Onion 12.04 and has been updated for Security Onion 14.04, but hasn't been heavily tested yet.

11.4.1 Traffic Flow and NIC offloading functions

The cloud client uses `daemonlogger` or `netsniff-ng` to copy all packets from eth0 to tap0 (OpenVPN). OpenVPN transports the packets to the cloud sensor, where tap0 is a member of bridge br0. The standard Security Onion stack sniffs br0. NIC offloading functions must be disabled on all of these interfaces (eth0 and tap0 on cloud client, and tap0 and br0 on cloud sensor) to ensure that Snort, Bro, etc. all see traffic as it appeared on the wire. This guide will walk you through disabling NIC offloading functions on eth0 and br0 via `/etc/network/interfaces` and tap0 via `/etc/openvpn/up.sh`.

11.4.2 Daemonlogger vs netsniff-ng

This guide is written using `daemonlogger` because it is more likely to be available on most cloud boxes. If `netsniff-ng` is available, it can provide higher performance (less packet loss), and you would just need to change the calls from daemonlogger to netsniff-ng and translate the options to the equivalent netsniff-ng options.

11.4.3 References and Thanks

This is based on Josh Brower's great work:

http://www.slideshare.net/DefensiveDepth/so-conference-2014

The OpenVPN configuration shown below is based on the following guides:

https://help.ubuntu.com/community/OpenVPN

https://help.ubuntu.com/lts/serverguide/openvpn.html

11.4.4 Install Packages

If you are installing from Ubuntu 16.04, make sure you install our packages before continuing with this procedure. For more information, please see the Getting Started section.

11.4.5 Security Onion Sensor

We start with our Security Onion sensor.

First, ensure that the bridge-utils package is installed:

```
sudo apt-get update
sudo apt-get install bridge-utils
```

Run Security Onion Setup Phase 1 (Network Configuration), allow it to write your /etc/network/interfaces file, but DON'T reboot at the end:

```
sudo sosetup
```

Add br0 to /etc/network/interfaces and disable offloading functions:

```
cat << EOF | sudo tee -a /etc/network/interfaces
# Bridge for OpenVPN tap0
auto br0
iface br0 inet manual
  bridge_ports none
  post-up for i in rx tx sg tso ufo gso gro lro; do ethtool -K \$IFACE \$i off; done
EOF
```

Reboot:

```
sudo reboot
```

Run Security Onion Setup Phase 2 and choose to monitor br0:

```
sudo sosetup
```

Setup has locked down the UFW firewall, so let's go ahead and allow OpenVPN port 1194:

```
sudo ufw allow 1194
```

Install OpenVPN:

```
sudo apt-get update
sudo apt-get install openvpn easy-rsa
```

Next, copy files to the /etc/openvpn/easy-rsa/ directory:

```
sudo mkdir /etc/openvpn/easy-rsa/
sudo cp -r /usr/share/easy-rsa/* /etc/openvpn/easy-rsa/
```

Edit /etc/openvpn/easy-rsa/vars:

```
sudo vi /etc/openvpn/easy-rsa/vars
```

Change these lines at the bottom so that they reflect the proper settings for your new CA:

```
export KEY_COUNTRY
export KEY_PROVINCE
export KEY_CITY
export KEY_ORG
export KEY_EMAIL
export KEY_CN
export KEY_NAME
export KEY_OU
```

Setup the CA and create the first server certificate:

```
cd /etc/openvpn/easy-rsa/ ## move to the easy-rsa directory
sudo chown -R root:sudo .  ## make this directory writable by the system
→administrators
sudo chmod g+w . ## make this directory writable by the system administrators
```

(continues on next page)

```
source ./vars ## execute your new vars file
./clean-all   ## Setup the easy-rsa directory (Deletes all keys)
./build-ca    ## generate the master Certificate Authority (CA) certificate and key
./build-key-server server ## creates a server cert and private key
./build-dh
cd keys
sudo cp server.crt server.key ca.crt dh2048.pem /etc/openvpn/
# The Certificate Authority is now setup and the needed keys are in /etc/openvpn/
```

Create a script that OpenVPN will call when the tunnel comes up to add tap0 to br0 and disable offloading functions on tap0:

```
cat << EOF | sudo tee -a /etc/openvpn/up.sh
#!/bin/sh

BR=\$1
DEV=\$2
/sbin/ip link set "\$DEV" up promisc on
/sbin/brctl addif \$BR \$DEV

for i in rx tx sg tso ufo gso gro lro; do ethtool -K \$DEV \$i off; done
EOF
```

Create a script that OpenVPN will call when the tunnel goes down:

```
cat << EOF | sudo tee -a /etc/openvpn/down.sh
#!/bin/sh

BR=\$1
DEV=\$2

/sbin/brctl delif \$BR \$DEV
/sbin/ip link set "\$DEV" down
EOF
```

Make both of these scripts executable:

```
sudo chmod +x /etc/openvpn/up.sh /etc/openvpn/down.sh
```

Create OpenVPN `server.conf`:

```
sudo cp /usr/share/doc/openvpn/examples/sample-config-files/server.conf.gz /etc/
↪openvpn/
sudo gzip -d /etc/openvpn/server.conf.gz
```

Modify `/etc/openvpn/server.conf`:

```
sudo sed -i 's|^dev tun$|;dev tun|g' /etc/openvpn/server.conf
sudo sed -i 's|^;dev tap|dev tap|g' /etc/openvpn/server.conf
sudo sed -i 's|^comp-lzo|;comp-lzo|g' /etc/openvpn/server.conf
sudo sed -i 's|^dh dh1024.pem|dh dh2048.pem|g' /etc/openvpn/server.conf


cat << EOF | sudo tee -a /etc/openvpn/server.conf

up "/etc/openvpn/up.sh br0"
```

```
down "/etc/openvpn/down.sh br0"
EOF
```

Restart OpenVPN server:

```
sudo service openvpn restart
```

Check log for errors:

```
sudo tail -f /var/log/syslog
```

Verify tap0 came up:

```
ifconfig
```

11.4.6 Generate client certs

Perform the steps in this section for each cloud client you want to monitor.

Generate client cert (replacing `client` with the name of the cloud client you want to add):

```
cd /etc/openvpn/easy-rsa/    ## move to the easy-rsa directory
source ./vars                ## execute the vars file
./build-key client
```

Copy generated files to cloud client (replacing `client` with the name of the cloud client you want to add):

```
scp /etc/openvpn/easy-rsa/keys/client* username@hostname:~/
scp /etc/openvpn/easy-rsa/keys/ca.crt username@hostname:~/
```

11.4.7 Cloud client

Perform the steps in this section on each cloud client you want to monitor.

Install `openvpn` and `daemonlogger`:

```
sudo apt-get update
sudo apt-get install openvpn daemonlogger
```

Copy crt files to `/etc/openvpn/`:

```
sudo cp client* /etc/openvpn/
sudo cp ca.crt /etc/openvpn/
```

Create OpenVPN `client.conf`:

```
sudo cp /usr/share/doc/openvpn/examples/sample-config-files/client.conf /etc/openvpn/
```

Modify `/etc/openvpn/client.conf`:

```
sudo sed -i 's|^dev tun$|;dev tun|g' /etc/openvpn/client.conf
sudo sed -i 's|^;dev tap|dev tap|g' /etc/openvpn/client.conf
sudo sed -i 's|^comp-lzo|;comp-lzo|g' /etc/openvpn/client.conf
```

(continued from previous page)

```
cat << EOF | sudo tee -a /etc/openvpn/client.conf

up "/etc/openvpn/up.sh"
down "/etc/openvpn/down.sh"
EOF
```

Find the "remote my-server-1 1194" line in `/etc/openvpn/client.conf` and replace my-server-1 with the hostname or IP address of your OpenVPN server.

Create a script that OpenVPN will call when the tunnel comes up to disable offloading functions on tap0 and start daemonlogger. The daemonlogger BPF at minimum should exclude the OpenVPN traffic on port 1194 ('not port 1194'). You may need to restrict this BPF even further if there is other traffic you do not wish to send across the OpenVPN tunnel.

```
cat << EOF | sudo tee -a /etc/openvpn/up.sh
#!/bin/sh

IN=eth0
OUT=\$1

daemonlogger -d -i \$IN -o \$OUT 'not port 1194'

for i in rx tx sg tso ufo gso gro lro; do ethtool -K \$OUT \$i off; done
EOF
```

Create a script that OpenVPN will call when the tunnel goes down:

```
cat << EOF | sudo tee -a /etc/openvpn/down.sh
#!/bin/sh

pkill daemonlogger
EOF
```

Make both of these scripts executable:

```
sudo chmod +x /etc/openvpn/up.sh /etc/openvpn/down.sh
```

Restart OpenVPN client:

```
sudo service openvpn restart
```

Check log for errors:

```
tail -f /var/log/syslog
```

Verify that tap0 came up:

```
ifconfig
```

Disable NIC offloading functions on main ethernet interface.
Add the following to your eth stanza in `/etc/network/interfaces` OR add to `/etc/openvpn/up.sh`:

```
post-up for i in rx tx sg tso ufo gso gro lro; do ethtool -K $IFACE $i off; done
```

Bounce the interface (you may lose access if connected remotely over ssh) or reboot the box.

11.4.8 Check traffic

Your Security Onion sensor should now be seeing traffic from your Cloud Client. Verify as follows:

```
sudo tcpdump -nnvvAi tap0
```

tap0 should be a member of br0, so you should see the same traffic on br0:

```
sudo tcpdump -nnvvAi br0
```

When you ran Setup phase 2 you configured Security Onion to monitor br0, so you should be getting IDS alerts and Bro logs.

11.4.9 Hardening

Once you get everything working properly, you should configure OpenVPN (server and client) and daemonlogger to run as a limited user.

11.4.10 Tuning

If your cloud box is seeing lots of traffic, daemonlogger may not be able to keep up, resulting in packet loss. You may need to switch to netsniff-ng for higher performance. Don't forget to run netsniff-ng as a limited user!

11.5 Connecting to Sguild

This article will show how to connect to the Sguil server to view security alerts in real-time.

11.5.1 Connecting to Sguild from an Analyst Machine

To directly connect to a Sguild server one must possess a working Sguil client. Sguil may not be easy or available for install on certain operating systems. Because of this we recommend installing Security Onion in a virtual machine on your workstation and use that to connect to sguild on your production Security Onion instance. For more information, please see the Analyst-VM section.

11.5.2 Connect to Sguild Locally (not recommended)

- Double-click the Sguil icon on the desktop of your Security Onion server.
- Set the Sguil Host to localhost, enter your credentials, and then click OK.
- After, choose which sensors you would like to monitor for this sguil session and then click Start Sguil.

11.5.3 Connect Remotely via SSH w/ X11 Forwarding

This method requires SSH and an X11 server installed on the machine from which you will be connecting from.

If you're using OSX install the XQuartz package, Windows try ciXwin, Linux and BSD family use Xorg.

Connect to the Security Onion server via SSH while passing the X11 forwarding option (-X).

```
ssh -X user@nsm
```

Once logged in as the normal user open the sguil client application. The display will be sent to your machine using the X11 protocol over SSH.

```
sguil.tk
```

Since we're only forwarding the application window, we're connected locally i.e. as if we were sitting at the server's console. Because of this we can use `localhost` as the Sguild Host.

Once logged in we will be able to select which sensors we would like to monitor.

Finally, select Start Sguil. Now you can view the alerts in real-time, perform advanced SQL queries, and pivot into a number of applications like Wireshark, Kibana, and NetworkMiner.

11.6 Disabling Desktop

You can disable the GUI after the system is fully configured:

```
sudo sed -i.bak 's|GRUB_CMDLINE_LINUX_DEFAULT="quiet splash"|GRUB_CMDLINE_LINUX_
↪DEFAULT="text"|g' /etc/default/grub
sudo update-grub
sudo systemctl enable multi-user.target --force
sudo systemctl set-default multi-user.target
sudo reboot
```

For more information, please see:

http://askubuntu.com/questions/16371/how-do-i-disable-x-at-boot-time-so-that-the-system-boots-in-text-mode.

11.7 DNS Anomaly Detection

Dr. Johannes Ullrich of the SANS Internet Storm Center posted a great DNS Anomaly Detection script based on the query logs coming from his DNS server. We can do the same thing with Bro's dns.log (where Bro captures all the DNS queries it sees on the network).

Please note that this script is only intended for standalone machines and will not work properly on distributed deployments.

This version of the script works on older installations using Bro TSV output:

```
#!/bin/bash

export PATH=/opt/bro/bin:$PATH
BRO_LOGS="/nsm/bro/logs"
TODAY=`date +%Y-%m-%d`
```

(continues on next page)

(continued from previous page)

```
YESTERDAY=`date -d yesterday +%Y-%m-%d`
OLD_DIRS=`ls $BRO_LOGS |egrep -v "current|stats|$TODAY|$YESTERDAY"`
TMPDIR=/tmp
OLDLOG=$TMPDIR/oldlog
NEWLOG=$TMPDIR/newlog
SUSPECTS=$TMPDIR/suspects

for DIR in $OLD_DIRS; do zcat $BRO_LOGS/$DIR/dns* |bro-cut id.resp_p query; done |
↪grep -v "^5353" | awk '{print $2}' | sort | uniq -c | sort -k2 > $OLDLOG
zcat $BRO_LOGS/$YESTERDAY/dns* |bro-cut id.resp_p query | grep -v "^5353" | awk '
↪{print $2}' | sort | uniq -c | sort -k2 > $NEWLOG
join -1 2 -2 2  -a 2 $OLDLOG $NEWLOG | egrep -v '.* [0-9]+ [0-9]+$' | sort -nr -k2 |
↪head -50 > $SUSPECTS

echo
echo "=================================="
echo "Top 50 First Time Seen DNS queries:"
echo "=================================="
cat $SUSPECTS
```

We've since changed Bro's default output to json (for faster Logstash parsing), so `senatorhotchkiss` on our mailing list updated the script, replacing `bro-cut` with `jq` as follows:

```
#!/bin/bash

export PATH=/opt/bro/bin:$PATH
BRO_LOGS="/nsm/bro/logs"
TODAY=`date +%Y-%m-%d`
YESTERDAY=`date -d yesterday +%Y-%m-%d`
OLD_DIRS=`ls $BRO_LOGS |egrep -v "current|stats|$TODAY|$YESTERDAY"`
TMPDIR=/tmp
OLDLOG=$TMPDIR/oldlog
NEWLOG=$TMPDIR/newlog
SUSPECTS=$TMPDIR/suspects

for DIR in $OLD_DIRS; do zcat $BRO_LOGS/$DIR/dns* | jq '{"id.resp_p"},{"query"}' ;
↪done  | grep -v "^5353" | awk '{print $2}' | sort | uniq -c | sort -k2 > $OLDLOG
zcat $BRO_LOGS/$YESTERDAY/dns* | jq '{"id.resp_p"},{"query"}' | grep -v "^5353" | awk
↪'{print $2}' | sort | uniq -c | sort -k2 > $NEWLOG
join -1 2 -2 2  -a 2 $OLDLOG $NEWLOG | egrep -v '.* [0-9]+ [0-9]+$' | sort -nr -k2 |
↪head -50 > $SUSPECTS

echo
echo "=================================="
echo "Top 50 First Time Seen DNS queries:"
echo "=================================="
cat $SUSPECTS
```

11.8 ICMP Anomaly Detection

At Security Onion Conference 2016, Eric Conrad shared some IDS rules for detecting unusual ICMP echo requests/replies and identifying C2 channels that may utilize ICMP tunneling for covert communication.

11.8.1 Usage

We can add the rules to `/etc/nsm/rules/local.rules` and the variables to `snort.conf` and/or `suricata.yaml` so that we can gain better insight into ICMP echoes or replies over a certain size, containing particularly suspicious content, etc.

11.8.2 Presentation

You can find Eric's presentation here:

http://www.ericconrad.com/2016/09/c2-phone-home-leveraging-securityonion.html

11.8.3 Download

You can download the rules here:

https://drive.google.com/file/d/0ByeHgv6rpa3gUDNuMUdobFBCNkk

11.9 MetaPackages

Security Onion consists of over 50 packages in a Launchpad PPA. You can install these packages individually or you can install one or more metapackages (groups of packages) depending on what functionality you need.

- securityonion-client (about 525MB)

    Sguil client, Wireshark, NetworkMiner, etc.

    ```
    sudo apt install securityonion-client
    ```

- securityonion-sensor (about 135MB)

    Snort, Suricata, Bro, netsniff-ng, Sguil agents, etc.

    ```
    sudo apt install securityonion-sensor
    ```

- securityonion-server (about 265MB)

    Sguil server, Squert, CapMe, etc.

    ```
    sudo apt install securityonion-server
    ```

- securityonion-elastic (about 5MB)

    Scripts and configuration files for the Elastic Stack (Elasticsearch, Logstash, and Kibana) and its associated log pipeline including syslog-ng. This package includes `so-elastic-download` which downloads the Docker images for the Elastic stack. You'll probably want to install syslog-ng-core explicitly to replace rsyslog.

    ```
    sudo apt install securityonion-elastic syslog-ng-core
    ```

- securityonion-all (about 930MB)

    all of the above plus syslog-ng

    ```
    sudo apt install securityonion-all
    ```

- securityonion-iso

all of the above plus bridge-utils, byobu, foremost, pinguybuilder, securityonion-desktop-gnome, securityonion-onionsalt, securityonion-samples-bro, securityonion-samples-markofu, securityonion-samples-mta, securityonion-samples-shellshock, xfsprogs

```
sudo apt install securityonion-iso
```

11.10 Adding a new disk

Before doing this in production, make sure you practice this on a non-production system!

There are at least 3 different ways to do this:

11.10.1 Method 1: LVM (Logical Volume Management)

If you chose the LVM option in the Ubuntu installer, then this should be the easiest way of adding disk space: https://wiki.ubuntu.com/Lvm

11.10.2 Method 2: Mount a separate drive to /nsm

This can be done in the Ubuntu installer, or after installation is complete. If doing this after running Setup, then you'll need to copy the existing data in /nsm to the new drive using something like this:

1. Comment out the cron job in /etc/cron.d/nsm-watchdog

2. Restart cron:

   ```
   sudo service cron restart
   ```

3. Stop all services:

   ```
   sudo service nsm stop
   sudo service syslog-ng stop
   sudo service apache2 stop
   sudo service mysql stop
   ```

4. Check for any ELSA perl processes which may need to be killed manually:

   ```
   ps aux |grep perl
   ```

5. Determine your new drive's path:

   ```
   sudo fdisk -l
   ```

6. Partition the new drive using `fdisk` or `parted`

7. Format the new partition using `mkfs`

8. Mount the new drive to a temporary location in the filesystem:

   ```
   sudo mount /dev/sdb2 /mnt
   ```

9. Copy the existing data from /nsm to the temporary location:

```
sudo cp -av /nsm/* /mnt/
```

10. Unmount the new drive from the temporary location:

```
sudo umount /mnt
```

11. Rename the existing /nsm:

```
sudo mv /nsm /nsm-backup
```

12. Update /etc/fstab to mount the new drive to /nsm:

```
sudo vi /etc/fstab
```

(You can use blkid to find your drive's UUID to write in /etc/fstab)

```
sudo blkid /dev/sdb2
```

13. Re-create nsm directory after it was renamed:

```
mkdir /nsm
```

14. Mount the new /nsm:

```
sudo mount /nsm
```

15. Start all services:

```
sudo service mysql start
sudo service apache2 start
sudo service syslog-ng start
sudo service nsm start
```

16. Uncomment the cron job in /etc/cron.d/nsm-watchdog

17. Restart cron:

```
sudo service cron restart
```

18. Test and verify that everything works

19. Reboot:

```
sudo reboot
```

20. Test and verify that everything works

11.10.3 Method 3: Make /nsm a symlink to the new logging location

If you do this, you'll need to do something like the following to avoid AppArmor issues:

Stop all services:

```
sudo service nsm stop
```

Copy existing data from /nsm to new mount point:

```
sudo cp -av /nsm/* /mnt/nsm
```

Rename existing `/nsm`:

```
sudo mv /nsm /nsm-backup
```

Make `/nsm` a symlink to the new logging location:

```
sudo ln -s /mnt/nsm /nsm
```

Go to `/etc/apparmor.d/local/`:

```
cd /etc/apparmor.d/local/
```

Edit `usr.sbin.mysqld`, copy the `/nsm` line(s), and change `/nsm` to the new location:

```
sudo vi usr.sbin.mysqld
```

Edit `usr.sbin.tcpdump`, copy the `/nsm` line(s), and change `/nsm` to the new location:

```
sudo vi usr.sbin.tcpdump
```

Restart apparmor:

```
sudo service apparmor restart
```

Start all services:

```
sudo service nsm start
```

11.10.4 Moving the MySQL Databases

In this section, we'll cover how to move the MySQL databases containing all of your important alert and event data to another place. This section assumes we'll be moving the databases to `/nsm`, though, any other location will do.

The MySQL databases are stored under `/var/lib/mysql`. We will need to move this folder and its sub-contents to the destination location. First, we must stop all processes that may be writing or using the databases.

```
sudo service nsm stop
sudo service mysql stop
sudo service sphinxsearch stop
```

Now, we need to make sure all other nsm-related processes are stopped. To double-check, run `lsof` on the nsm mount point to list any processes that have open file descriptors. Kill everything, or nearly everything, that comes up in the list.

```
lsof /nsm
```

Next, let's copy the data over to the new location leaving the original intact. You can use `cp` or `rsync` or another similar tool but be sure to preserve permissions (-p) and copy recursively (-r). Both examples are listed below, choose one:

```
sudo cp -rp /var/lib/mysql /nsm
sudo rsync -avpr var/lib/mysql /nsm
```

Once that's finished, rename or backup the original just in case something goes wrong.

```
sudo mv /var/lib/mysql /var/lib/mysql.bak
```

Next, create a symbolic link from `/var/lib/mysql` to the new location:

```
sudo ln -s /nsm/mysql /var/lib/mysql
```

Ubuntu uses AppArmor to add an additional layer of security to running applications. We must tell apparmor about the new mysql database locations otherwise it will prevent the system from using it.

```
sudo service apparmor stop
```

Edit `/etc/apparmor.d/usr.sbin.mysqld` to reflect the following patch which adds the new location:

```
sudo vim /etc/apparmor.d/usr.sbin.mysqld
```

```
--- a/apparmor.d/usr.sbin.mysqld
+++ b/apparmor.d/usr.sbin.mysqld
@@ -19,8 +19,8 @@

/etc/hosts.allow r,
/etc/hosts.deny r,

+   /nsm/mysql/ r,
+   /nsm/mysql/** rwk,
+   /nsm/elsa/data/mysql/ r,
+   /nsm/elsa/data/mysql/** rwk,
/etc/mysql/*.pem r,
/etc/mysql/conf.d/ r,
/etc/mysql/conf.d/* r,
```

Finally, start all the processes back up:

```
sudo service apparmor start
sudo service mysql start
sudo service sphinxsearch start
sudo service nsm start
```

11.11 PCAPs for Testing

Security Onion 16.04 comes with several pcap samples in `/opt/samples/`.

11.11.1 Links

- http://www.malware-traffic-analysis.net/
- http://digitalcorpora.org/corpora/network-packet-dumps
- http://www.netresec.com/?page=PcapFiles
- http://www.netresec.com/?page=MACCDC
- https://github.com/bro/bro/tree/master/testing/btest/Traces
- http://www.ll.mit.edu/mission/communications/cyber/CSTcorpora/ideval/data/
- https://wiki.wireshark.org/SampleCaptures

- https://stratosphereips.org/category/dataset.html
- http://old.honeynet.org/scans/
- http://cctf.shmoo.com/
- http://ee.lbl.gov/anonymized-traces.html
- https://redmine.openinfosecfoundation.org/projects/suricata/wiki/Public_Data_Sets
- http://forensicscontest.com/puzzles
- https://www.evilfingers.com/repository/pcaps.php
- http://www.honeynet.org/node/504
- https://github.com/markofu/hackeire/tree/master/2011/pcap
- http://www.defcon.org/html/links/dc-ctf.html
- https://archive.wrccdc.org/
- https://github.com/chrissanders/packets

11.11.2 tcpreplay

You can use `tcpreplay` to replay any of these pcaps on your Security Onion sensor. For example, please see https://blog.securityonion.net/2011/01/introduction-to-sguil-and-squert-part-3.html for a quick, easy use-case and what you should see in the Sguil console.

11.11.3 so-replay

`so-replay` will use `tcpreplay` to replay **all** pcap samples in `/opt/samples` to your sniffing interface.

11.11.4 so-import-pcap

A drawback to using tcpreplay is that it's replaying the pcap as new traffic and thus the timestamps that you see in Kibana, Squert, and Sguil do not reflect the original timestamps from the pcap. To avoid this, a new tool was developed called so-import-pcap.

11.12 Removing a Sensor

There may come a time when you need to disable a sensor interface, delete a sensor's configuration, or get rid of an entire sensor and its data altogether. The steps below outline what is required to accomplish each objective.

11.12.1 Disable sensor interface

To disable a sensor interface:

- stop all sensor processes:

```
sudo so-sensor-stop
```

- edit `/etc/nsm/sensortab` and comment out the sensor interface line
- edit `/opt/bro/etc/node.cfg` and comment out the sensor interface stanza

- start all sensor processes:

```
sudo so-sensor-start
```

11.12.2 Delete sensor configuration

- To delete the configuration for a sensor, run `/usr/sbin/nsm_sensor_del` on the sensor box for which you wish to delete the configuration.

11.12.3 Wipe sensor configuration and data

- To completely wipe sensor configuration and data, run `sudo sosetup` on the sensor box for which you wish to wipe the data and configuration.

11.12.4 Remove sensor reference from master server

- In MySQL database `securityonion_db`, edit `sensor` table (you can simply set active='N'), then restart sguild.
- Stop sguild `sudo so-sensor-stop`
- Show sensor entries:

```
sudo mysql --defaults-file=/etc/mysql/debian.cnf -Dsecurityonion_db -e 'select * from
↪sensor';
```

- Set sensor as inactive:

```
sudo mysql --defaults-file=/etc/mysql/debian.cnf -Dsecurityonion_db -e "update sensor
↪set active='N' where sid in (<SID1>,<SID2>)";
```

- Start sguild:

```
sudo so-sensor-start
```

- If running salt, remove the sensor from `/opt/onionsalt/salt/top.sls` and then delete the key from salt:

```
sudo salt-key -d sensor_key_name
```

- PLEASE NOTE: This step is only required if you are still running ELSA. ELSA reached EOL on October 9, 2018. On the master server, edit `/etc/elsa_web.conf`, remove the sensor from the `peers` section, then restart Apache (`sudo service apache2 restart`).

11.12.5 Remove storage node reference from Master server Elasticsearch _cluster/settings

From Kibana, navigate to `Dev Tools` and paste the following text into the window (modifying `nodename` to match the name of your node):

```
PUT _cluster/settings
{
  "persistent": {
    "search": {
      "remote": {
        "nodename": {
          "skip_unavailable": null,
          "seeds":null
        }
      }
    }
  }
}
```

Click the play button to send the request to Elasticsearch.

11.13 Salt

From https://docs.saltstack.com/en/latest/:

> Salt is a new approach to infrastructure management built on a dynamic communication bus. Salt can be used for data-driven orchestration, remote execution for any infrastructure, configuration management for any app stack, and much more.

11.13.1 OnionSalt

OnionSalt is a set of Salt scripts created to manage multiple Security Onion sensors.

https://github.com/TOoSmOotH/onionsalt

11.13.2 Best Practices

If you're using our ISO image, `securityonion-onionsalt` is pre-installed, and Salt is configured by default when choosing `Production Mode` and then Best Practices during Setup.

11.13.3 Salt and OnionSalt are optional packages

If you choose to install Security Onion via PPA without installing `securityonion-iso syslog-ng-core`, please note that Salt is totally optional. If you're happy with your current method of sensor management, then you don't have to install `securityonion-onionsalt`, and nothing will change for you. Otherwise, install `securityonion-onionsalt` before running setup to enable Salt for your deployment.

11.13.4 Firewall Requirements

Sensors need to be able to connect to the master server on ports `4505/tcp` and `4506/tcp`:

http://docs.saltstack.com/topics/tutorials/firewall.html

11.13.5 Installation

For new deployments, Best Practices (Production Mode) checks to see if the `securityonion-onionsalt` package is installed and, if so, enables Salt by default. If choosing the "Custom" configuration option (Production Mode), simply answer "Yes" at the prompt (where applicable), and setup will configure salt-master and/or salt-minion services and open firewall ports as necessary.

For existing deployments, please see the Existing Deployment section.

11.13.6 Checking Status

Want to verify all your sensors are up?

```
sudo salt '*' test.ping
```

11.13.7 Remote Execution

Want to execute a command on all your sensors at once?

```
sudo salt '*' cmd.run 'InsertYourCommandHere'
```

11.13.8 Features

When you install and enable securityonion-onionsalt, the following data will replicate from the master server out to the sensors every 15 minutes:

- NIDS rules in /etc/nsm/rules/ (Snort/Suricata/barnyard will automatically restart as necessary)
- HIDS rules in /var/ossec/rules/local_rules.xml (Wazuh will automatically restart as necessary)
- Bro scripts in /opt/bro/share/bro/policy/
    - Bro does not restart automatically, but you can easily use salt on your master server to tell all your Bro instances to update and restart:

    ```
    # Force all Salt minions to update Bro scripts
    sudo salt '*' state.highstate
    # Restart Bro
    sudo salt '*' cmd.run 'so-bro-restart'
    ```

- Bro intel in /opt/bro/share/bro/intel/
    - You'll need to restart Bro as shown above if you add any intel files to the default intel.dat. After that initial Bro restart, Bro should be watching the intel files with the Input framework which should automatically notice if the files ever change (new intel is added). In many cases, you won't need to restart Bro if you're just adding intel to the existing intel file(s).
- user accounts and sudoers in /opt/onionsalt/pillar/users/init.sls
- user ssh keys in /opt/onionsalt/salt/users/keys/
    - For each user account in /opt/onionsalt/pillar/users/init.sls, you can add an SSH Public Key to `/opt/onionsalt/salt/users/keys/USERNAME.id_rsa.pub` (replacing `USERNAME` with the user's actual username)

In addition, Salt is a full configuration management system, so you can script anything that you want to deploy across your army of sensors.

11.13.9 Using Salt to Install Updates Across Your Entire Deployment

You can use Salt and Soup to install updates across your entire deployment, but please remember to always update your master server first:

```
# Update Master first
# If MySQL and/or kernel updates are installed, it will reboot
sudo soup -y

# After Master server is fully updated, now update the rest of the deployment
# If MySQL and/or kernel updates are installed, the sensors will reboot
sudo salt '*' cmd.run 'soup -y'
```

Also, please keep in mind that occasionally Ubuntu will release updates that prompt for user input which would cause that last command to hang. If you experience this, you should be able to ssh to each sensor and run `soup` interactively. For more information, please see https://github.com/Security-Onion-Solutions/security-onion/issues/1108.

11.13.10 Modifying Salt config files

If you need to modify the values in `/etc/salt/master` or `/etc/salt/minion`, please pay attention to this note at the top of each file:

```
# /etc/salt/master
# Per default, the master will automatically include all config files
# from master.d/*.conf (master.d is a directory in the same directory
# as the main master config file)
#default_include: master.d/*.conf
```

```
# /etc/salt/minion
# Per default the minion will automatically include all config files
# from minion.d/*.conf (minion.d is a directory in the same directory
# as the main minion config file).
#default_include: minion.d/*.conf
```

Instead of modifying /etc/salt/master or /etc/salt/minion directly, please add your custom settings in `/etc/salt/master.d/*.conf` or `/etc/salt/minion.d/*.conf`, respectively.

11.13.11 Changing Minion ID

If you need to change the ID for a minion, do the following.

On the minion machine:

```
# Stop salt-minion
sudo service salt-minion stop

# Edit /etc/salt/minion_id, modifying the ID as necessary.

# Start salt-minion
sudo service salt-minion start
```

On the master machine:

```
# Restart salt-master
sudo service salt-master restart

# List the salt keys
sudo salt-key -L

# Accept the new key for the modified minion
sudo salt-key -A

# Delete the old minion key
sudo salt-key -d OLD_MINION_NAME

# Test the configuration -- minion should return "TRUE"
sudo salt "MINION_NAME" test.ping
```

11.13.12 Salting an Existing Deployment

Configure the Master Server first

```
# Make sure the necessary packages are installed and updated
sudo apt-get update && sudo apt-get install securityonion-onionsalt

# Create a starting /opt/onionsalt/pillar/users/init.sls and /opt/onionsalt/salt/top.
↪sls file from the template.
sudo cp /opt/onionsalt/salt/top.sls.template /opt/onionsalt/salt/top.sls
sudo cp /opt/onionsalt/pillar/users/init.sls.template /opt/onionsalt/pillar/users/
↪init.sls

# Edit /opt/onionsalt/salt/top.sls and add your master as a "backend".
# For example, if your SO master server's hostname is so-master, then replace:
    # My Onion Backend:
    'C*':
        - backend
with:
    # My Onion Backend:
    'so-master':
        - backend

# Open salt ports in firewall:
# sudo ufw allow salt
# OR preferably just allow from your sensor IP addresses like this:
# sudo ufw allow proto tcp from a.b.c.d to any port 4505,4506
# Also see our Firewall page:
# https://securityonion.net/docs/Firewall

# Configure minion
echo "master: localhost" | sudo tee -a /etc/salt/minion.d/onionsalt.conf

# Allow salt-master and salt-minion to start on boot if they had previously been
↪disabled
[ -f /etc/init/salt-master.DISABLED ] && sudo mv /etc/init/salt-master.DISABLED /etc/
↪init/salt-master.conf
[ -f /etc/init/salt-master.override ] && sudo rm -f /etc/init/salt-master.override
[ -f /etc/init/salt-minion.DISABLED ] && sudo mv /etc/init/salt-minion.DISABLED /etc/
↪init/salt-minion.conf
```

(continues on next page)

```
[ -f /etc/init/salt-minion.override ] && sudo rm -f /etc/init/salt-minion.override

# Restart minion
sudo service salt-minion restart

# list the salt keys:
sudo salt-key -L

# You should see an unaccepted salt key for the minion, add it:
sudo salt-key -a '*'

# Verify that the master can communicate with the minion:
sudo salt '*' test.ping

# Tell salt to do an update
sudo salt '*' state.highstate
```

Now configure salt-minion on a Sensor

```
# Make sure the necessary packages are installed and updated
sudo apt-get update && sudo apt-get install securityonion-onionsalt

# Stop the running salt-master
sudo service salt-master stop

# Disable salt-master
[ -f /etc/init/salt-master.conf ] && echo "manual" | sudo tee /etc/init/salt-master.
↪override

# Allow salt-minion to start on boot if it had previously been disabled
[ -f /etc/init/salt-minion.DISABLED ] && sudo mv /etc/init/salt-minion.DISABLED /etc/
↪init/salt-minion.conf
[ -f /etc/init/salt-minion.override ] && sudo rm -f /etc/init/salt-minion.override

# Configure minion
MASTER=`grep SENSOR_SERVER_HOST /etc/nsm/*/sensor.conf |head -1 |cut -d\" -f2`
echo "master: $MASTER" | sudo tee -a /etc/salt/minion.d/onionsalt.conf

# Restart minion
sudo service salt-minion restart
```

Now return to the Master and accept the new minion

```
# Edit /opt/onionsalt/salt/top.sls and add the new minion as a "sensor"

# list the salt keys:
sudo salt-key -L

# You should see an unaccepted salt key for the sensor, add it:
sudo salt-key -a '*'

# Verify that the master can communicate with all minions:
sudo salt '*' test.ping
```

```
# Tell all minions to do an update
sudo salt '*' state.highstate
```

11.13.13 Maximum Event Size

Salt-master uses a default `max_event_size` of **1048576** bytes (1 Mebibyte). For some Security Onion deployments, this may need to be change to a larger value to avoid receiving a `VALUE_TRIMMED` error (if the output of a command run on a minion is too large to be passed back to the master).

See: https://docs.saltstack.com/en/latest/ref/configuration/master.html#max-event-size

This setting should be changed in `/etc/salt/master.d/onionsalt.conf`, as opposed to directly in `/etc/salt/master`.

On a distributed Security Onion deployment `/etc/salt/master.d/onionsalt.conf` (on the master) should look like the following:

```
file_roots:
  base:
    - /opt/onionsalt/salt
pillar_roots:
  base:
    - /opt/onionsalt/pillar
max_event_size: YOUR_NEW_VALUE
```

After making changes, ensure salt-master has been started/restarted:

```
sudo service salt-master restart
```

11.13.14 Additional Reading

http://www.geekempire.com/2014/09/onionsalt-saltstack-cheat-sheer.html

11.14 Sensor Stops Seeing Traffic

If you want an alert when your sensor stops seeing traffic, there are a few options:

11.14.1 Wazuh

Wazuh checks your sniffing interfaces every 10 minutes. If no packets have been received within that 10 minute window, then Wazuh will generate an alert. This alert can be found in Sguil, Squert, and Kibana. If you'd like Wazuh to email you, then configure it for email as shown in the Email section.

11.14.2 Bro

Bro will automatically email you when it stops seeing traffic on an interface. All you have to do is configure Bro per the Email section.

11.15 SSH

11.15.1 Changing the default ssh listening port

By default secure shell (ssh) listens on `tcp port 22`. If you want to obfuscate it by changing the listening port from `port 22` to something else like `port 31337`, you can do so in `/etc/ssh/sshd_config`.

You can use your favorite text editor (e.g., `vi`, `gedit`, `nano`, `emacs`) to edit `/etc/ssh/sshd_config`, but for the purpose of this example `vi` will be used.

```
sudo vi /etc/ssh/sshd_config
```

Change the `Port` setting from `22` to `31337`. Then restart the ssh daemon so that it will now start listening on port 31337:

```
sudo killall -HUP sshd
```

Verify that ssh is listening on the new port:

```
netstat -nltp | grep sshd
```

Allow the new ssh port in the firewall:

```
sudo ufw allow 31337/tcp
```

11.16 UTC and Time Zones

When you run Security Onion Setup, it sets the timezone to UTC/GMT because that is the recommended/required setting for Sguil:

http://osdir.com/ml/security.sguil.general/2008-09/msg00003.html

https://forums.snort.org/forums/linux/topics/barnyard-sguil-time-problem

Trying to use a non-UTC timezone can result in the following:

- Time zones that have daylight saving time have a one-hour time warp twice a year. This manifests itself in Sguil not being able to pull transcripts for events within that one-hour time period. This is avoided by using UTC, since there is no daylight saving time.
- Something similar can happen on a daily basis under certain conditions. If there is a discrepancy between the OS timezone and the Sguil UTC settings, then Sguil will be unable to pull transcripts for events in a window of time around midnight coinciding with the timezone's offset from UTC.

Additionally, UTC comes in quite handy when you have sensors in different time zones and/or are trying to correlate events with other systems or teams.

Kibana by default will render timestamps in the timezone of your local browser and Squert allows you to set your timezone.

11.16.1 How do I change the timezone for Ubuntu?

When you run our Setup wizard, it should automatically set your OS timezone to UTC. If you've already run Setup and then manually changed your timezone to non-UTC and would like to switch back to UTC, you can execute `sudo` `dpkg-reconfigure tzdata`. Scroll to the bottom of the Continents list and select `None of the above`. In the second list, select `UTC`. (http://askubuntu.com/questions/138423/how-do-i-change-my-timezone-to-utc-gmt)

CHAPTER 12

Services

Services are controlled by the use of Security Onion scripts (so-<noun>-<verb>) which act as wrappers to other lower-level scripts. You can see a list of all of these scripts with the following command:

```
ls /usr/sbin/so-*
```

These scripts are detailed below.

12.1 All services

You can control all services with the so-<verb> scripts as follows.

Check status of all services:

```
sudo so-status
```

Start all services:

```
sudo so-start
```

Stop all services:

```
sudo so-stop
```

Restart all services:

```
sudo so-restart
```

The three main categories of services are server, sensor, and elastic.

12.2 Server services

Check status of sguild (Sguil server):

```
sudo so-sguild-status
```

Start sguild:

```
sudo so-sguild-start
```

Stop sguild:

```
sudo so-sguild-stop
```

Restart sguild:

```
sudo so-sguild-restart
```

12.3 Sensor services

Sensor services are controlled with `so-sensor-*`.

The following examples are for Bro, but you could substitute whatever sensor service you're trying to control (nids, pcap, etc.).

Check status of Bro:

```
sudo so-bro-status
```

Start Bro:

```
sudo so-bro-start
```

Stop Bro:

```
sudo so-bro-stop
```

Restart Bro:

```
sudo so-bro-restart
```

12.4 Elastic services

Elastic services are controlled with `so-elastic-*`.

Check status of the Elastic stack:

```
sudo so-elastic-status
```

Start the Elastic stack:

```
sudo so-elastic-start
```

Stop the Elastic stack:

```
sudo so-elastic-stop
```

Restart the Elastic stack:

```
sudo so-elastic-restart
```

CHAPTER 13

Utilities

This section covers some of the main utilities in Security Onion.

13.1 jq

From https://stedolan.github.io/jq/:
> jq is like sed for JSON data - you can use it to slice and filter and map and transform structured data with the same ease that sed, awk, grep and friends let you play with text.

13.1.1 Usage

If you have Bro configured to write logs in JSON format and you want to parse those logs from the command line, then you can use `jq`. Here's a basic example:

```
jq '.' /nsm/bro/logs/current/conn.log
```

This command will parse all of the records in `/nsm/bro/logs/current/conn.log`. For each of the records, it will then output every field and its value.

13.1.2 More Information

For more information about `jq`, please see https://stedolan.github.io/jq/.

13.2 Setup

After installing Security Onion, double-click the `Setup` icon on the desktop (or run `sudo sosetup` from a terminal) to configure your system. In most cases, you'll run Setup to do network configuration, reboot, and then run Setup again for service configuration.

13.2.1 Automating Setup

You can automate the Setup process using `sosetup.conf`.

13.2.2 Starting from scratch

There are a few example files in `/usr/share/securityonion/`. Copy one of these example files to your home directory:

```
cp /usr/share/securityonion/sosetup.conf ~
```

Edit your new `sosetup.conf` using `nano` or your favorite text editor:

```
nano ~/sosetup.conf
```

Then run Setup with the `-f` switch and the path to this file:

```
sudo sosetup -f ~/sosetup.conf
```

13.2.3 sosetup -w

`sosetup` also supports a `-w` switch that allows you to answer the standard Setup questions and have it write out your custom `sosetup.conf`. For example:

```
# Configure sosetup to write out a new configuration file called sosetup.conf
sosetup -w ~/sosetup.conf

# Answer all questions in Setup

# Run sosetup with the new configuration file
sudo sosetup -f ~/sosetup.conf
```

13.3 so-allow

Setup locks down the firewall by default. If you need to open ports for OSSEC agents, syslog devices, or analyst VMs, you can run `so-allow` and it will walk you through this process. `so-allow` also provides an option to add firewall rules for sensors although you shouldn't need this under normal circumstances since they should automatically add their own rules.

```
This program allows you to add a firewall rule to allow connections from a new IP
↪address.

What kind of device do you want to allow?

[a] - Analyst - ports 22/tcp, 443/tcp, and 7734/tcp
[b] - Logstash Beat - port 5044/tcp
[c] - apt-cacher-ng client - port 3142/tcp
[e] - Elasticsearch REST endpoint - port 9200
[f] - Logstash forwarder - standard - port 6050/tcp
[j] - Logstash forwarder - JSON - port 6051/tcp
[l] - Syslog device - port 514
[n] - Elasticsearch node-to-node communication - port 9300
```

(continues on next page)

```
                                                            (continued from previous page)
[o] - OSSEC agent - port 1514
[s] - Security Onion sensor - 22/tcp, 4505/tcp, 4506/tcp, and 7736/tcp

If you need to add any ports other than those listed above,
you can do so using the standard 'ufw' utility.

For more information, please see:
https://securityonion.net/docs/Firewall

Please enter your selection (a - analyst, c - apt-cacher-ng client, l - syslog, o -
↪ossec, or s - Security Onion sensor, etc.):
```

13.3.1 so-allow-view

To view existing rules granted through the use of `so-allow`, use the following command:

```
so-allow-view
```

13.3.2 Wazuh Whitelist

If you choose the `analyst` option, `so-allow` will also add the `analyst` IP address to the Wazuh Whitelist. This will prevent Wazuh Active Response from blocking the `analyst` IP address.

13.4 so-import-pcap

`so-import-pcap` is a quick and dirty EXPERIMENTAL script that will import one or more pcaps into Security Onion and preserve original timestamps.

It will do the following:

- stop and disable Curator to avoid closing old indices
- stop and disable all active sniffing processes (Bro, Snort, Suricata, and netsniff-ng)
- stop and disable ossec_agent
- reconfigure and restart sguild, syslog-ng, and Logstash where necessary
- generate IDS alerts using Snort or Suricata
- generate Bro logs
- store IDS alerts and Bro logs with original timestamps
- split traffic into separate daily pcaps and store them where sguil's pcap_agent can find them

Requirements:

- You must be running at least Security Onion 16.04.

Warnings:

- Do NOT run this on a production deployment. It is designed for standalone systems designated for so-import-pcap.
- If you're running in a VM with snapshot capability, you might want to take a snapshot before this program makes changes.

Reverting System Changes:

- If you take a VM snapshot before this program makes changes, then just revert to snapshot.
- Otherwise, you can re-run Setup and it should overwrite all modified files to revert the system to normal operation.

13.4.1 Usage

Please supply at least one pcap file.

For example, to import a single pcap named `import.pcap`:

```
so-import-pcap import.pcap
```

To import multiple pcaps:

```
so-import-pcap import1.pcap import2.pcap
```

13.4.2 Example

For a detailed walk-through with screenshots, please see https://taosecurity.blogspot.com/2018/02/importing-pcap-into-security-onion.html.

13.4.3 Warning

Please note that so-import-pcap will make changes to your system! It will warn you before doing so and will prompt you to press Enter to continue or Ctrl-c to cancel.

If you want to bypass the "Press Enter to continue" prompt, you can do something like this:

```
echo | sudo so-import-pcap /opt/samples/markofu/ie*
```

CHAPTER 14

Help

Having problems? Try the suggestions below.

- Are you running the latest version of Security Onion?
- Check the FAQ.
- Search the Security Onion Mailing List.
- Search the documentation and mailing lists of the tools contained within Security Onion: Tools
- Run `sostat` for some diagnostics:

```
sudo sostat | less
```

- If any of the NSM processes show up as failed, try restarting them:

```
sudo service nsm restart
```

- Check log files in /var/log/nsm/ or other locations for any errors or possible clues:
    - Setup /var/log/nsm/sosetup.log
    - Daily Log / PCAPs /nsm/sensor_data/{ HOSTNAME-INTERFACE }/dailylogs
    - sguil /var/log/nsm/securityonion/sguild.log
    - Suricata /var/log/nsm/{ HOSTNAME-INTERFACE }/suricata.log
    - barnyard2 /var/log/nsm/ { HOSTNAME-INTERFACE }/barnyard2.log
    - netsniff-ng /var/log/nsm/{ HOSTNAME-INTERFACE }/netsniff-ng.log
    - Bro /nsm/bro/logs/current
    - snort_agent /var/log/nsm/{ HOSTNAME-INTERFACE }/snort_agent.log
    - Elasticsearch /var/log/elasticsearch/<hostname>.log
    - Kibana /var/log/kibana/kibana.log
    - Logstash /var/log/logstash/logstash.log

- Elastalert `/var/log/elastalert/elastalert_stderr.log`
- If this is a sensor sending alerts to master server, is autossh running?

```
sudo so-autossh-status
```

- Having trouble with MySQL? Check all databases to see if any tables are are marked as crashed or corrupt.

```
sudo mysqlcheck -A
```

- Check specific MySQL databases by running something similar to the following:

```
sudo mysqlcheck -c securityonion_db
```

- Are you able to duplicate the problem on a fresh Security Onion installation?
- Check the Known Issues to see if this is a known issue that we are working on.
- If all else fails, please send an email to our security-onion mailing list.
- Need training or commercial support? https://www.securityonionsolutions.com

14.1 FAQ

Install / Update / Upgrade
Users / Passwords
Support / Help
Error messages
IDS engines
Security Onion internals
Tuning
sostat output
Miscellaneous

14.1.1 Install / Update / Upgrade

Why won't the ISO image boot on my machine?

Please see the TroubleBooting section.

What's the recommended procedure for installing Security Onion?

Please see the Installation Procedure section.

Why does the installer crash when selecting a non-English language?

We only support the English language at this time:
Installation#language

Why can't I see the Continue button on the Keyboard Layout screen of the installer?

The Keyboard Layout screen may be larger than your screen resolution and so the Continue button may be off the screen to the right(as shown in https://launchpadlibrarian.net/207213663/Screenshot_wilyi386deskmanual_2015-05-22_13%3A05%3A41.png). You can simply slide the window over until you see the Continue button. For more information, please see https://bugs.launchpad.net/ubuntu/+source/ubiquity/+bug/1458039.

How do I install Security Onion updates?

Please see the Upgrade Procedure section.

Why do I get `Snort/Suricata/Bro` errors after upgrading the `kernel` and `pfring` packages?

Please see the Updating section.

What do I need to do if I'm behind a proxy?

Please see the Proxy Configuration section.

Ubuntu is saying that my kernel has reached EOL (End Of Life). Should I update to the newer HWE stack?

Please see the HWE section.

Why does my VMware image rename `eth0` to `eth1`?

Usually this happens when you clone a VM. VMware asks if you moved it or copied it. If you select "copied", it will change the MAC address to avoid duplication. At the next boot, Ubuntu's udev will see a new MAC address and create a new network interface (eth1). To fix this:

```
sudo rm /etc/udev/rules.d/70-persistent-net.rules
sudo reboot
```

Can I run Security Onion on Raspberry Pi or some other non-x86 box?

No, we only support 64-bit Intel/AMD architectures. Please see the hardware section.

What's the difference between a `server` and a `sensor`?

box
Definition: A physical or virtual machine running the Security Onion operating system.

server

Definition: A set of processes that receive data from sensors and allow analysts to see and investigate that data. The set of processes includes sguild, mysql, and optionally the Elastic stack (Elasticsearch, Logstash, Kibana) and Curator. The server is also responsible for ruleset management.

Naming convention: The collection of server processes has a server name separate from the hostname of the box. Security Onion always sets the server name to `securityonion`.

Configuration files: `/etc/nsm/securityonion/`

Controlled by: `/usr/sbin/nsm_server`

server box

Definition: A machine running the server processes. May optionally be running sensor processes.

Example 1: User runs Quick Setup on machine with hostname securityonion and two ethernet interfaces. Setup creates a server and two sensors (`securityonion-eth0` and `securityonion-eth1`).

Example 2: User runs Advanced Setup and chooses Server. Setup creates a server only (no sensor processes).

sensor

Definition: A set of processes listening on a network interface. The set of processes currently includes Snort/Suricata, netsniff-ng, and bro (although this is in constant flux as we add new capabilities and find better tools for existing capabilities).

Naming convention: `$HOSTNAME-$INTERFACE`

Configuration files: `/etc/nsm/$HOSTNAME-$INTERFACE/`

Example: `sensor1-eth0`

Controlled by: `/usr/sbin/nsm_sensor`

sensor box

Definition: A machine having one or more sensors that transmit to a central server. Does not run server processes. Pulls ruleset from server box.

Example: A machine named `sensor1` having sensors `sensor1-eth0` and `sensor1-eth1`.

back to top

14.1.2 Users / Passwords

What is the password for `root/mysql/Sguil/Squert/Kibana`?

Please see the Passwords section.

How do I add a new user account for logging into Sguil/Squert/Kibana?

Please see the Adding Sguil accounts section.

back to top

14.1.3 Support / Help

Where do I send questions/problems/suggestions?

security-onion Google Group

I submitted a message to the security-onion Google Group. Why isn't it showing up?

Please see the Moderation section.

Is commercial support available for Security Onion?

Yes! Please see https://securityonionsolutions.com.

back to top

14.1.4 Error messages

Why does rule-update fail with Error 400 when running behind a proxy?

Please see the Proxy#pulledpork section.

Why does rule-update fail with an error like "Error 404 when fetching s3.amazonaws.com/snort-org/www/rules/community/community-rules.tar.gz.md5"?

The Snort Community ruleset has moved to a different URL. You can run the following command to update the Snort Community URL in `pulledpork.conf`:

```
sudo sed -i 's\rule_url=https://s3.amazonaws.com/snort-org/www/rules/community/
↪|community-rules.tar.gz|Community\rule_url=https://snort.org/downloads/community/
↪|community-rules.tar.gz|Community\g' /etc/nsm/pulledpork/pulledpork.conf
```

For more information, please see:

https://blog.snort.org/2015/10/are-you-getting-404-errors-attempting.html

Why does `soup` fail with an error message like "find: '/usr/lib/python2.7/dist-packages/salt/': No such file or directory"?

This is a bug in the salt packages that can manifest when skipping salt versions. Resolve with the following:

```
sudo mkdir -p /usr/lib/python2.7/dist-packages/salt/
sudo apt-get -f install
sudo soup
```

Why does barnyard2 keep failing with errors like "Returned signature_id is not equal to updated signature_id"?

Please see:

https://blog.securityonion.net/2014/06/new-securityonion-rule-update-package.html

I just updated Snort and it's now saying 'ERROR: The dynamic detection library "/usr/local/lib/snort_dynamicrules/chat.so" version 1.0 compiled with dynamic engine library version 2.1 isn't compatible with the current dynamic engine library "/usr/lib/snort_dynamicengine/libsf_engine.so" version 2.4.'

Run the following:

```
sudo rule-update
```

For more information, please see:

https://blog.securityonion.net/2014/12/new-version-of-securityonion-rule.html

I get periodic MySQL crashes and/or error code 24 "out of resources" when searching in Sguil. How do I fix that?

Modern versions of Setup should set MySQL's `open-files-limit` to 90000 to avoid this problem.

For more information, please see:

http://nsmwiki.org/Sguil_FAQ#I.27m_seeing_error_code_24_from_MySQL._How_do_I_fix_that.3F

Barnyard2 is failing with an error like "ERROR: sguil: Expected Confirm 13324 and got: Failed to insert 13324: mysqlexec/db server: Duplicate entry '9-13324' for key 'PRIMARY'". How do I fix this?

Sometimes, just restarting Barnyard will clear this up:

```
sudo so-barnyard-restart
```

Other times, restarting Sguild and then restarting Barnyard will clear it up:

```
sudo so-sguild-restart
sudo so-sensor-restart --only-barnyard2
```

If that doesn't work, then try also restarting mysql:

```
sudo service mysql restart
sudo so-sguild-restart
sudo so-sensor-restart --only-barnyard2
```

If that still doesn't fix it, you may have to perform MySQL surgery on the database `securityonion_db` as described in the Sguil FAQ: http://nsmwiki.org/Sguil_FAQ#Barnyard_dies_at_startup.2C_with_.22Duplicate_Entry.22_error

Why does Snort segfault every day at 7:01 AM?

7:01 AM is the time of the daily PulledPork rules update. If you're running Snort with the Snort Subscriber (Talos) ruleset, this includes updating the SO rules. There is a known issue when running Snort with the Snort Subscriber (Talos) ruleset and updating the SO rules: https://groups.google.com/d/topic/pulledpork-users/1bQDkh3AhNs/discussion

After updating the rules, Snort is restarted, and the segfault occurs in the OLD instance of Snort (not the NEW instance). Therefore, the segfault is merely a nuisance log entry and can safely be ignored.

Why does the pcap_agent log show "Error: can't read logFile: no such variable"?

This usually means that there is an unexpected file in the dailylogs directory. Run the following:

```
ls /nsm/sensor_data/*/dailylogs/
```

You should see a bunch of date stamped directories and you may see some extraneous files. Remove any extraneous files and restart pcap_agent:

```
sudo so-pcap-agent-restart
```

Why does Chromium display a black screen and/or crash?

This is a known issue with certain versions of VMware. You can either:

- go into the VM configuration and disable 3D in the video adapter OR
- upgrade the VM hardware level (may require upgrading to a new version of VMware)

Why does Bro log `Failed to open GeoIP database` and `Fell back to GeoIP Country database`?

The GeoIP CITY database is `not free` and thus we cannot include it in the distro. Bro fails to find it and falls back to the GeoIP COUNTRY database (which is free). As long as you are seeing some country codes in your conn.log, then everything should be fine. If you really need the CITY database, see this thread for some options: https://groups.google.com/d/topic/security-onion-testing/gtc-8ZTuCi4/discussion

Why does soup tell me I need a Secure Boot key?

Please see the Secure Boot section.

back to top

14.1.5 IDS engines

I'm currently running `Snort`. How do I switch to `Suricata`?

Please see the NIDS#switching-from-snort-to-suricata section.

I'm currently running `Suricata`. How do I switch to `Snort`?

Please see the NIDS#switching-from-suricata-to-snort section.

Can Security Onion run in `IPS` mode?

Please see the NIDS#NIPS section.

back to top

14.1.6 Security Onion internals

Where can I read more about the tools contained within Security Onion?

Please see the Tools section.

What's the directory structure of `/nsm`?

Please see the /nsm Directory Structure section.

Why does Security Onion use `UTC`?

Please see the UTC and Time Zones section.

Why are the `timestamps` in Kibana not in UTC?

Please see the UTC and Time Zones section.

Why is my disk filling up?

Sguil uses netsniff-ng to record full packet captures to disk. These pcaps are stored in `nsm/sensor_data/$HOSTNAME-$INTERFACE/dailylogs/`. `/etc/cron.d/sensor-clean` is a cronjob that runs every minute that should delete old pcaps when the disk reaches your defined disk usage threshold (90% by default). It's important to properly size your disk storage so that you avoid filling the disk to 100% between purges.

I just rebooted and it looks like the services aren't starting automatically.

Older versions of Security Onion waited 60 seconds after boot to ensure network interfaces are fully initialized before starting services. Starting in 16.04, services should start automatically as soon as network interfaces are initialized.

Why do apt-get and the Update Manager show `tcl8.5 as held back`?

Please see the tcl section.

back to top

14.1.7 Tuning

What do I need to tune if I'm monitoring VLAN tagged traffic?

Please see the VLAN Traffic section.

How do I configure email for alerting and reporting?

Please see the Email section.

How do I configure a `BPF` for `Snort/Suricata/Bro/netsniff-ng/prads`?

Please see the BPF section.

How do I filter traffic?

Please see the BPF section.

How do I exclude traffic?

Please see the BPF section.

What are the default firewall settings and how do I change them?

Please see the Firewall section.

What do I need to modify in order to have the log files stored on a different mount point?

Please see the Adding a New Disk for /nsm section.

How do I disable the graphical `Network Manager` and configuring networking from the command line?

Please see the Network Configuration section.

How do I enable/disable processes?

Please see the Disabling Processes section.

I disabled some Sguil agents but they still appear in Sguil's `Agent Status` tab.

Please see the Disabling Processes section.

What can I do to decrease the size of my `securityonion_db` (sguild) MySQL database?

You can lower the `DAYSTOKEEP` setting in `/etc/nsm/securityonion.conf`.
Also see `UNCAT_MAX`:
https://blog.securityonion.net/2015/01/new-version-of-sguil-db-purge-helps.html

How do I change the fonts in the Sguil client?

Please see the Sguil#customize-sguil-client section.

14.1. FAQ

Can I be alerted when an interface stops receiving traffic?

Please see the Interface stops receiving traffic section.

How do I boot Security Onion to text mode (CLI instead of GUI)?

Please see the Disabling Desktop section.

I'm running Security Onion in a VM and the screensaver is using lots of CPU. How do I change/disable the screensaver?

back to top

14.1.8 sostat output

What does it mean if `sostat` show a high number of `Sguil Uncategorized Events`?

`Sguild` has to load uncategorized events into memory when it starts and it won't accept connections until that's complete. You can either:

- wait for sguild to start up (may take a LONG time), then log into Sguil, and `F8` LOTS of events OR
- stop sguild

  ```
  sudo so-sguild-stop
  ```

  and manually categorize events using `mysql`
  (see http://taosecurity.blogspot.com/2013/02/recovering-from-suricata-gone-wild.html)
  OR
  lower your `DAYSTOKEEP` setting in `/etc/nsm/securityonion.conf` and run

  ```
  sudo sguil-db-purge
  ```

  To keep `Uncategorized Events` from getting too high, you should log into Sguil/Squert on a daily/weekly basis and categorize events.

back to top

14.1.9 Miscellaneous

Where can I find the version information for Security Onion?

If the machine was built with the Security Onion 16.04 ISO image, version information can be found in `/etc/PinguyBuilder.conf`.

Where can I find interesting pcaps to replay?

Please see the Pcaps section.

Why is Security Onion connecting to an IP address on the Internet over port 123?

Please see the NTP section.

Should I backup my Security Onion box?

Network Security Monitoring as a whole is considered "best effort". It is not a "mission critical" resource like a file server or web server. Since we're dealing with "big data" (potentially terabytes of full packet capture), backups would be prohibitively expensive. Most organizations don't do any backups and instead just rebuild boxes when necessary.

How can I add and test local rules?

Please see the Adding local rules and testing them with scapy section.

Where can I get the source code?

You can download the full source code for any of our packages like this:

```
apt-get source PACKAGE-NAME
```

where `PACKAGE-NAME` is usually something like `securityonion-snort`. Here's a list of all of our packages: |
https://launchpad.net/~securityonion/+archive/stable

How can I remote control my Security Onion box?

A few options:
"ssh -X" - any program started in the SSH session will be displayed on your local desktop (requires a local X server)
xrdp - sudo apt-get install xrdp - requires an rdp client

Why isn't Squert showing GeoIP data properly?

If the Squert map is not showing the country for IPs, try running the following:

```
sudo /usr/bin/php -e /var/www/so/squert/.inc/ip2c.php 0'/
```

Why do I get segfaults when booting on VMware ESX?

This is a known issue with Ubuntu 10.04 and ESXi 4.1 and is unrelated to Security Onion. Please see:
http://ubuntuforums.org/showthread.php?t=1674759
https://bugs.launchpad.net/ubuntu/+source/linux/+bug/659422

How do I run `ntopng` on Security Onion?

Please see the Deploying NtopNG section.

How do I open rar files?

We're not allowed to redistribute the unrar plugin, so you'll need to install it manually:

```
sudo apt-get update
sudo apt-get install unrar
```

How do I perform "X" in Ubuntu?

Security Onion is based on Ubuntu, but we don't provide community support for the Ubuntu OS itself. If you have questions about Ubuntu, you should check the Ubuntu website, forums, and Google.

back to top

14.2 Directory Structure

14.2.1 /nsm Directory Structure

14.2.2 /nsm

Backup, Bro, sensor (if configured as sensor), and server (if configured as server) data.

14.2.3 /nsm/bro

Bro IDS logs.

14.2.4 /nsm/elasticsearch

Elasticsearch data.

14.2.5 /nsm/sensor_data

Sensor data including IDS alerts and full pcap organized by sensor name ($HOSTNAME-$INTERFACE).

14.2.6 /nsm/server_data

Server data including IDS rulesets.

14.3 Tools

Security Onion would like to thank the following open-source projects for their contribution to our community!

barnyard2

http://www.securixlive.com/barnyard2/

"Barnyard2 is an open source interpreter for Snort unified2 binary output files. Its primary use is allowing Snort to write to disk in an efficient manner and leaving the task of parsing binary data into various formats to a separate process that will not cause Snort to miss network traffic."

Bro (Zeek)

https://zeek.org/

"Bro is a powerful network analysis framework that is much different from the typical IDS you may know."

chaosreader

http://chaosreader.sourceforge.net/

"Chaosreader is a freeware tool to fetch application data from snoop or tcpdump logs. Supported protocols include TCP, UDP, IPv4, IPv6, ICMP, telnet, FTP, HTTP, SMTP, IRC, X11, and VNC."

Daemonlogger

http://www.snort.org/snort-downloads/additional-downloads#daemonlogger

"Daemonlogger™ is a packet logger and soft tap developed by Martin Roesch."

driftnet

http://www.ex-parrot.com/~chris/driftnet/

"Driftnet is a program which listens to network traffic and picks out images from TCP streams it observes."

dsniff

http://www.monkey.org/~dugsong/dsniff/

"dsniff is a collection of tools for network auditing and penetration testing. dsniff, filesnarf, mailsnarf, msgsnarf, urlsnarf, and webspy passively monitor a network for interesting data (passwords, e-mail, files, etc.). arpspoof, dnsspoof, and macof facilitate the interception of network traffic normally unavailable to an attacker (e.g, due to layer-2 switching). sshmitm and webmitm implement active monkey-in-the-middle attacks against redirected SSH and HTTPS sessions by exploiting weak bindings in ad-hoc PKI."

Elastic Stack

https://www.elastic.co/

The Elastic Stack consists of Elasticsearch, Logstash, and Kibana and replaces ELSA.

hping

http://www.hping.org/

"hping is a command-line oriented TCP/IP packet assembler/analyzer. The interface is inspired to the ping(8) unix command, but hping isn't only able to send ICMP echo requests. It supports TCP, UDP, ICMP and RAW-IP protocols, has a traceroute mode, the ability to send files between a covered channel, and many other features."

hunt

"Advanced packet sniffer and connection intrusion. Hunt is a program for intruding into a connection, watching it and resetting it. Note that hunt is operating on Ethernet and is best used for connections which can be watched through it.

However, it is possible to do something even for hosts on another segments or hosts that are on switched ports."

labrea

http://labrea.sourceforge.net/labrea-info.html

"LaBrea takes over unused IP addresses, and creates virtual servers that are attractive to worms, hackers, and other denizens of the Internet. The program answers connection attempts in such a way that the machine at the other end gets "stuck", sometimes for a very long time."

mergecap

http://www.wireshark.org/docs/man-pages/mergecap.html

"Mergecap is a program that combines multiple saved capture files into a single output file specified by the -w argument. Mergecap knows how to read libpcap capture files, including those of tcpdump, Wireshark, and other tools that write captures in that format."

netsed

"The network packet altering stream editor NetSED is small and handful utility designed to alter the contents of packets forwarded thru your network in real time. It is really useful for network hackers in following applications: black-box protocol auditing - whenever there are two or more proprietary boxes communicating over undocumented protocol (by enforcing changes in ongoing transmissions, you will be able to test if tested application is secure), fuzz-alike experiments, integrity tests - whenever you want to test stability of the application and see how it ensures data integrity, other common applications - fooling other people, content filtering, etc etc - choose whatever you want to. It perfectly fits ngrep, netcat and tcpdump tools suite."

netsniff-ng

http://netsniff-ng.org/

"netsniff-ng is a free, performant Linux networking toolkit."

NetworkMiner

http://www.netresec.com/?page=NetworkMiner

"NetworkMiner is a Network Forensic Analysis Tool (NFAT) for Windows. NetworkMiner can be used as a passive network sniffer/packet capturing tool in order to detect operating systems, sessions, hostnames, open ports etc. without putting any traffic on the network. NetworkMiner can also parse PCAP files for off-line analysis and to regenerate/reassemble transmitted files and certificates from PCAP files."

ngrep

http://ngrep.sourceforge.net/

"ngrep strives to provide most of GNU grep's common features, applying them to the network layer. ngrep is a pcap-aware tool that will allow you to specify extended regular or hexadecimal expressions to match against data payloads of packets. It currently recognizes IPv4/6, TCP, UDP, ICMPv4/6, IGMP and Raw across Ethernet, PPP, SLIP, FDDI, Token Ring and null interfaces, and understands BPF filter logic in the same fashion as more common packet sniffing tools, such as tcpdump and snoop."

p0f

http://lcamtuf.coredump.cx/p0f3/

"P0f is a tool that utilizes an array of sophisticated, purely passive traffic fingerprinting mechanisms to identify the players behind any incidental TCP/IP communications (often as little as a single normal SYN) without interfering in any way. Version 3 is a complete rewrite of the original codebase, incorporating a significant number of improvements to network-level fingerprinting, and introducing the ability to reason about application-level payloads (e.g., HTTP)."

Reassembler

http://isc.sans.edu/diary.html?storyid=13282

"If you provide reassembler.py with a pcap that contains fragments, it will reassemble the packets using each of the 5 reassembly engines and show you the result."

scapy

http://www.secdev.org/projects/scapy/

"Scapy is a powerful interactive packet manipulation program. It is able to forge or decode packets of a wide number of protocols, send them on the wire, capture them, match requests and replies, and much more. It can easily handle most classical tasks like scanning, tracerouting, probing, unit tests, attacks or network discovery (it can replace hping, 85% of nmap, arpspoof, arp-sk, arping, tcpdump, tethereal, p0f, etc.). It also performs very well at a lot of other specific tasks that most other tools can't handle, like sending invalid frames, injecting your own 802.11 frames, combining technics (VLAN hopping+ARP cache poisoning, VOIP decoding on WEP encrypted channel, ...), etc."

sguil

http://sguil.sourceforge.net/

"Sguil (pronounced sgweel) is built by network security analysts for network security analysts. Sguil's main component is an intuitive GUI that provides access to realtime events, session data, and raw packet captures. Sguil facilitates the practice of Network Security Monitoring and event driven analysis. The Sguil client is written in tcl/tk and can be run on any operating system that supports tcl/tk (including Linux, BSD, Solaris, MacOS, and Win32)."

Sniffit

http://sniffit.sourceforge.net/

"SniffIt is a Distribted Sniffer System, which allows users to capture network traffic from an unique machine using a graphical client application. This feature is very useful in switched networks, where traditional sniffers only allow users to sniff their own network traffic."

Snort

http://www.snort.org/

"Snort® is an open source network intrusion prevention and detection system (IDS/IPS) developed by Sourcefire. Combining the benefits of signature, protocol, and anomaly-based inspection, Snort is the most widely deployed IDS/IPS technology worldwide. With millions of downloads and nearly 400,000 registered users, Snort has become the de facto standard for IPS."

Squert

http://www.squertproject.org/

"Squert is a web application that is used to query and view event data stored in a Sguil database (typically IDS alert data). Squert is a visual tool that attempts to provide additional context to events through the use of metadata, time series representations and weighted and logically grouped result sets. The hope is that these views will prompt questions that otherwise may not have been asked."

ssldump

http://www.rtfm.com/ssldump/

"ssldump is an SSLv3/TLS network protocol analyzer. It identifies TCP connections on the chosen network interface and attempts to interpret them as SSLv3/TLS traffic. When it identifies SSLv3/TLS traffic, it decodes the records and displays them in a textual form to stdout. If provided with the appropriate keying material, it will also decrypt the connections and display the application data traffic."

sslsniff

http://www.thoughtcrime.org/software/sslsniff/

"sslsniff is designed to create man-in-the-middle (MITM) attacks for SSL/TLS connections, and dynamically generates certs for the domains that are being accessed on the fly. The new certificates are constructed in a certificate chain that is signed by any certificate that is provided. sslsniff also supports other attacks like null-prefix or OCSP attacks to achieve silent interceptions of connections when possible."

Suricata

http://www.openinfosecfoundation.org/index.php/download-suricata

"The Suricata Engine is an Open Source Next Generation Intrusion Detection and Prevention Engine. This engine is not intended to just replace or emulate the existing tools in the industry, but will bring new ideas and technologies to the field."

tcpdump

http://www.tcpdump.org/

"Tcpdump prints out a description of the contents of packets on a network interface that match the boolean expression. It can also be run with the -w flag, which causes it to save the packet data to a file for later analysis, and/or with the -r flag, which causes it to read from a saved packet file rather than to read packets from a network interface. In all cases, only packets that match expression will be processed by tcpdump."

tcpick

http://tcpick.sourceforge.net/

"tcpick is a textmode sniffer libpcap-based that can track, reassemble and reorder tcp streams. Tcpick is able to save the captured flows in different files or displays them in the terminal, and so it is useful to sniff files that are transmitted via ftp or http. It can display all the stream on the terminal, when the connection is closed in different display modes like hexdump, hexdump + ascii, only printable charachters, raw mode and so on. Available a color mode too, helpful to read and understand better the output of the program. Actually it can handle several interfaces, including ethernet cards and ppp. It is useful to keep track of what users of a network are doing, and is usable with textmode tools like grep, sed, awk."

tcpreplay

http://tcpreplay.synfin.net/

"Tcpreplay is a suite of GPLv3 licensed tools written by Aaron Turner for UNIX (and Win32 under Cygwin) operating systems which gives you the ability to use previously captured traffic in libpcap format to test a variety of network devices. It allows you to classify traffic as client or server, rewrite Layer 2, 3 and 4 headers and finally replay the traffic back onto the network and through other devices such as switches, routers, firewalls, NIDS and IPS's. Tcpreplay supports both single and dual NIC modes for testing both sniffing and inline devices."

tcpslice

http://sourceforge.net/projects/tcpslice/

"tcpslice is a tool for extracting portions of packet trace files generated using tcpdump's -w flag. It can combine multiple trace files, and/or extract portions of one or more traces based on time."

tcpstat

http://www.frenchfries.net/paul/tcpstat/

"tcpstat reports certain network interface statistics much like vmstat does for system statistics. tcpstat gets its information by either monitoring a specific interface, or by reading previously saved tcpdump data from a file."

tcpxtract

http://tcpxtract.sourceforge.net/

"tcpxtract is a tool for extracting files from network traffic based on file signatures."

tshark

http://www.wireshark.org/docs/man-pages/tshark.html

"TShark is a network protocol analyzer. It lets you capture packet data from a live network, or read packets from a previously saved capture file, either printing a decoded form of those packets to the standard output or writing the packets to a file. TShark's native capture file format is libpcap format, which is also the format used by tcpdump and various other tools."

u2boat

http://www.snort.org/

Part of Snort, u2boat converts unified2 files to pcaps.

u2spewfoo

http://www.snort.org/

Part of Snort, u2spewfoo converts unified2 files to text.

Wazuh

https://wazuh.com/

"Wazuh is a free, open source and enterprise-ready security monitoring solution for threat detection, integrity monitoring, incident response and compliance."

Wireshark

http://www.wireshark.org/

"Wireshark is a GUI network protocol analyzer. It lets you interactively browse packet data from a live network or from a previously saved capture file. Wireshark's native capture file format is libpcap format, which is also the format used by tcpdump and various other tools."

14.4 Passwords

14.4.1 OS root account

Like other Ubuntu-based distributions, there is no root password. Your default user account has been given sudo permissions. Graphical utilities requesting administrative access should prompt for password; enter your user password. Command-line utilities that require administrative access can be prefixed with `sudo`. For example, to add an OS user account:

```
sudo adduser mynewuseraccount
```

14.4.2 Sguil

Log into Sguil using the username and password you created in the Setup wizard.

You can add accounts as follows (please note that Sguil usernames must be alphanumeric):

```
sudo so-user-add
```

You can change passwords using the Sguil client (`File -> Change Password`) or as follows:

```
sudo so-user-passwd
```

You can disable accounts as follows:

```
sudo so-user-disable
```

14.4.3 Squert

Squert authenticates against the Sguil user database, so you should be able to login to Squert using the same username and password you use to login to Sguil.

14.4.4 Kibana

When you access Kibana, you are prompted to login using Apache Single Sign On (SSO). This SSO authenticates against the Sguil user database, so you should be able to login to Kibana using the same username and password you use to login to Sguil.

14.4.5 MySQL

The MySQL root password is randomized. MySQL only allows connections from localhost. If you need to look at the database manually, you can do so like this:

```
sudo mysql --defaults-file=/etc/mysql/debian.cnf
```

14.5 Support

14.5.1 Commercial Support

If you need private and/or priority support, please consider purchasing commercial support:

https://securityonionsolutions.com

14.5.2 Free Support

If you need free support, please use our public security-onion mailing list:

MailingLists

14.6 Mailing Lists

14.6.1 Check Documentation First

Before sending an email to our mailing list, check to see if your question has already been answered by one of the following:

Help

FAQ

14.6.2 Moderation

Please keep in mind that our Google Groups are moderated, so your email will have to be approved before it is published to the list. If at first you don't see your email appear in the mailing list, there is no need to re-send your email. It has been queued and will be approved if appropriate.

14.6.3 Etiquette

Please be courteous and respectful. Disrespectful emails can result in being banned from the Google Group.

14.6.4 Questions/Problems

Start a new thread instead of replying to an old one

Please search the mailing list to see if you can find similar issues that may help you. However, please do not reply to old threads with your new issue. Instead, please start a new thread and provide a hyperlink to the related discussion at https://groups.google.com/forum/#!forum/security-onion.

Avoid generic Ubuntu questions

Security Onion is based on Ubuntu. Quite often, folks ask the Security Onion mailing list for help with Ubuntu issues not strictly related to Security Onion. In order to keep the signal-to-noise ratio as high as possible, the Security Onion mailing list should only be used for questions directly relating to Security Onion itself. If you have questions about Ubuntu, you should check the Ubuntu website, forums, and Google.

Provide sufficient technical info

In order to be as effective and efficient as possible, please consider the following when posing your question/problem to the group:

http://www.chiark.greenend.org.uk/~sgtatham/bugs.html

Include sostat-redacted output

Please run the following command:

```
sudo sostat-redacted
```

There will be a lot of output, so you may need to increase your terminal's scroll buffer OR redirect the output of the command to a file:

```
sudo sostat-redacted > sostat-redacted.txt 2>&1
```

`sostat-redacted` will automatically redact any IPv4/IPv6/MAC addresses, but there may be additional sensitive info that you still need to redact manually.

Attach the output to your email in plain text format (.txt) OR use a service like http://pastebin.com.

14.6.5 Security-Onion mailing list

Once you've read and understand all of the above, you can send your question to our security-onion mailing list. It is hosted by Google Groups, so you can send via email or by posting in the web interface:

http://groups.google.com/group/security-onion

14.7 Help Wanted

Folks frequently ask how they can give back to the Security Onion community. Here are a few of our community teams that you can help with.

14.7.1 Marketing Team

We need more folks to help spread the word about Security Onion by blogging, tweeting, and other social media.

14.7.2 Support Team

If you'd like help out other Security Onion users, please join the security-onion mailing list and/or IRC channel and start answering questions!

https://groups.google.com/forum/#!forum/security-onion

14.7.3 Testing/QA Team

If you'd like to do testing/QA, please join the security-onion-testing mailing list.

https://groups.google.com/forum/#!forum/security-onion-testing

14.7.4 Documentation Team

If you find that some information in our Documentation is incorrect or lacking, please feel free to submit Pull Requests via GitHub!

https://github.com/Security-Onion-Solutions/securityonion-docs

14.7.5 Core Development

Most of our code is on GitHub. Please feel free to submit pull requests!

https://github.com/Security-Onion-Solutions

14.7.6 Thanks

The following folks have made significant contributions to Security Onion over the years. Thanks!

- Wes Lambert
- Mike Reeves
- Phil Plantamura

- Dustin Lee
- Josh Brower
- Kevin Branch
- Scott Runnels
- Brad Shoop
- Liam Randall
- Paul Halliday
- Eric Ooi
- Lawrence Abrams
- Mark Hillick
- Joe Hargis
- Dennis Distler
- Jon Schipp
- Josh More
- Jack Blanchard

CHAPTER 15

Integrations

There are many different ways that we can integrate Security Onion into other systems. However, please note that we don't provide free support for third party systems, so this section will be just a brief introduction to how you would accomplish this. If you need commercial support, please see https://www.securityonionsolutions.com.

15.1 AlienVault-OTX

We can easily pull in Alienvault OTX pulses into Security Onion and have Bro utilize them for the Intel Framework by leveraging Stephen Hosom's work with Alienvault OTX integration.

15.1.1 Warning

Please keep in mind we do not officially support use of this script, so installation is at your own risk.

15.1.2 Installation

In order to do begin, we will need to make sure we satisfy a few prerequisites:

Alienvault OTX API key - can be obtained for free at: https://otx.alienvault.com
Security Onion standalone/sensor (running Bro)
External internet access - to retrieve updated pulses (https://otx.alienvault.com/api/v1/pulses/subscribed)

Download the installation script:

```
wget https://raw.githubusercontent.com/weslambert/securityonion-otx/master/
↪securityonion-otx
```

Run the script:

```
sudo bash securityonion-otx
```

After using the above script, `/opt/bro/share/bro/policy/bro-otx` will house all necessary files, etc (including `otx.dat`, the intel file where all pulses will be fed).

We can test our configuration by adding another piece of intel to the end of `/opt/bro/share/bro/policy/bro-otx/otx.dat`. For example:

```
google.com[literal tab]Intel::DOMAIN[literal tab]Test-Google-Intel[literal tab]https:/
↪/google.com[literal tab]T
```

As long as our syntax is correct, we should not need to restart Bro. We can check for errors in `/nsm/bro/logs/current/reporter.log`.

Let's see if we can get an intel hit by doing the following:

```
curl google.com
```

Next, we need to check `/nsm/bro/logs/current/intel.log` for entries in regard to our indicator:

```
grep google /nsm/bro/logs/current/intel.log
```

We should have received a Bro Notice as well, so lets check that:

```
grep google /nsm/bro/logs/current/notice.log
```

After successful testing, we can remove our addition from `/opt/bro/share/bro/policy/bro-otx/otx.dat` or just run `/opt/bro/share/bro/policy/bro-otx/bro-otx.py` again.

By default, pulses will be retrieved on an hourly basis. To change this to a different value, simply alter the interval in `/etc/cron.d/bro-otx`.

15.2 Etherpad

We can add Etherpad to Security Onion to allow us to take notes during investigations and share those with our team.

Simply run the following commands from a fresh Security Onion install (master server/or standalone):

Download:

```
wget https://raw.githubusercontent.com/weslambert/securityonion-etherpad/master/
↪install_etherpad
```

Execute:

```
sudo bash ./install_etherpad
```

Follow the prompts.

You should then be able to access Etherpad at the destination defined in the setup script.

Be sure to configure DNS or client hosts file(s) with the appropriate information and then run so-allow and allow port 443 for analysts:

```
sudo so-allow
```

15.3 FIR

From: https://github.com/certsocietegenerale/FIR:

> FIR (Fast Incident Response) is an cybersecurity incident management platform designed with agility and speed in mind. It >allows for easy creation, tracking, and reporting of cybersecurity incidents.
>
> FIR is for anyone needing to track cybersecurity incidents (CSIRTs, CERTs, SOCs, etc.). It's was tailored to suit our >needs >and our team's habits, but we put a great deal of effort into making it as generic as possible before releasing it >so that >other teams around the world may also use it and customize it as they see fit.

We can add FIR to Security Onion as a Docker container to enhance its current capabilities and leverage the great work from the folks at CERT Societe Generale.

15.3.1 Warning

Please keep in mind we do not officially support FIR, so installation is at your own risk.

15.3.2 Installation

To install FIR on Security Onion, use the following steps.

Get the install script:

```
wget https://raw.githubusercontent.com/weslambert/securityonion-fir/master/install_fir
```

Run the script:

```
sudo bash ./install_fir
```

Follow the prompts, and once finished, you should be able to navigate to FIR via `https://domain.you.specified`. (Note this address in also referenced in `/etc/apache2/sites-available/fir.conf`.)

Keep in mind, FIR is still accessible at `http://localhost:8001`, so you will want to make sure only port 443 is allowed externally, or alter your web server settings appropriately.

Also note, to access FIR by the above name you will need to:

- configure a hosts file on your local host or
- create a DNS record pointing to it.

For more information on the FIR, see here:
https://github.com/certsocietegenerale/FIR

15.4 GRR

From: https://github.com/google/grr:

> GRR Rapid Response: remote live forensics for incident response

We can add GRR to Security Onion as a Docker container to enhance its current capabilities and leverage the great work from the folks at Google.

15.4.1 Warning

Please keep in mind we do not officially support GRR, so installation is at your own risk.

15.4.2 Installation

To install GRR on Security Onion:

Get the install script:

```
wget https://raw.githubusercontent.com/weslambert/securityonion-grr/master/install_grr
```

Run the script:

```
sudo bash ./install_grr
```

Follow the prompts, and once finished, you should be able to navigate to GRR via `https://domain.you.specified`. (Note this address in also referenced in `/etc/apache2/sites-available/grr.conf`.)

Keep in mind, GRR is still accessible at `http://localhost:8000`, so you will want to make sure only port 443 is allowed externally, or alter your web server settings appropriately.

Also note, to access GRR by the above name you will need to:

- configure a hosts file on your local host OR
- create a DNS record pointing to it.

15.4.3 Firewall Rules

You can add firewall rules using so-allow and choosing the `Analyst` option:

```
sudo so-allow
```

OR

```
sudo ufw allow proto tcp from REMOTE_IP to any port 443
```

GRR Client IP:

```
sudo iptables -I DOCKER-USER ! -i docker0 -o docker0 -s ClIENT_IP -p tcp --dport 8080 -j ACCEPT
```

15.4.4 Management

If you would like to add another user, aside from the default, you can follow the instructions here:
https://grr-doc.readthedocs.io/en/latest/maintaining-and-tuning/user-management/index.html

For more information on the GRR Docker image, see here:
https://grr-doc.readthedocs.io/en/latest/

15.5 TheHive

15.5.1 Elastalert Rules

We can send events to an instance of the TheHive, as Elastalert includes the TheHive alerter (Nclose-ZA).

Simply modify the following rule as desired, and place the rule in `/etc/elastalert/rules`, on your Security Onion box (master server if running Distributed Deployment).

```
# hive.yaml
# Elastalert rule to forward IDS alerts from Security Onion to a specified TheHive
↪instance.
#
es_host: elasticsearch
es_port: 9200
name: TheHive - New IDS Alert!
type: frequency
index: "*:logstash-ids*"
num_events: 1
timeframe:
    minutes: 10
buffer_time:
    minutes: 10
allow_buffer_time_overlap: true

filter:
- term:
    event_type: "snort"

alert: hivealerter

hive_connection:
  hive_host: http(s)://YOUR_HIVE_INSTANCE
  hive_port: YOUR_HIVE_INSTANCE_PORT
  hive_apikey: APIKEY

hive_proxies:
  http: ''
  https: ''

hive_alert_config:
  title: '{rule[name]} -- {match[alert]}'
  type: 'external'
  source: 'SecurityOnion'
  description: '{match[message]}'
  severity: 2
  tags: ['elastalert, SecurityOnion']
  tlp: 3
  status: 'New'
  follow: True

hive_observable_data_mapping:
  - ip: '{match[source_ip]}'
  - ip: '{match[destination_ip]}'
```

15.6 MISP

15.6.1 NIDS Rules

Not long ago, the MISP project announced the ability to export NIDS rules created from events/indicators: https://www.circl.lu/doc/misp/automation/#get-eventsnids-nids-rules-export

We can leverage this functionality by quickly and easily setting up an automated mechanism to pull NIDS rules from a MISP instance and add them to our local rules for Security Onion. To do so, we just need to follow the simple steps below.

15.6.2 Warning

Please keep in mind we do not officially support this integration, so installation is at your own risk. Additionally, the current version of MISP seems to have an issue with Bro Intel export, therefore, this particular functionailty may not work as intended (depending on the version of MISP you are using).

See: https://github.com/MISP/MISP/issues/4050 for more details.

15.6.3 Installation

Clone the repo:

```
git clone https://github.com/weslambert/securityonion-misp
```

Run the setup script:

```
sudo securityonion-misp/so-misp-setup
```

Update rules (if desired):

```
sudo rule-update
```

Confirm rules in place:

```
grep -i misp /etc/nsm/rules/downloaded.rules
```

You should now be up and running!

MISP rules will be downloaded via cron-job at the interval specified in `/etc/cron.d/download-misp`.

15.6.4 Elastalert

If we want to send events to TheHive based on the MISP NIDS rules we've pulled into Security Onion, we can implement an Elastalert rule like the following, filtering on the `alert` field for NIDS alerts:

```
# misp-nids-hive.yaml
# Elastalert rule to forward IDS alerts generated by MISP NIDS rules from Security
↪Onion
# to a specified TheHive instance.
#
```

(continues on next page)

(continued from previous page)

```
es_host: elasticsearch
es_port: 9200
name: MISP NIDS Rule Match
type: frequency
index: "*:logstash-ids*"
num_events: 1
timeframe:
     minutes: 1
filter:
- query:
    query_string:
       query: "alert: MISP"

alert:
- "hivealerter"

hive_connection:
    hive_host: http(s)://YOUR_HIVE_INSTANCE
    hive_port: YOUR_HIVE_INSTANCE_PORT
    hive_apikey: APIKEY

hive_proxies:
  http: ''
  https: ''

hive_alert_config:
    title: '{match[alert]}'
    type: 'external'
    source: 'SecurityOnion'
    description: '{match[message]}'
    severity: 2
    tags: ['elastalert, SecurityOnion, MISP, NIDS']
    tlp: 3
    status: 'New'
    follow: True

hive_observable_data_mapping:
    - ip: '{match[source_ip]}'
    - ip: '{match[destination_ip]}'
    - other: '{match[interface]}'
    - other: '{match[sid]}'
```

Simply fill in the pertinent TheHive instance connection details above, and place this rule in `/etc/elastalert/rules` as `misp-nids-hive.yaml`.

As a result, you will receive alerts in TheHive for any matching events in the `logstash-ids-*` index. The following observables will be generated for the alert:

- Source/Destination IP from alert
- Sensor interface from IDS alert
- Signature ID (sid) from alert

15.7 NtopNG

The latest-stable version of ntopng can now be installed on the latest-stable version of Security Onion.

Installer script maintained here:
https://github.com/branchnetconsulting/so-ntopng-installer

15.8 RITA

From: https://github.com/activecm/rita

> RITA is an open source framework for network traffic analysis.
>
> The framework ingests Bro Logs, and currently supports the following analysis features:
>
> Beaconing: Search for signs of beaconing behavior in and out of your network
> DNS Tunneling Search for signs of DNS based covert channels
> Blacklisted: Query blacklists to search for suspicious domains and hosts
> URL Length Analysis: Search for lengthy URLs indicative of malware
> Scanning: Search for signs of port scans in your network

We can add RITA to Security Onion to enhance its current capabilities and leverage the great work from the folks at Active Countermeasures. They've done a fantastic job of allowing RITA to be easy to integrate with Security Onion.

15.8.1 Warning

Please keep in mind we do not officially support RITA, so installation is at your own risk.

Additionally, RITA currently only supports use of Bro logs in `TSV` format. If you are running the latest version of Security Onion, you will need to switch from `JSON` to `TSV` format by following the steps here:

Bro#tsv

15.8.2 Installation

To install RITA on Security Onion:

Download the install script:

```
wget https://raw.githubusercontent.com/activecm/rita/master/install.sh
```

Run the installer:

```
sudo bash ./install.sh
```

Start MongoDB:

```
sudo service mongod start
```

15.8.3 Usage

You can then import logs with:

```
rita import /nsm/bro/logs dataset1
```

Then have RITA analyze the imported data:

```
rita analyze
```

To see the most visited URLs:

```
rita show-most-visited-urls dataset1
```

To see long connections, type:

```
rita show-long-connections dataset1
```

To see beacons, type:

```
rita show-beacons dataset1
```

Finally, you can issue an HTML report (viewable in browser) by typing:

```
rita html-report
```

See other available commands with:

```
rita --help
```

15.8.4 Configuration

If you don't want to specify your the path for your Bro logs, you'll want to change the value for `ImportDirectory` in `/etc/rita/config.yaml` to `/nsm/bro/logs`.

For additional information, see:
https://github.com/activecm/rita

15.9 Strelka

From https://github.com/target/strelka:

> Strelka is a real-time file scanning system used for threat hunting, threat detection, and incident response. Based on the design established by Lockheed Martin's Laika BOSS and similar projects (see: related projects), Strelka's purpose is to perform file extraction and metadata collection at huge scale.

15.9.1 Warning

Please keep in mind we do not officially support Strelka, so installation is at your own risk.

15.9.2 Installation

For installation instructions, please see https://github.com/weslambert/securityonion-strelka.

15.10 Syslog Output

Please keep in mind that we don't provide free support for third party systems, so this section will be just a brief introduction to how you would send syslog to external syslog collectors. If you need commercial support, please see https://www.securityonionsolutions.com.

15.10.1 How do I send Bro and Wazuh logs to an external syslog collector?

Configure /etc/syslog-ng/syslog-ng.conf with a new destination to forward to your external syslog collector and then restart syslog-ng.

15.10.2 How do I send IDS alerts to an external system?

2 options:

- Edit ALL /etc/nsm/HOSTNAME-INTERFACE/barnyard2*.conf files on ALL sensors with a new output to send IDS alerts to your external systems and then restart all barnyard2 instances:

```
sudo so-barnyard-restart
```

OR

- On your master server (running sguild), configure /etc/syslog-ng/syslog-ng.conf with a new source to monitor /var/log/nsm/securityonion/sguild.log for Alert Received lines and a new destination to send to your external system, and then restart syslog-ng. To do this modify /etc/syslog-ng/syslog-ng.conf and add the following lines:

This line specifies where the sguild.log file is located, and informs syslog-ng to tail the file, the program_override inserts the string sguil_alert into the string:

```
source s_sguil { file("/var/log/nsm/securityonion/sguild.log"
program_override("sguil_alert")); };
```

This line filters on the string "Alert Received":

```
filter f_sguil { match("Alert Received"); };
```

This line tells syslog-ng to send the data read to the IP address of 10.80.4.37, via UDP to port 514:

```
destination d_sguil_udp { udp("10.80.4.37" port(514)); };
```

This log section tells syslog-ng how to structure the previous 'source / filter / destination' and is what actually puts them into play:

```
log {
source(s_sguil);
filter(f_sguil);
destination(d_sguil_udp);
};
```

Please note that this option requires `set DEBUG 2` in `/etc/sguild/sguild.conf`.

CHAPTER 16

Security

If you have any security concerns regarding Security Onion or believe you have uncovered a vulnerability, please follow these steps:

- send an email to security@securityonion.net
- include a description of the issue and steps to reproduce
- please use plain text format (no Word documents or PDF files)
- please do not disclose publicly until we have had sufficient time to resolve the issue

Note that this security address should be used only for undisclosed vulnerabilities. Dealing with fixed issues or general questions on how to use Security Onion should be handled regularly via the security-onion Google Group.

CHAPTER 17

Appendix

This appendix covers the process of upgrading older 14.04/ELSA boxes.

17.1 ELSA to Elastic

The Elastic Stack typically requires more CPU and more RAM than ELSA. In addition, you will most likely want SSD storage for Elastic data if at all possible. For best results, we recommend performing a fresh installation on new hardware designed to meet these requirements. If your ELSA hardware already meets these requirements and you really need to perform an in-place upgrade from ELSA to Elastic, this page will provide an overview of steps necessary.

17.1.1 Warning

The in-place upgrade process is still considered EXPERIMENTAL and so the usual warnings and disclaimers apply:

- This is BLEEDING EDGE and TOTALLY UNSUPPORTED!
- If this breaks your system, you get to keep both pieces!
- This may result in nausea, vomiting, or a burning sensation.

17.1.2 Exporting Data from ELSA

By default, this process does NOT export data from ELSA. If you need the data that is in ELSA, there is an experimental script called `so-elsa-export` that can export data from ELSA to raw logs in the filesystem. Before running this script, please check your disk space as this will duplicate all your logs. Once exported, you may want to move these logs off to a separate system for archival. They are standard cleartext logs so you can use standard command line tools such as `grep`, `awk`, and `sed` to search through them if necessary.

17.1.3 Importing Data to Elastic

The export script provides information on how to import the data into Elastic. However, please note the following caveats:

- this creates yet another copy of the data and so it is essential that you have plenty of free space
- Logstash only has parsers for the current version of Bro, so older Bro logs may not parse correctly

17.1.4 Upgrade Process

Standalone

For a single standalone box that doesn't have any separate sensor boxes connected to it:

Install all updates:

```
sudo soup
```

Reboot:

```
sudo reboot
```

Install and configure Elastic:

```
sudo apt update
sudo apt install securityonion-elastic
sudo so-elastic-download
sudo so-elastic-configure
```

Distributed Deployment

For distributed deployments consisting of a master server and one or more sensor boxes, start the upgrade process with the master server. Once the master server has been fully converted to the Elastic Stack, then start updating sensors one at a time.

Master Server

Before initiating the upgrade process on the master server, run sostat:

```
sudo sostat
```

At the very end of the sostat output, look for the section entitled "ELSA Log Node SSH Tunnels". Save the information in this section as you will need it later in this procedure.

Install all updates:

```
sudo soup
```

Reboot:

```
sudo reboot
```

Install and configure Elastic:

```
sudo apt update
sudo apt install securityonion-elastic
sudo so-elastic-download
sudo so-elastic-configure
```

For each sensor ssh account, add lines to `/etc/ssh/sshd_config` like the following (replacing `$SSH_USERNAME` with the actual sensor ssh account):

```
Match User $SSH_USERNAME
    GatewayPorts clientspecified
```

Restart `sshd`:

```
sudo service ssh restart
```

Sensors

Perform the following steps on each sensor box, one at a time (finish the first sensor before starting the second sensor, etc.).

Install all updates:

```
sudo soup
```

Reboot:

```
sudo reboot
```

Install and configure Elastic:

```
sudo apt update
sudo apt install securityonion-elastic
sudo so-elastic-download
echo "KIBANA_ENABLED=no" | sudo tee -a /etc/nsm/securityonion.conf
echo "ELASTALERT_ENABLED=no" | sudo tee -a /etc/nsm/securityonion.conf
sudo so-elastic-configure
sudo so-autossh-restart
```

Check to make sure the old ELSA autossh tunnel is not still running – if it is, it could cause problems starting our new one for Elasticsearch:

```
ps aux | grep autossh
```

If you see something like the following, you'll need to kill it and run `so-autossh-start` again:

```
4356  0.0  0.0  4356   92 ?        Ss   18:26  0:00 /usr/lib/autossh/autossh -M 0
↪  -q -N -o ServerAliveInterval 60 -o ServerAliveCountMax 3 -i /root/.ssh/
↪securityonion -L 3306:127.0.0.1:3306 -R 50000:localhost:3154 sensor@192.168.1.3

sudo kill -9 4356
ps aux | grep autossh (verify no process)
sudo so-autossh-start
```

Checking again with `ps aux | grep autossh`, we see the correct connection information:

```
17707  0.0  0.0  4356   92 ?        Ss   18:50  0:00 /usr/lib/autossh/autossh -M 0
↪    -q -N -o ServerAliveInterval 60 -o ServerAliveCountMax 3 -i /root/.ssh/
↪securityonion -R 172.18.0.1:50000:localhost:9300 sensor@192.168.1.3
```

(continues on next page)

(continued from previous page)

Next we'll want to check to make sure `$REVERSE_PORT` was correctly set in `/root/.ssh/securityonion_ssh.conf`:

```
sudo cat /root/.ssh/securityonion_ssh.conf
```

We should get something like the following:

`SSH_USERNAME=sensor SERVERNAME=192.168.1.3 REVERSE_PORT=50000`

Next, we'll manually add transport settings to `/etc/elasticsearch/elasticsearch.yml` (replacing `$REVERSE_PORT` with the actual reverse port):

```
transport.bind_host: 0.0.0.0
transport.publish_host: 172.18.0.1
transport.publish_port: $REVERSE_PORT.
```

`transport.publish_host` should ALWAYS be set to `172.18.0.1`

Restart Elasticsearch:

```
sudo docker restart so-elasticsearch
```

Back to the master server

Next, we'll need to add the correct information for UFW and Elasticsearch so that we can query the sensor's Elasticsearch instance via Cross Cluster Search:

For each sensor, add a firewall rule (replacing `5000X` with the actual reverse port):

```
sudo ufw allow proto tcp from 172.18.0.0/24 to 172.18.0.1 port 5000X
```

Log into Kibana, click Dev Tools, paste the following, and then click the green triangle to send the request:

```
GET _cluster/settings
```

The output pane on the right will then display `_cluster/settings` which will list the master server and any remote nodes.

If any of your hostnames have capital letters, you'll want to lowercase those letters when adding these settings, given that our new standard is to use lowercase. Paste the following into Dev Tools with the actual node name and $REVERSE_PORT you'd like to add:

```
PUT _cluster/settings
{
  "persistent": {
    "search": {
      "remote": {
        "sensorname": {
          "seeds": [ "172.18.0.1:5000X" ],
          "skip_unavailable": true
        }
      }
    }
  }
}
```

Next, we can do the following from within Kibana Dev Tools to check our configuration:

```
GET _cluster/settings
```

If everything worked, then you should see the new sensor listed in the output.

Last, check the Kibana Overview Dashboard or Discover and search for logs from the new sensor.

17.2 Upgrading from 14.04 to 16.04

Please read through this entire page before beginning!

17.2.1 Disclaimers

- We offer no guarantees that this upgrade process will work perfectly.

17.2.2 Warnings

- Before upgrading production sensors, you should fully test this upgrade process on test sensors in a test environment that closely matches your production environment.
- Argus, Pads, Prads, and ELSA are no longer supported – these software packages will be removed upon upgrade and will not be supported in future releases.
- If you were previously running ELSA, please ensure your system has been converted to Elastic before upgrading.

17.2.3 Pre-upgrade Notes

- If you are behind a proxy, make sure that you've configured your proxy settings. In the commands below that use sudo, you may need to use `sudo -i` so that your proxy settings are applied to the sudo environment.
- The upgrade process will take at **least** 1-2 hours (per server/sensor), depending on the speed of your server hardware and Internet connection. Please plan accordingly.
- If you're upgrading a distributed deployment, you'll need to perform the steps below on the master server and all sensors, but make sure you **start with the master server first!**
- If you're upgrading a master server and you have a large ip2c table, you may want to truncate it and populate fresh data before initiating the 16.04 upgrade:

```
sudo mysql --defaults-file=/etc/mysql/debian.cnf -Dsecurityonion_db -e 'truncate
↪table ip2c;'
sudo so-squert-ip2c
```

- After upgrading the master server, ensure all sensors are upgraded as soon as possible to minimize disruption and/or incompatibility issues. Mixed-release (14.04 + 16.04) environments are currently untested and unsupported.

17.2.4 Preparation

- Start with a fully configured Security Onion 14.04 (Elastic Stack) installation.
- If running in a VM, create a snapshot so that you can revert if necessary.

- You may want to record a transcript of the full upgrade so you can refer back to it in case of any errors. For more information, please see https://www.debian.org/releases/stable/i386/release-notes/ch-upgrading.en.html#record-session.

- **NON-MASTER MACHINES ONLY** - If the master server has already been upgraded, on each forward node, heavy node, or storage node, do the following:

  ```
  sudo rm /etc/apt/sources.list.d/securityonion-ubuntu-stable-xenial.list
  sudo service salt-minion stop
  ```

- Ensure all 14.04 updates are installed:

  `sudo soup`

- If soup prompted to reboot, go ahead and do that. If it didn't, go ahead and reboot anyway:

  `sudo reboot`

- Review sostat output to make sure system is healthy before continuing:

  `sudo sostat`

- **IMPORTANT!** Backup Bro config since it will be removed when Ubuntu removes the package:

  ```
  sudo sed -i 's|PREV="pre-.*$|PREV="pre-upgrade-to-16.04"|g' /var/lib/dpkg/info/
  ↪securityonion-bro.preinst
  sudo /var/lib/dpkg/info/securityonion-bro.preinst install
  ```

- Verify that Bro config was backed up to /opt/bro/etc_pre-upgrade-to-16.04/ (you should have files in this directory):

  `ls -alh /opt/bro/etc_pre-upgrade-to-16.04/`

- You may want to backup any other files that you've manually modified.

17.2.5 Upgrade from Ubuntu 14.04 to Ubuntu 16.04

- Configure Ubuntu to look for the 16.04 upgrade:

  `sudo sed -i 's|Prompt=never|Prompt=lts|g' /etc/update-manager/release-upgrades`

- Kill xscreensaver (otherwise, do-release-upgrade in the next step will prompt you to do so):

  `sudo pkill xscreensaver`

- Initiate upgrade to Ubuntu 16.04:

  `sudo do-release-upgrade`

- If you receive a message like `No new release found.`, then you'll need to ensure you can reach the Ubuntu changelogs site:

  `curl http://changelogs.ubuntu.com/meta-release-lts`

  If you can't reach the site, try checking for connectivity, or your firewall to see if it is being blocked.

- If you receive a prompt to restart services during the upgrade, choose `Yes`.

- If you receive a prompt to allow non-superusers to capture packets (Wireshark), choose `No`.

- If you receive a prompt in regard to grub configuration, choose `keep local GRUB configuration`.

- Follow the prompts. If you receive a prompt regarding xscreensaver, select OK. You may receive prompts regarding files that have changed like the following:

file	answer
/etc/sudoers	Y
/etc/default/grub	N
/etc/apt/apt.conf.d/01autoremove	N
/etc/apt/apt.conf.d/99update-notifier	N
/etc/apache2/mods-available/ssl.conf	Y
/etc/apache2/apache2.conf	Y
/etc/apache2/ports.conf	Y
/etc/syslog-ng/syslog-ng.conf	N
/etc/php5/apache2/php.ini	Y
/etc/xdg/menus/gnome-flashback-applications.menu	N
/etc/redis/redis.conf	N
/etc/pulse/default.pa	N

- These are files that Security Onion modifies, and you may receive prompts for additional files that you have modified. The safest option for each of these is to choose to install the package maintainer's version (Y, where applicable), with the exception of the prompt in regard to syslog-ng.conf. Choosing the installation of the package maintainer's version will back up the existing file in case you need to review it later for any custom modifications you had made.

- **IMPORTANT!** If you receive a prompt regarding syslog-ng.conf, press N to keep your currently-installed version.

- If you receive an error message in regard to mysql-server, please disregard and continue with the upgrade.

- When prompted to restart, press Y to continue.

17.2.6 Add back Security Onion packages

- After rebooting, log back in.

- If running in a VM, perform a snapshot.

- Open a terminal, remove the old PPA, and add our stable PPA:

```
sudo rm /etc/apt/sources.list.d/*
sudo add-apt-repository -y ppa:securityonion/stable
sudo apt-get update
```

- Add back any missing Security Onion packages by installing the `securityonion-iso` metapackage. If you didn't install from our ISO and instead installed from your preferred flavor of Ubuntu and added our PPA and packages, then you may not necessarily need to install the `securityonion-iso` metapackage. In the command below, you can replace `securityonion-iso` with the same Security Onion metapackage(s) you originally installed (`securityonion-server`, `securityonion-sensor`, `securityonion-all`, etc).:

```
sudo apt-get install securityonion-iso syslog-ng-core
```

- **IMPORTANT!** If you receive a prompt regarding `syslog-ng.conf`, press N to keep your currently-installed version.

- If you encounter an error in regard to `mod_passenger.so`, try disabling the module as follows:
  `sudo a2dismod passenger`

- Copy backed up Bro config back to `/opt/bro/etc`:
  `sudo cp /opt/bro/etc_pre-upgrade-to-16.04/* /opt/bro/etc`

- Copy OSSEC config back in place:

```
sudo cp /var/ossec/etc/ossec.conf-2.8 /var/ossec/etc/ossec.conf
sudo /var/ossec/bin/ossec-control enable client-syslog
```

- Stop salt-minion and salt-master before running soup:
  ```
  sudo service salt-minion stop
  sudo service salt-master stop
  ```
- Update all packages that are currently installed:
  ```
  sudo soup -y
  ```
- Soup should prompt for a reboot. After reboot, run the following to enable `securityonion.service`:
  ```
  sudo systemctl enable securityonion.service
  ```
- NON-MASTER MACHINES ONLY:

  run the following to disable MySQL:
  ```
  sudo systemctl disable mysql
  ```

  run the following to disable salt-master:
  ```
  sudo systemctl disable salt-master
  ```

  run the following to disable Redis:
  ```
  sudo systemctl disable redis
  ```

- Reboot again:
  ```
  sudo reboot
  ```
- MASTER ONLY - If sguild does not start after reboot, try running `sguil-db-purge`:
  ```
  sudo sguil-db-purge
  ```

17.2.7 Clean Up

- Review your Snort/Suricata/Bro/other configuration for any local customizations that you may need to re-apply.
- Clean up old UFW file:
  ```
  sudo rm /etc/ufw/applications.d/apache2.2-common
  ```
- Remove old Security Onion init file:
  ```
  sudo rm /etc/init/securityonion.conf
  ```
- Remove any unnecessary packages:
  ```
  sudo apt-get autoremove
  ```
- Reboot:
  ```
  sudo reboot
  ```

17.2.8 Verify

- After rebooting, log back in.

- Verify that `/etc/update-manager/release-upgrades` has `Prompt=never` to avoid prompts to upgrade to 18.04 (not supported right now).
- Keep in mind, Logstash may take a few minutes to initialize, so you may want to wait a few minutes before continuing.
- Verify services are running:
  `sudo so-status`
- Run sostat and look for anything out of the ordinary:
  `sudo sostat`
- Check log files for anything out of the ordinary.

17.2.9 MySQL root password

- We will need to set a randomized root password for MySQL. We can do so by doing the following:

Reset debian.cnf:

```
sudo rm /etc/mysql/debian.cnf
sudo dpkg-reconfigure --frontend noninteractive mysql-server-5.7
```

If root password is blank, set random password:

```
if echo "quit" | sudo mysql -uroot 2>/dev/null; then
    PASSWORD=$(LC_ALL=C </dev/urandom tr -dc '[:alnum:]' | head -c 32)
    sudo mysql --defaults-file=/etc/mysql/debian.cnf -e "ALTER USER 'root'@'localhost
↪' IDENTIFIED WITH mysql_native_password BY
    '$PASSWORD';"
fi
```

17.2.10 Optional

- Switch to pure GNOME desktop:
  `sudo so-desktop-gnome`
- If you disabled the GUI previously, you'll need to re-apply similar configuration to boot into text mode:

```
sudo systemctl enable multi-user.target --force
sudo systemctl set-default multi-user.target
sudo reboot
```

Security Onion

Configuration Files

Configuration	File
General Settings	/etc/nsm/securityonion.conf
Sensor Settings	/etc/nsm/<hostname-interface>/sensor.conf
Maintenance Scripts	/etc/cron.d, /usr/sbin
Snort	/etc/nsm/<hostname-interface>/snort.conf
Suricata	/etc/nsm/<hostname-interface>/suricata.yaml
Bro	/opt/bro
Bro Config	/opt/bro/etc/networks.cfg, node.cfg
Bro Local Policy/Scripts/Intel	/opt/bro/share/bro/site/local.bro (config) /opt/bro/share/bro/policy (scripts) /opt/bro/share/bro/intel/intel.dat (intel)
Elasticsearch Config	/etc/elasticsearch/elasticsearch.yml /etc/elasticsearch/jvm.options (heap size)
Logstash Config	/etc/logstash/logstash.yml /etc/logstash/jvm.options (heap size) /etc/logstash/conf.d (standard pipeline config) /etc/logstash/custom (custom pipeline config and custom templates)
Kibana Config	/etc/kibana/kibana.yml
Curator Config	/etc/curator/config/curator.yml
Syslog-NG	/etc/syslog-ng/syslog-ng.conf
Wazuh	/var/ossec/etc/ossec.conf
Sguil (Server)	/etc/nsm/securityonion/sguild.conf
Sguil (Client)	/etc/sguil/sguil.conf
Sguil (Email)	/etc/nsm/securityonion/sguild.email
Onionsalt	/opt/onionsalt

Log Files

Scope	File
Bro	/nsm/bro/logs/current/stderr.log (errors), reporter.log (errors/warnings), loaded_scripts.log (loaded scripts)
Elastalert	/var/log/elastalert/elastalert_stderr.log
Elasticsearch	/var/log/elasticsearch/<hostname>.log
Logstash	/var/log/logstash/logstash.log
Kibana	/var/log/kibana/kibana.log
OSSEC	/var/ossec/logs/ossec.log
Sensor Logs	/var/log/nsm/<hostname-interface>/snortu-n.log, barnyard2-n.log, suricata.log, netsniff-ng.log
Sguild	/var/log/nsm/securityonion/sguild.log

Performance Tuning

Target	Parameter/File
Bro	lb_procs in /opt/bro/etc/node.cfg
Snort/Suricata	IDS_LB_PROCS in /etc/nsm/<hostname-interface>/sensor.conf
PF_RING	min_num_slots in /etc/modprobe.d/pf_ring.conf
Netsniff-NG	PCAP_OPTIONS, PCAP_SIZE, PCAP_RING_SIZE in /etc/nsm/<hostname-interface>/sensor.conf

Rule Management

Configuration	File
IDS Rules (Downloaded)	/etc/nsm/rules/downloaded.rules
IDS Rules (Custom)	/etc/nsm/rules/local.rules
Rule Thresholds	/etc/nsm/rules/threshold.conf
Disabled Rules	/etc/nsm/pulledpork/disablesid.conf
Modified Rules	/etc/nsm/pulledpork/modifysid.conf
PulledPork Config	/etc/nsm/pulledpork/pulledpork.conf
Wazuh Rules	/var/ossec/rules
Wazuh Rules (Custom)	/var/ossec/rules/local_rules.xml
Elastalert	/etc/elastalert/rules

Packet Filtering

Scope	File
Server (Entire Deployment)	/etc/nsm/rules/bpf.conf
Sensor-Specific	/etc/nsm/<hostname-interface>/bpf.conf
Component-Specific	/etc/nsm/<hostname-interface>/bpf-bro.conf, bpf-ids.conf, etc.

DATA

Data Directories

Data	Directory
Packet Capture (Sensor)	/nsm/sensor_data/<hostname-interface>/dailylogs
Alert Data (Sensor)	/nsm/sensor_data/<hostname-interface>
Alert Data (Master)	/var/lib/mysql/securityonion_db
Bro (Archived) (Sensor)	/nsm/bro/logs/yyyy-mm-dd
Bro (Current Hr) (Sensor)	/nsm/bro/logs/current
Bro Extracted Files (Sensor)	/nsm/bro/extracted (only EXEs extracted, by default)
Elasticsearch (Master/Heavy/Storage)	/nsm/elasticsearch/nodes/x/indices

COMMON TASKS

General Maintenance

Task	Command
Check Service Status	so-status
Start/Stop/Restart All Services	so-start|stop|restart
Start/Stop/Restart Server Services	so-sguild-start|stop|restart
Start/Stop/Restart Sensor Services	so-sensor-start|stop|restart
Start/Stop/Restart Docker	docker start|stop|restart
Start/Stop All Docker Containers	so-elastic-start|stop
Start/Stop Specific Container/Service	so-<noun>-verb Ex: so-logstash-start|stop
Add Analyst (Sguil/Squert/Kibana) User	so-user-add
Change Analyst User Password	so-user-passwd
Add/View Firewall Rules (Analyst, Beats, Syslog, etc.)	so-allow so-allow-view
Update SO (and Ubuntu)	soup
Update Rules	rule-update
Generate SO Statistics	sostat
Check Redis Queue Length	redis-cli llen logstash:redis

Salt Commands (from Master Server)

Task	Command
Execute Command	salt '*' cmd.run '<command>'
Verify Minions Up	salt '*' test.ping
Sync Minions	salt '*' state.highstate
Update Entire Deployment	soup && salt '*' cmd.run 'soup -y'

Port/Protocols/Services (Distributed Deployment)

Port/Protocol	Service/Purpose
22/tcp (Sensor/Master)	SSH access/AutoSSH tunnel from sensor(s) to Master
4505-4506/tcp (Master)	Salt comm from sensor(s) to Master
7736/tcp (Master)	Sguild comm from sensor(s) to Master

Support

Mailing List
https://securityonion.net/docs/mailinglists

Reddit
https://www.reddit.com/r/securityonion/

Docs
https://securityonion.readthedocs.io

Blog
https://blog.securityonion.net

Training, Professional Services, Hardware Appliances
https://securityonionsolutions.com

Originally Designed by: Chris Sanders - http://www.chrissanders.org - @chrissanders88
Updated by: Security Onion Solutions - https://securityonion.net - @securityonion
Security Onion Version: 16.04.6.1
Last Modified: 05.14.2019

Printed in Great Britain
by Amazon